AF207193

THE ATLANTIC BLUEFIN TUNA...
Yesterday, Today and Tomorrow.

THE ATLANTIC BLUEFIN TUNA…
Yesterday, Today and Tomorrow

Captain Al Anderson

THE FISHERMAN LIBRARY
by Ocean Sport Fishing
1620 Beaver Dam Road
Point Pleasant, NJ 08742

Printed in the United States of America

Library of Congress Cataloging-in-Publication data

ISBN 0-923155-11-2

THE FISHERMAN LIBRARY
Ocean Sport Fishing
1620 Beaver Dam Road
Point Pleasant, NJ 08742

Copy Editing . . . . Linda Barrett
Production . . . . Matt Muzslay
Art Direction . . . . Steve and Terri Goione

PHOTO CREDITS

All photos are by the author except following:

Atlantic Tuna Club pp. 88, 89, 125U
Pete Barrett pp. 128, 167
Staff Carroll pp. 41, 56, 60, 84, 93, 94, 121, 151, 158, 170, 182, 202
Donald Cianciolo pp. 40, 228
Bob Downie p. 99
Pete Fisher p. 179
Lucy Fox p. 181
Barry Gibson p. 244U
Earl H. Goodison p. 102
International Game Fish Association pp. 246, 247
Forest Johnson p. 112
Frank J. Mather, III p. 244L
Ed Murray pp. 66, 110
Providence Journal Company p. 46
Robert Rakovic pp. 177, 194
Jean Reese pp. 211, 214, 215
Richard Turner p. 28
Al Ristori pp. 10, 34, 62, 70, 72, 74, 79, 80, 156, 160, 168, 178, 216, 242, 250
Florence E. Young p. 218

DEDICATION

To Frank J. Mather, III, Scientist Emeritis, Woods Hole Oceanographic Institute. His career work earned him the title "Dean of studies on Atlantic bluefin tuna," and he started the first successful tagging program on bluefin tuna in 1954. Today, this same program, the Cooperative Game Fish Tagging Program is now under the auspices of the National Marine Fisheries Service, Southeast Fisheries Center, Miami, Florida. This program has contributed significantly to our understanding of bluefin tuna and has been responsible for the development of conservation measures for this species through the International Commission for the Conservation of Atlantic tuna.

ACKNOWLEDGEMENTS

As this book began to take shape, I became encouraged by the assistance and enthusiasm of many people. Although some chapters may appear critical of occurring changes, they simply reflect the attitudes and opinions of those involved in the transition of the Atlantic bluefin tuna fishery.

The late photojournalist, John C. "Staff" Carroll did more than anyone to record recent rod and reel fishing in Rhode Island waters, notably that for giant bluefin tuna, and many of the photographs are his.

Special thanks to Al Ristori who provided background on giant tuna fishing outside of New England waters and for background on Ed and Frank Murray.

Also thanks to Len Belcaro, Dave Borden, Don Cianciolo, Al Conti, Tom Crafford, Jay DeNoia, Brigs Endt, Ron Feuring, Web Goodwin, E.K. Harry, Roger Hillhouse, George Hilton, N.W. Knuckey, Bill Kreuger, Dick Lema, Bob Linton, Frank Mather, Tom Meade, Bob Meloccaro, Ed Murray, Kathi Rodrigues, Mike Roffer, Ed Scott, Don Slater, Les Smith, Bob Tobin and Ralph Watson.

Finally, a special thank you to my wife Daryl Anne, whose patience, help and encouragement allowed me to complete this effort.

INTRODUCTION

Imagine, after a day's fishing that a 600 pound giant bluefin tuna worth close to $10,000 lies in the cockpit. Some catch, right?

This book chronicles the recent history of this fishery as it changed from a traditional rod and reel sport into today's commercial activity. Twenty-five years ago there really was not much you could do after landing a giant bluefin other than take a few pictures. These trophy fish were considered poor tablefare and had little or no market value. If you couldn't find someone locally to buy it for five to ten cents a pound, you either had to pay to have it hauled to the dump or you took it back out to sea.

But times change and today, as a result of the Japanese export market, a giant bluefin tuna may be worth upwards of $20 a pound or more. Japan's craving for tuna fish has been partially responsible for this change in value with regional entrepreneurs capitalizing on this demand. Whether sliced and served raw (sashimi), or with rice (sushi), or rolled in seaweed (tekamaki), the demand for jumbo maguro (clovefin) is high. So high, in fact, Japan trains and sends tuna buyers to the United States to assay fish quality and offer a purchase price to the boats.

Fish that arrive at the dock cool and bled usually bring a good price. Bulky fish, those with a high fat content and more flavorful to the Japanese palate, bring the highest prices on the floors of the major fish auctions. Fish can arrive there only a few days after their capture.

Today, there is little or no sportfishing for bluefin tuna as a great deal of money can be made in taking even a single fish. Regulation tackle and the use of gaffs have given way to heavy lines and electrified harpoons. Just a few shorts years ago, the greatest numbers of giant bluefin tuna were landed by rod and reel. Today, the harpoon, longline and seine fishery landings far outstrip rod and reel landings. As you might imagine, there was a rapid evolution in both tackle and equipment from earlier days to take these fish. Unfortunately, a considerable change in the attitude of those who went tuna fishing also occurred. In an attempt to capture these valuable levithans, boats today frequently employ light aircraft to spot fish for them.

Presently, government officials and scientists from 23 nations that fish for these animals are joined together to study the fish and, if necessary, create conservation and management measures for this valuable resource, in an organization called International Commission for the Conservation of Atlantic Tuna, better known as ICCAT. Despite their efforts, however, there has been a steady decline in the bluefin tuna stocks. It appears this will continue unless drastic measures are taken to curtail harvesting of this resource.

Those of us who tuna fished years ago never would have envisioned this decline in the resource, as there were fish everywhere, or so it seemed. Hopefully, money and greed will not devastate this resource and it will be allowed to recover before it is too late.

What does the future hold in store for the bluefin? Quite possibly, but highly unlikely, ICCAT could mandate a complete, total moratorium with no quota for scientific purpose in the western North Atlantic. Many in the political and scientific community are doubtful this will happen. If for some reason the giant bluefin tuna became much less valuable and those actively pursuing these fish ceased their efforts, there is the possibility the stocks could rebound. It's an interesting scenario but highly unlikely.

There have been a number of major changes in the bluefin tuna fishery in these last three decades. Previously published articles by the author serve as the nucleus for this book which profiles those changes as seen by a charterboat captain actively fishing Rhode Island waters during this time.

TABLE OF CONTENTS

1 THE BLUEFIN TUNA

Identification And Background

"Hey…Prowler boat. Drop what you're doing and come to the radio."

The remote speaker of the VHF radio in the electronics box above the console carried the voice of Captain Fritz Hubner aboard his **Mistress Too** out of Montauk, New York. Fishing alone this day, with no mate to assist, I was tending to tackle and gear in the cockpit. Anchor line was being coiled back into a fish tote as we idled away from the fleet on the West Bank of the Butterfish Hole.

"Go ahead, Captain. What's the problem?" I replied.

"You know, I've been catching these fish for years but I have no idea how old they are," admitted the speaker. "One fellow in the party wants to know how old the fish is that he caught today."

Fishing this late September day for school bluefin tuna had been, without a doubt, packed with action and many boats were leaving the grounds "limited out" as we say. We had decided to tag a few fish, extending our fishing till early afternoon. With a long run back to Pt. Judith, I was anxious to get going.

"Well, I'm flattered to have you think I know something about the age and size of Atlantic bluefin tuna," I told the other captain. "I've got a rough idea, but it's only a guess."

"Well, the mate's got the fish on the deck now, looks between 35 to 45 pounds," described my new friend. "Any idea how old it is? The mate estimates at least five or six years old."

"Could be, but maybe not," I explained. More like two or three years old. It's tough to be sure. Tell you what, this coming winter when I've got a little time on my hands, I'll put together some information for you on age and size of bluefin."

"Sounds good, I'll tell this guy it's only a baby tuna, a 'flunked-out' school tuna," answered the voice on the other end.

This fall, prior to his annual retreat to Florida, I managed to persuade Frank J. Mather, III, Scientist Emeritus, Woods Hole Oceanographic Institute (WHOI) to send me some of the scientific literature that profiles age and growth in Atlantic bluefin tuna. This gentleman is considered to be the dean of studies on Atlantic bluefin tuna and the man who started the first successful tagging program on Atlantic bluefin tuna years ago at the WHOI.

The package that arrived was bulky and heavy containing a wealth of information on studies that had been done over the years by many trained fishery biologists. One study in particular dealt with length, weight and age in young western North Atlantic bluefin tuna. Other studies dealt with information on older fish. On the basis of some data presented in these studies, the accompanying table describes the average length and weight in bluefin tuna up to 30 years of age.

In its first summer of adventure and travel, bluefin migrate up the coast from southerly waters. By the time they reach New England waters and still just several months old, a young bluefin tuna has already grown rapidly. Arriving in mid to late August, the fish are believed to have migrated northward along the inshore edge of the slope waters of the Continental Shelf. Depending on what part of the coast you fish, these school fish may be within 10 miles of the beach or 50 miles. The Hatteras and Virginia boats see young of the year and school bluefin in May, the south Jersey boats look for them in June. They arrive in New England waters by late July.

Probably spawned in the blue waters of the Gulf of Mexico or the Straits of Florida back in April, these fish may range from 9 to 18 inches. Come late summer, their average length is about 13 inches. Their weight could range from a half pound but 3.5 pounds is average.

Returning to the New England summering grounds in their second year, late summer finds them now averaging 24 inches in length and weighing about 9 pounds. However, depending on food availability, these fish could range in weight from 5 to 13 pounds. In their third summer, these gamesters again push into the New York Bight and New England area in late July through August. The schools reach the grounds south of Martha's Vineyard by August.

Studies done on the migration of small bluefin seem to indicate these fish follow the 20 degrees Centigrade (68.0 degree Fahrenhite) isotherm as they move northward over the Continental Shelf south of New England. These tightly schooled predators constantly chase juvenile mackerel and butterfish, squid, sand

TABLE ON AGE AND SIZE OF ATLANTIC BLUEFIN TUNA

AGE	Aver. LENGTH (Inches)	WEIGHT (Lbs.)
Young School Tuna		
0	13	2
1	24	9
School Tuna		
2	32	22
3	39	40
4	47	69
5	55	100
Medium Tuna		
6	62	140
7	67	185
8	73	240
9	78	290
Giant Tuna		
10	83	340
15	98	600-800
20	106	700-950
25	112	800-1100
30	118	1200-1500

The author holding up a freshly caught four year old school bluefin tuna with an estimated weight of 70 to 80 pounds.

eels and other bait fish they may find. By late September or early October, these same fish may now weigh anywhere from 14 to 30 pounds with an average weight of 22 pounds. Studies indicate the late summer and early fall months are the time in which these fish put on the most weight with fat content in body tissues at the highest levels.

New York to New England fishermen benefit greatly from the biological needs of the bluefin tuna. Without the cold waters north of Cape Cod acting as a thermal barrier, the bluefin would swim right by these famous fishing areas. The fishing opportunities off more southern grounds, such as Hatteras, Virginia and south Jersey are often brief as the fish migrate past these areas in search of food and ideal water temperature. This presents some great fishing opportunities for northern boats that frequently "limit out" and even tag a few.

For many years it has been well known that few, if any, juvenile Atlantic bluefin tuna make their way into the summertime waters of the Gulf of Maine. Instead, the grounds south of Block Island, Montauk, Shinnecock, and east of the Jersey Highlands in late summer offer good fishing. Studies now seem to indicate the juvenile bluefin lack the ability to thermoregulate body temperature (elevate blood and body tissue temperatures above that of the environment). Waters north of Cape Cod are just too cold to support body metabolism in these young fish.

However, as they age and put on weight, they appear to further develop their blood circulatory mechanism that allows them to maintain body temperatures above that of a cold environment. A giant Atlantic bluefin can easily invade the cold, food-rich waters of the Canadian Maritimes with little or no concern for thermal gradients in the water column. Scientists indicate that giant bluefin will invade water as cold as 6 degrees C (42.8 degrees F) and still actively feed.

The bluefin lying on the deck of the **Mistress Too**, weighing between 35 to 40 pounds was probably a three year old fish on the basis of its weight. However, scientific studies have shown that the length of a bluefin is a much better indicator of age than is its weight. While the weights of the bluefin vary substantially depending on the availability of food, the length of the fish as it grows is much more predictable, particularly in older fish.

However, the accompanying **INSTANT FISH WEIGHT CHART and FORMULA** can very accurately predict what the weight of a bluefin might be based on length and girth of the fish.

This table is very accurate for bluefin and bigeye, and reasonably accurate for yellowfin and longfin albacore.

INSTANT FISH WEIGHT CHART

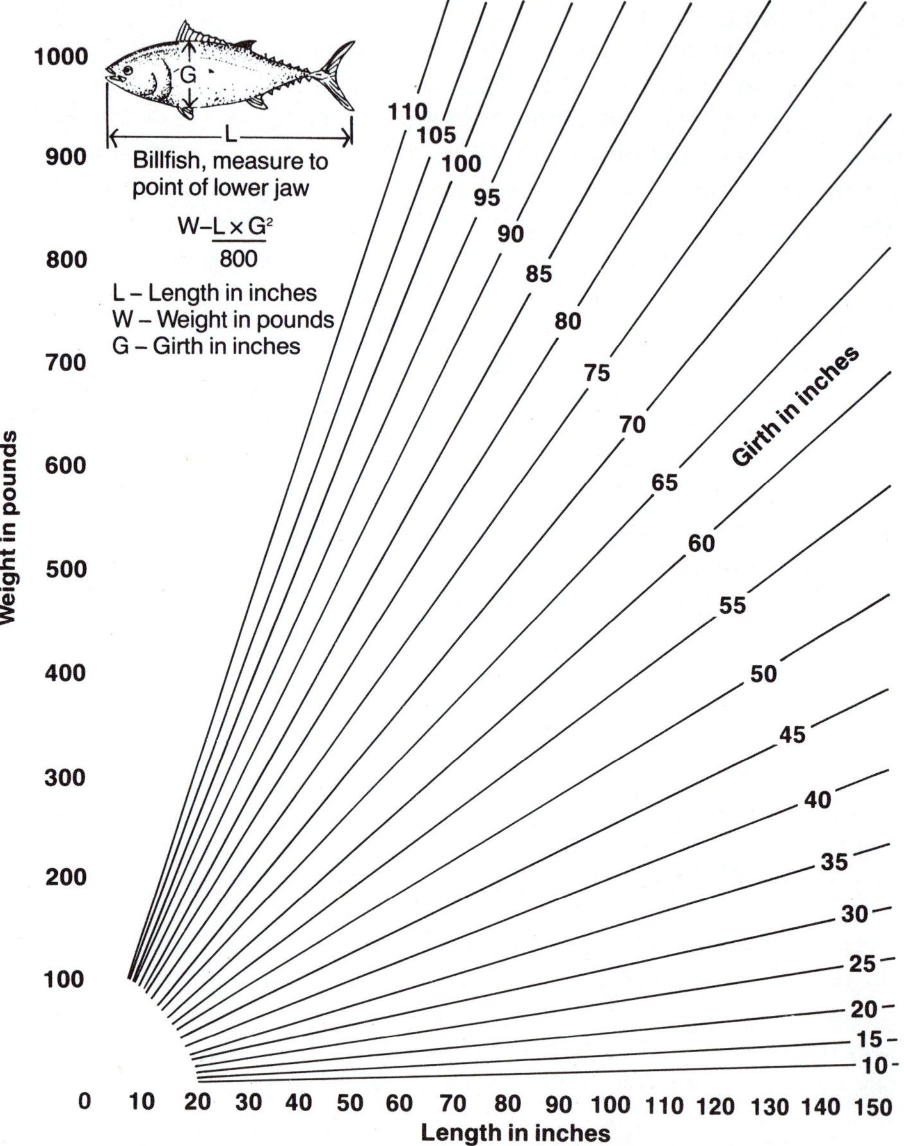

Find point where vertical length line and girth diagonal cross. Read weight at left.

Knowing the length and weight of the bluefin you catch will also enable you to make a very accurate guess about the age of the fish. The growth rates of other tuna species varies greatly from that of the bluefin so the chart will only be accurate for the bluefin.

Let's take a quick look at the **FORMULA** and see how it works. From a point at the fish's jaw to a point through an imaginary line at the outermost tips of the tail, determine total length in inches. Then, from a point at the anterior dorsal fin measure the largest circumference of the fish, called its girth, in inches. Multiply this number times itself (squared). The result is then multiplied by the length, then divided by 800 to achieve the approximate weight of the fish in pounds.

$$\text{Weight} = \frac{\text{Length X Girth}^2}{800}$$

The length and girth are measured in inches, the weight will be in pounds. With this **FORMULA**, tape measure and a handy pocket calculator aboard the boat next summer, you can quickly predict the weight and probable age of a bluefin or any other tuna species.

On the ride back to Pt. Judith the day I talked to Captain Hubner, talk again turned to the age and size of bluefin tuna. "How big and how old do these fish get?" one of my charter fares asked.

"No one knows for sure but they do grow substantially over 1,000 pounds." The charter customer whistled. "I remember a very large fish taken in the Maritimes some years back," I continued. "World record fish I believe."

Pulling the latest IGFA World Record Gamefish book from a forward drawer in the cabin, we soon learned that the largest bluefin taken by rod and reel pulled the scales down to 1,496 pounds. It was landed at Aulds Cove, Nova Scotia, by Ken Fraser in 1979. That particular fish had an overall length exceeding 119 inches and had an estimated age of over 30 years. In fact, scientists suspect that bluefin in the 1,400 to 1,500 pound range captured in traps off Sardinia were well in excess of 30 years of age.

It is interesting to note that in bluefin tuna, unlike most other fish species, the males tend to outweigh the females as they age. Usually it's the females that grow larger so they can carry more eggs and reproduce their own kind in ever greater numbers.

"Hey Captain, what's a school bluefin tuna?" came another question.

"Well, that's an easy one to answer. According to the rules and regulations on Atlantic bluefin tuna printed annually in the Federal Register, and administered by the National Marine Fisheries Service, there are two classes of school tuna; the young schoolies and the schoolies. A young school bluefin tuna is a fish of less than 14 pounds, whereas a school tuna is a bluefin 14 pounds or more but less than 135 pounds. These are fish ranging in age from one to five years."

"As these fish grow and age," I continued, "the class size designation changes. A medium tuna is a bluefin weighing 135 pounds or more but less than 310 pounds. This class of fish range from 6 to 9 years. A giant tuna is a bluefin of 77 inches in length, or greater, and weighing 310 pounds or more. It is 10 years of age or older."

The regulations change. In 1989, Federal Regulations allowed the keeping of four school bluefin tuna per person per day. Young of the year fish could also be taken by anglers. It didn't happen too frequently, but some days a few boats had action on medium bluefins. The Regulations said a vessel could have possession of no more than four fish in this class size. As for giants, one fish per day for vessels is permitted in the General Category. As we'll see further on in this book, the regulations may change from time to time as the bluefin population is monitored to be sure we don't over-fish these great fish.

Usually by its tenth year, a bluefin tuna is classified as a giant by weight and length. Growth rates in these fish are rapid, as documented by scientific evidence. Young school bluefin can increase their body weight ten fold in a period of four months! The information on growth in school bluefin is more qualified than on growth rates in the larger fish. Studies done in Nova Scotia indicate that giants can gain up to 200 pounds of body weight within a year when generously fed in captivity. Another study suggests that giant bluefin gain, on the average, about 50 pounds of body weight a year. With the information on hand, the accompanying table compares the probable age, length and weight of older fish.

As one can easily see, the range in weights of the older fish vary considerably. Obviously, the history of each fish over a span of 15 to 30 years has a lot to do with its total weight. However, knowing a fish's weight, or even more precisely, its overall length in inches, can give you a fairly good idea as to its age. So, keep a copy of this book on your boat and the next time a question arises on the age and size of an Atlantic bluefin tuna, you'll have the answer. With a tape measure in hand, you can go to work to make an accurate guess as to the weight and age of the fish.

1 THE BLUEFIN TUNA

1989 National Marine Fisheries Service Atlantic Bluefin Tuna Report

Each year the **NATIONAL MARINE FISHERIES SERVICE** (NMFS) releases a report on the status of the giant Atlantic bluefin tuna landings of the previous year. In this book I'm reviewing the report covering the period 1/1/89 through 12/15/89. As I write this, with charter fishing aboard the **PROWLER** over for the season, I've had a chance to look closely at the data furnished in this years report. Some information has also been provided on landings of Medium (135 to 310 lbs.) bluefin tuna, by rod and reel angling, and will also be discussed. However, focus is primarily on giant Atlantic bluefin tuna landings, and comparisons will be made to data from the previous year (1988), as well as data going back to 1984, in an attempt to profile the ongoing trends in this valuable fishery. This report gives many insights into the plight of the Atlantic bluefin tuna today and what the future holds.

In 1989, a total of 27,313 vessels were on record as having been issued a NMFS permit to land giant Atlantic bluefin tuna. This represents an increase of about 4 percent over the previous year, when approximately 26,300 vessels had NMFS giant Atlantic bluefin tuna permits.

In 1989, less than 3% of the permitted vessels took fish, with a total of over 4,400 giant Atlantic bluefin tuna landed. Compared to 1988, that's a dramatic increase of over 16% in the landings (3,797 fish in 1988). However, compared to 1984, when 4,750 giant Atlantic bluefin tuna were landed, this is a decline of approximately 7 percent.

This past season the General Category (Harpoon, Rod & Reel, Handline) took a total of 2,054 giant Atlantic bluefin tuna, a tremendous increase over last year of 58 percent. Unlike the last few seasons, this reverses the trend of a declining catch total for this Category. Compared to the previous year (1988), the total percentage of landings for this Category jumped from 34% in 1988 to 46% in 1989, a very significant increase. In 1989, the average weight of fish landed in this Category again decreased over that of the last season, maintaining a continued downward trend, with average fish weight down from 554 pounds in 1988 to 503 pounds in 1989. As in previous years, younger, smaller fish are becoming a greater percentage of the catch for this Category.

In the Harpoon Category for 1989, the number of giant Atlantic bluefin tuna harvested declined compared to the previous year, down 13 percent with a total of 308 fish. Again for 1989, the average weight of each fish landed decreased, down from 462 pounds in 1988 to 441 pounds in 1989. This Fishery Category was closed on July 14th by the NMFS Regional Director due to near quota attainment.

Data for the Incidental Category indicated a decrease in landings compared to 1988, when a total of 534 giant Atlantic bluefin tuna were landed. For 1989, 478 giant Atlantic bluefin tuna were harvested, with average fish weight decreasing somewhat, basically due to a shift in landings from catch areas. Unlike the previous year when 98 percent of the fish landed were southern longline fish, this year only 63 percent of the landings came from the Gulf of Mexico. The southern fishery area was closed on February 19, 1989, and the northern fishery area closed on November 15, 1989. Again for 1989, the average weight of longline caught giant Atlantic bluefin tuna decreased from 625 pounds in 1988 to 514 pounds in 1989.

In the Purse Seine Category, a total of 1,583 giant Atlantic bluefin tuna were landed, very close to the number landed in 1988 of 1,608. However, the average fish weight increased slightly over the previous year from 525 pounds to 537 pounds. Fishing in this Category came to an end in early October just shy of quota attainment.

For the fourth year in a row, in the General Category, the daily catch rate was allowed to increase from one fish per day to two fish per day in late season. Federal regulations continue to provide for an increase in the catch rate if the fishery is slow and does not approximate estimated tonnage of landings. The increased catch rate for this Category remained in effect until deteriorating Fall weather brought an end to the fishery in this Category. This Category again in 1989 did not attain tonnage quota, hence a closure was not necessitated. However, the fishing for young school, school and medium fish closed on October 21st due to the landings of 139 Short Tons in the Angling Category of Medium and school fish. This was the first time such a closure occured in the General Category, brought upon by the season-long harvesting of medium sized fish from both the south Cape and New York bight areas.

A comparison of landings data in all Categories since 1984 indicates a definite shift in the size, and hence age class, of Atlantic bluefin tuna being harvested. With the exception of the Purse Seine Category, the average weight of fish landed in 1989 again decreased over the previous year. One does not have to be a trained fishery Biologist to recognize that the number of older, larger giant Atlantic bluefin tuna have declined significantly and that younger, smaller fish are a growing percentage of the annual harvest.

A record number of permits were issued by the NMFS to land giant Atlantic Bluefin Tuna in 1989. 27,313 vessels were permitted. This is an increase of about 4 percent over the previous year and a whopping 148 percent increase since 1983 when approximately 11,000 vessels had permits to land fish. This past year there were over 6 times as many permit holders as there were giant bluefin tuna landed, a far cry from six years ago.

Let's take a quick look to see how these permits were dispersed: General Category; 25,466, Harpoon Category; 236, Incidental Category; 1,604, Purse Seine Category; 5.

However, in all fairness, not all permitted vessels may have entered the fishery last year and a good number of permit holders are suspected to be no longer fishing. If you plan on fishing for giant bluefin tuna this coming season, and you do not hold a federal fisheries permit, contact the National Marine Fisheries Service (NMFS) at:

> NMFS
> FEDERAL FISHERIES PERMIT OFFICE
> Northeast Region
> One Blackburn Drive
> Gloucester, Mass. 01930

The accompanying table summarizes some of the data presented by the 1989 NMFS giant Atlantic bluefin tuna report. On the basis of this latest information, a number of trends are evident:

(1) The number of NMFS permits issued annually continues to increase, undoubtedly due to the very high value of the fish in the overseas (Japan) market place. With dockside prices averaging $10.00 to $14.00 a pound, dressed weight, in late season, with some fish bringing as much as $30.00 a pound, the Japanese demand

has maintained a "fever" of catch effort and continues to draw new vessels into the fishery annually.

(2) Less there be any doubt in your mind, fishing for giant Atlantic bluefin tuna is being done under a moratorium, with the U.S. share presently 1,440 short tons. This quota allocation is for scientific data assessment purposes. For the fourth year in a row, quota attainment was not reached. For 1989, 1,306 of the allocated 1,440 short tons was landed for all Categories, basically as a result of vessels in the General Category failing to catch their alloted quota. In fact, only 516 tons of the allocated 650 tons (79%) was landed in this Category. Interestingly enough, the Harpoon Category was shy of its quota allotment by nearly 7 tons and the Incidental Category (longline) was shy by nearly 28 tons this past season.

(3) The Purse Seine Category continues to do very well at harvesting the allowable giant Atlantic bluefin tuna resource. In fact, since 1984 this Category has landed over one third of the tonnage quota annually. Over the last five years fishing was being done by only four or five permitted vessels, which enjoy licensing that allow them to create a significant impact on the western North Atlantic bluefin tuna stocks. This past year, the Purse Seine Category landed 36% of the total catch, down somewhat from last year as a result of a larger harvest by vessel in the General Category. For the first time since 1984 they landed a fish with a greater average weight of 537 pounds compared to the other Categories.

(4) For the fourth year in a row, vessels in the General Category failed to catch their alloted quota, however the trend of declining catch was reversed this past season, with a total of 753 more giant Atlantic bluefin tuna landed this year than last. All Divisions within this Category enjoyed a significant increase in landings when compared to the previous year. Handline landings increased 61%, rod and reel landings increased 47%, and harpoon landings increased over 65%. Keep in mind the General Category accounts for the greatest number of bluefin permits, approximately 93% of the total. Whether in the New York bight area or north of Cape Cod, attempts to land fish typically begin in June for permit holders and extends well into the Fall season. The summer of 1989 saw extended periods of excellent weather and this no doubt contributed to increased catch effort and subsequent increased landings.

(5) This season again saw the Harpoon Boat Category reaching near quota attainment earlier than ever. Approximately one month after fishing actively began here in New England, the 75 short ton quota was nearly reached on July 14th. Never before has this Category harvested their alloted quota in such a short period of time, although falling short by nearly 7 tons. Interestingly enough,

this frenzied effort occurs when the fish are ''lean'' and have relatively low economic value.

Asked why holders of Harpoon Boat permits don't wait until later in the season to take a somewhat more valuable fish, the common reply is ''someone else will beat 'em to it if they wait.'' Don't be surprised if this Category fails to see their alloted quota again next year, mainly as a result of the lag in reporting by fish buyers. Interestingly enough, if you combined the number of fish taken by both the Harpoon Boat Category and Harpoon Division of the General Category, for 1989, the numbers of total fish landed is second only to that by vessels in the Purse Seine Category. It appears that unless the use of aircraft for spotting fish for vessels in this Category is prohibited, this trend will continue.

(6) Not too many years ago, the most common technique for harvesting giant Atlantic bluefin tuna was rod and reel fishing. Basically with the chumming method, one waited for the fish to come to the bait, a passive technique with success due to high numbers of fish. Today, high levels of success are reached by those who actively search for fish, either with high speed vessels or aircraft.

(7) In 1989, the handliner and longliner continued to land a significantly larger fish than those caught by rod and reel. Basically their tackle is heavier and fish for longer periods of time, frequently employing refined antichaffing gear. This past season saw a closure of the Incidental Longline Category in the Gulf of Mexico in mid February, and that for the area north of 36⁰ N latitude in November. For whatever reasons, the allotted 145 short ton quota for this Category was not attained, falling short by approximately 22 tons.

(8) 1989 again witnessed a growing effort in landing medium sized bluefin of 130 to 310 pounds, largely from areas south of Cape Cod. A total of 1,585 fish with an average weight of 188 pounds were landed, primarily by rod and reel fishermen. Compared to the previous year, 1988, when only 625 fish were landed, this represents an increase of over 150 percent. Many conversations this past season by experienced anglers focused on the apparent increased numbers of this class of fish and continuing efforts to land them. This resulted in a closure in October of the fisheries for school and medium size fish. This created some confusion in the minds of many anglers, particularly as landings of giant Atlantic bluefin tuna remained open in the General Category. Although mediums have much less value per pound compared to a giant, their value is still significant, particularly when as many as four fish can be harvested daily by a permit holder. No doubt this catch effort increase was fueled by the continued relatively high dockside prices. It is obvious a

change in regulations is needed if the future of this fishery is to continue. Accelerated harvesting of this class of fish, which have yet to contribute to spawning stocks, as they are sexually immature, can only impact the future of this commercially valuable resource.

(9) As this is written, efforts are presently underway in Congress to include all tuna under the reauthorization of the Magnuson Act, popularly known as the 200 Mile Limit Act. As this Act is being amended, the House of Representatives has passed the resolution to include Tuna and we await the decision in the Senate. However, at the present time the responsibility of conserving and managing tuna stocks is in the hands of the International Commission for the Conservation of Atlantic Tuna (ICCAT). The decision reached at the last meeting in September of 1989 in Madrid, Spain was to again allow harvesting in 1990, without any quota change recommendations, for purposes of scientific monitoring. Should present trends in this fishery continue, this coming season should again see quota attainment being reached by late summer in all but the General Category and we can expect to see a continued decline in the average weight of fish landed, as older and heavier fish have declined in abundance.

Should the market value of this resource escalate to even higher levels in 1990, this will prompt an increase in cach efforts. With release of the NMFS landings data for giant Atlantic bluefin tuna this season, present trends can continue to be profiled. Those concerned with the future of the bluefin stay tuned...

1989 NMFS GIANT ATLANTIC BLUEFIN TUNA REPORT
SUMMARY TABLE

CATEGORY	NO. OF FISH	AVERAGE WEIGHT	PERCENTAGE
GENERAL:	2,054	503 lbs.	46%
HANDLINE	795	535 lbs.	18%
ROD & REEL	654	506 lbs.	15%
HARPOON	605	458 lbs.	14%
HARPOON:	308	441 lbs.	7%
INCIDENTAL:	487	514 lbs.	11%
LONGLINE			
NORTH	178	385 lbs.	
SOUTH	298	592 lbs.	
OTHER	2	468 lbs.	
PURSE SEINE:	1,583	537 lbs.	36%
TOTAL:	4,421	GIANT ATLANTIC BLUEFIN LANDED	
TOTAL:	1,585	MEDIUM ATLANTIC BLUEFIN LANDED	
GRAND TOTAL:	6,006		

1 THE BLUEFIN TUNA

Why All The Regulations?

Back in February of 1989, I attended the Atlantic Fisherman Expo at the Sheraton Islander Inn in Newport, Rhode Island. I had been invited to attend as a guest of the Atlantic Offshore Fisherman's Association, as I had authored a piece on giant bluefin tuna for their magazine and the previous year had given a seminar on tuna behavior. I was particularly interested in hearing the National Marine Fisheries Service (NMFS) persentation on bluefin tuna stock assessment and management by Dave Crestin, who is the Chief of the Fisheries Management Division. Because he was unable to attend, Kathi Rodrigues spoke in his place. She's been with NMFS for ten years and is currently responsible for managing the Atlantic bluefin tuna program.

In her presentation, she indicated the first attempt to put bluefin tuna under the endangered species act was in 1973. The attempt was unsuccessful and did not occur. Two years later, in 1975, the Atlantic Tuna Convention Act was passed. That legislation gave NMFS the authority to implement the recommendations of the International Commission for the Conservation of Atlantic Tuna (ICCAT). With ICCAT having existed for a number of years, the recommendation was made to limit fishing mortality to recent levels and prohibit the taking of juvenile young school bluefin under 14 pounds. Since then, bluefin tuna have been limited to catch quotas and season closures in the western North Atlantic.

The first thing NMFS did was implement quotas for the purse seiners, allowing them 1,100 tons of school tuna and 200 tons of giant tuna. All other categories shared a quota of 2,250 giants. Also, a limit of four school tuna per person per day was implemented, and is still in effect today.

The next year, with continued decline of the bluefin tuna stocks, ICCAT requested the U.S. reduce the quotas slightly. The purse seiners were reduced by 100 tons, giant tuna by 20 tons, school tuna by 100 tons and the General Category by 250 giant tuna. In light of what was to follow a few years later, those were only slight reductions and add virtually nothing to stem the tide of over-fishing.

Bag limits were established of one giant tuna per vessel per day, which is still in effect today. Back then, fishermen complained that the season didn't last long enough and there were still plenty of fish around when quota attainment ended. Fishermen wanted to see the season run the traditional time of June to October.

The year 1980 was a big one for regulations as an attempt was made to stop the development of a directed longline fishery. The reason behind this was that longlining was not a traditional, historical fishery for bluefin tuna. It was felt that longlining would increase the catch rate considerably and that was contrary to the ICCAT proposal of decreasing fishing effort and mortality.

Regulations in affect at that time allowed longliners to take two giant tuna per trip south of Hatteras and two percent by weight per trip north of Hatteras.

Further, a limit on the numbers of purse seiners in the fishery was established. Only those vessels in the fishery at that time would be allowed to fish, limiting the total number of seiners to five. Along with that, the tonnage of school fish in their quota was reduced.

Also in 1980, NMFS established a Harpoon boat category, allowing multiple fish catch. NMFS felt that these fishermen required optimal weather conditions to take fish and could not, therefore, take fish on a daily basis.

In 1982 the "roof caved in" and a moratorium was recommended as a result of the four-fold drop in fish stocks which occurred since the 1960s and early 1970s. The quota for the U.S. prior to the moratorium was 2,393 tons and was now reduced to 667 tons of bluefin tuna. This was a drastic reduction and NMFS eliminated the purse seine category quota, allowing, however, for an incidental catch. The allocation for the General Category quota was reduced to 310 tons, which happens to be slightly under what is being caught today.

In 1983, ICCAT decided the U.S. moratorium quota was insufficient to monitor the status of the bluefin stock because too few fish were caught to tell what was going on with the stocks. As a result, a recommendation was made to basically double the existing quota, but still with a moratorium. With that, the tuna seiner came back.

That's the situation today and many people simply do not realize they are fishing under a moratorium. The U.S. share is presently

WEST ATLANTIC BLUEFIN TUNA CATCH (MT)
estimated from ICCAT catch at length

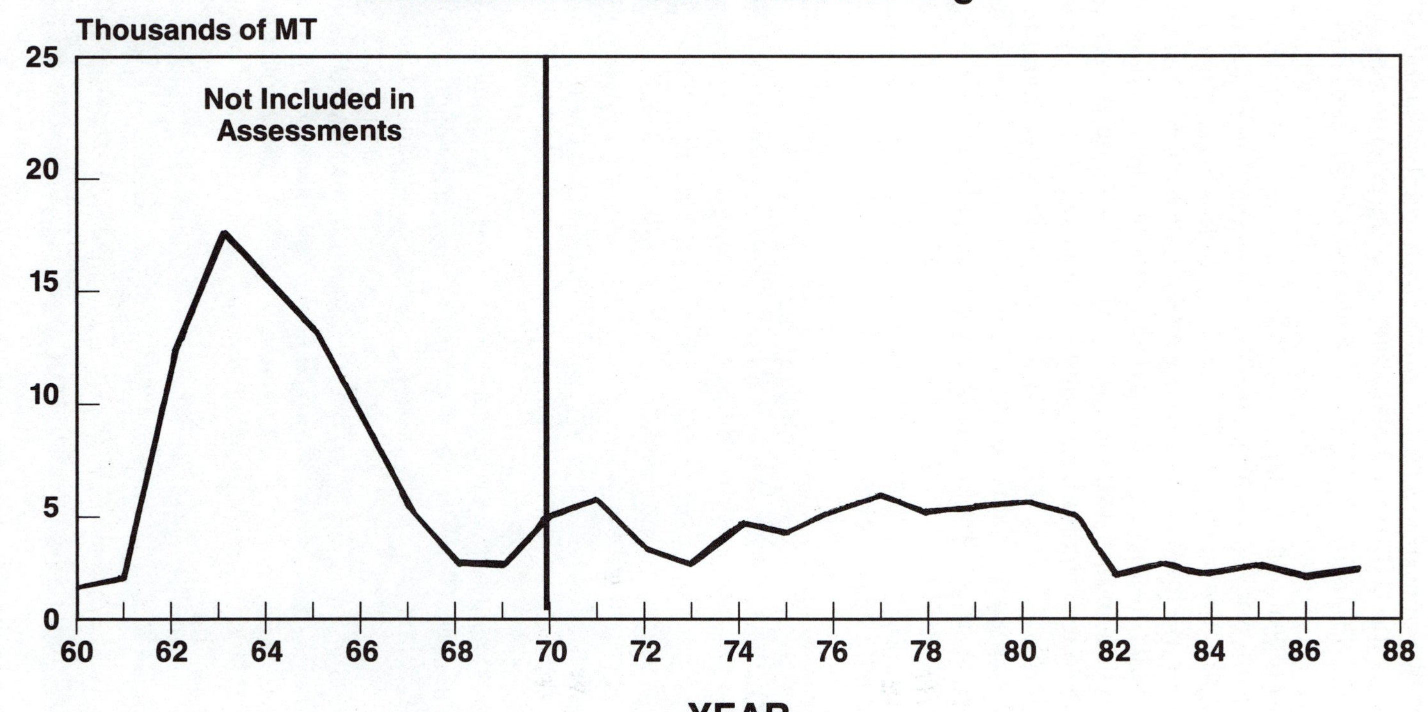

1,520 tons and that quota allocation is for scientific data assessment. Since the late 1970s, the prevailing scientific opinion suggests the U.S. should be fishing as near as possible to zero.

During her presentation, Kathi Rodrigues showed several NMFS graphs on various age groups of Atlantic bluefin tuna. Those graphs are reproduced here.

One doesn't have to be a trained fishery biologist to see that in Figure 1, Atlantic bluefin tuna aged 10 to 30 years, the stocks of older fish have been in decline since the mid 1970s and today are in serious trouble. The line drawn between 1985 and 1986 indicates caution should be used with this information as these last years are the least reliable data points in a population analysis. However, allowing that the information is accurate, it appears the population of Atlantic bluefin tuna ages 10 to 30 in 1988 was only 26 percent of that in the early 1970s. If the proposed NMFS theory of sexual maturity of Atlantic bluefin tuna at age 10 is accurate, then since the early 1970s the spawning population has been reduced by approximately 74 percent.

This early 1950s photo shows large numbers of schooled adult bluefin, which unfortunately are not seen today.

ATLANTIC BLUEFIN TUNA
AGES 10-30
Thousands
160
140
120
100
80
60
40
20
0
70 71 72 73 74 75 76 77 78 79 80 81 82 83 84 85 86 87 88
YEAR
NUMBER OF FISH

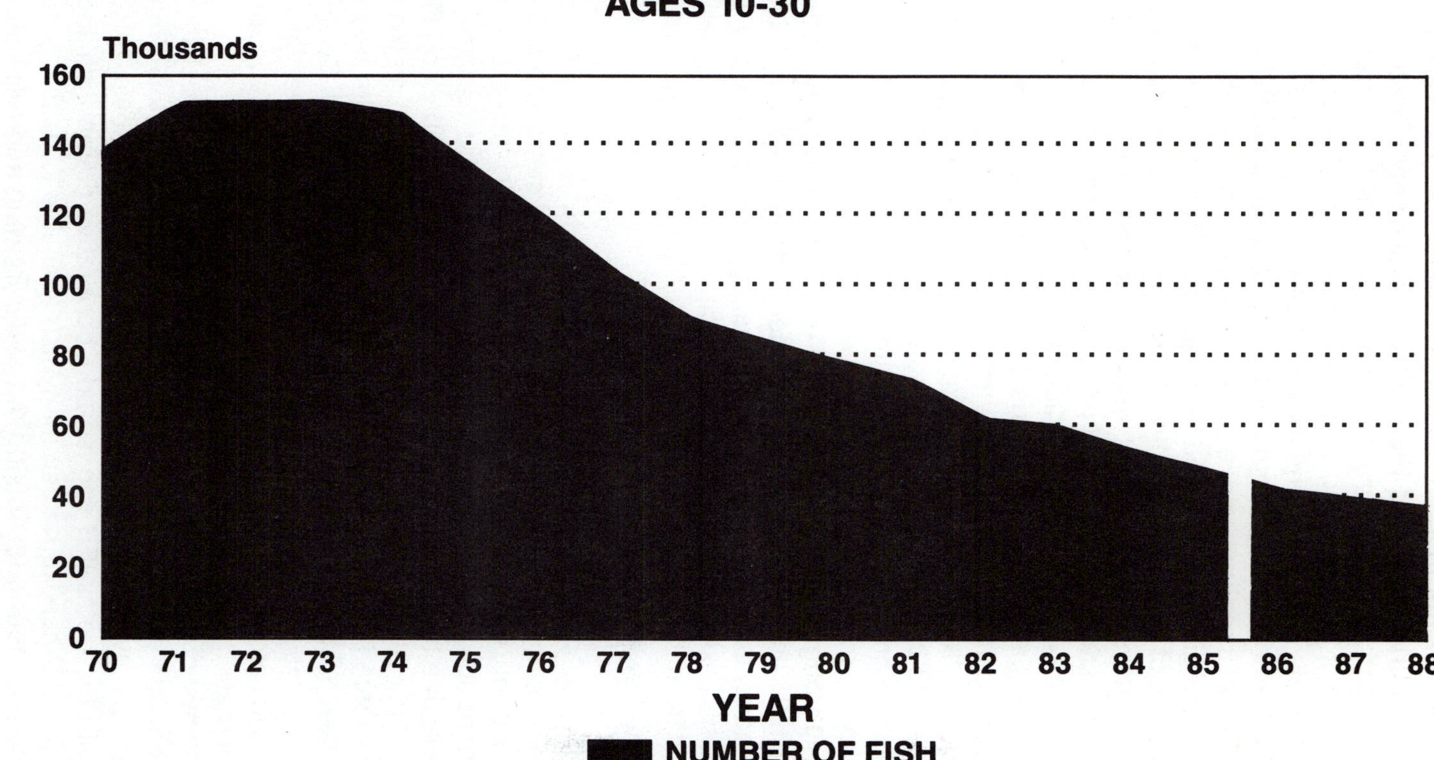

Figure No. 1

In Figure 2, Atlantic bluefin tuna aged 6 to 9 years, those fish we classify as medium bluefin, appear to have reached a low point in number during 1982 and 1983. In those years, only 33 percent of the population of that age group existed compared to the period 1969 and 1970. It is interesting to note the drastic decline in number of medium sized fish over the four-year period 1978 to 1982.

On the bright side, there appears to be a slight increase in the number of mediums since 1986. However, with a decline in the number of giants, it's a good bet attention will turn to harvesting this age class of fish, particularly if the demand and price paid by tuna buyers stays high. Present regulations allow the taking of four medium sized fish per vessel per day, so the potential for reduction in the number of this class of fish is high.

Figure 3, Atlantic bluefin tuna ages 1 to 5 years, shows that this age group represents the greatest number of bluefin tuna in existence. If the latest stock assessment figures are accurate, there appears to be over 300,000 animals, based on 1987 figures, in the western North Atlantic. These animals represent the future of the fishery and regulations to conserve and manage the stocks must carry through with this class of fish until sexual maturity occurs.

In 1981 and 1982, the data provided indicates a low point in the number of school Atlantic bluefin tuna, approximately 19 percent of what had existed in 1970. This 80 percent reduction could very well result from the decline in spawning fish. Since 1982, the data is encouraging, and suggests a rebound in the number of school size fish. One, of course, asks how this is possible with the continued decline of supposedly sexually mature fish. Much of the stock assessment data comes from the recreational sector (so called) of the fishing industry and since the early 1980s there has been tremendous increase in the popularity of offshore fishing in our waters due to the increased availability of longfin albacore, (Thunnus alalunga) and yellowfin tuna (Thunnus albacores). In the summer months, school bluefin tuna traditionally work their way up to the New York bight area and waters south of Cape Cod. Could it be this increase in offshore tuna fishing effort has resulted in an increased catch rate of school bluefin tuna, creating the appearance of increased numbers of young bluefin?

Interestingly enough, in 1981, one of the years that stock levels of school Atlantic bluefin tuna reached a recent all-time low, I managed to talk my clients into tagging and releasing well over 70 school bluefin for the NMFS sponsored Cooperative Game Fish Tagging Program. Since we had so many fish available to us that summer, many days found us limiting out early. Tagging and releasing was one way to extend the fishing day.

ATLANTIC BLUEFIN TUNA
AGES 6-9

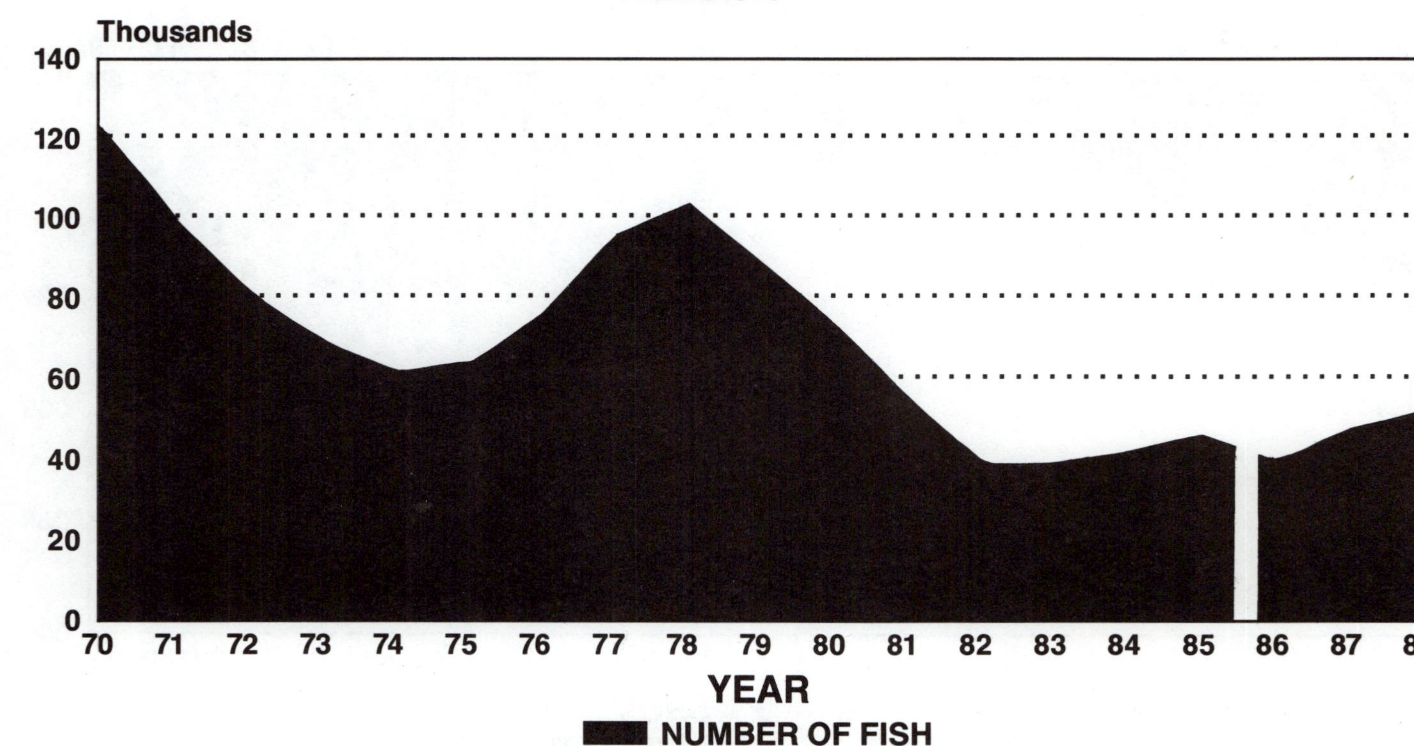

Figure No. 2

ATLANTIC BLUEFIN TUNA
AGES 1-5

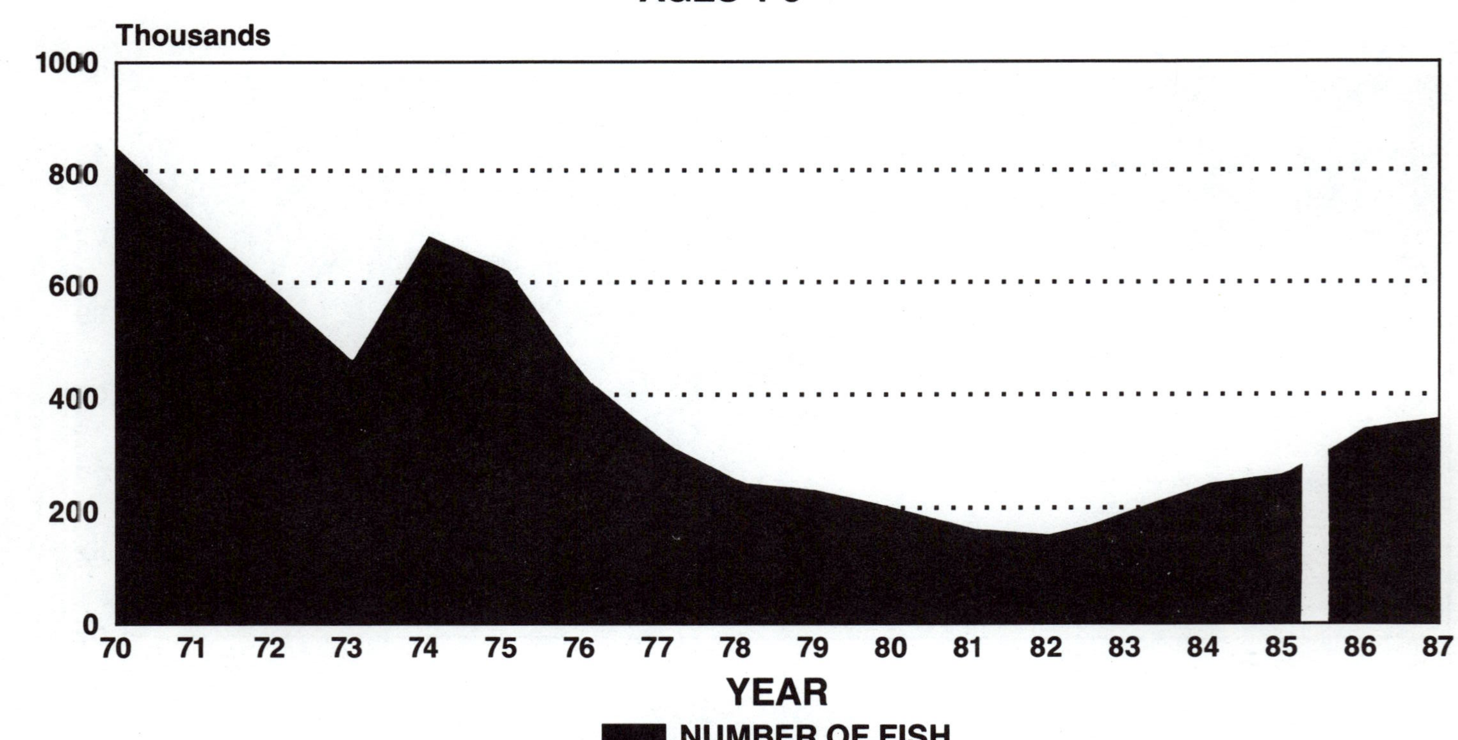

Figure No. 3

Before you are quick to question the accuracy of stock assessment figures, I must mention that I was of the opinion we were fishing on the "mother load," as talking with numerous other charter captains fishing other areas indicated little or no success with bluefin that size. Hard to believe, I'm sure, but was it possible most of the school fish that season in our area were swimming in just one spot?

With no changes scheduled for the bluefin quotas monitored by NMFS, it is doubtful the 2,660 metric tonnage quota set by ICCAT will be reached, the 6th year in a row. Under the present regulations, it appears impossible for the bluefin stocks to increase. Instead, we may see a collapse in the spawning population, which could lead to a severe reduction in recruitment fish for as long as a decade or more.

The present quota for "scientific monitoring" simply allows continued fishing for profit and assists with stock assessment only by profiling the continuing decline of this resource.

BASS
TUNA

2 SPORT FISHING FOR BLUEFIN TUNA

Some Opinions And Insights

My charter fishing career spans a good number of years and as a result I've had the opportunity to make some observations regarding changing attitudes by those who giant tuna fish. For some in the charter fishing industry, as these fish became more valuable, there was a tendency to place a higher value on the fish than on the client booking the boat. In most cases, it depended on how busy or how many bookings a boat captain had, as well as whether they had an inshore or offshore oriented business. It mattered little if the party was satisfied and returned to fish another day. Instead, focus was on the excitement and glamour of catching a giant bluefin and its financial reward.

Little thought was given to the increasing competition on the fishing grounds due to escalating fish value. Nor to the rapidly decreasing resource and the vagaries of haphazard bait supply, fish movements and the ever changing weather.

However, before I initiate criticism and am accused of having a holier than thou attitude, I must confess to going along with several widely accepted policy changes and activities that developed in the last few years. Let's take a look at what has happened as seen through my eyes.

In the early 1970s, with a newly built charter boat, I purchased various tackle and equipment to expand the range of fishing activities I could make available to my clients. Prior to this time I was fishing almost exclusively for striped bass. This new tackle for school, medium and giant bluefin was purchased for the fun and enjoyment of the customer in my rapidly growing business of charter fishing.

Compared to today, many captains just entering the charter business have purchased tackle and equipment directly for the catch and sale of these fish. This usually prompts the frequently asked question, "If we catch a tuna, who gets to keep it?" Certainly a valid question, and some charter boats have a policy of keeping all the tuna boated; schoolies, mediums and giants.

Being familiar with the operation of several local tackle shops, it's no surprise major changes have occurred in this business as a result of escalating tuna prices. Simply put, tuna tackle is no longer purchased just for fun but for making serious profit as well. In the last few years, landings of giant bluefin tuna have fallen severly but tuna tackle sales continue as never before due to the growing popularity of offshore fishing and the sale of other tuna species. Expensive items such as a complete bent butt outfit can be readily paid for by the sale of tuna, especially a giant bluefin. With the tremendous demand for hooks, line, lures, leader material, rods, reels, harnesses, gaffs and harpoons, some tackle shops have almost forsaken the general angler and now specialize in tuna equipment. Retail sales have skyrocketed in this realm, with many shops becoming specialized havens to the profit minded rod and reel fisherman.

Were it not for the monies handed over in the sale of giant bluefin tuna, and tuna in general, retail boat sales along some parts of the coast would have nowhere near the profits earned today. A long-time friend in the manufacturing and retail sportfishing boat buiness has time and again indicated the purchase of his boat for potential profit making, as well as fun and enjoyment-frequently in that order of priority.

In fact, advertisements by a major boat manufacturer promoted the catch and sale of tuna as a means to pay for boat and fishing expenses! This Michigan boat manufacturer seized the concept of profit making and employed "tuna hysteria" in its advertising sales pitch. On the flip side of the coin, another major boat manufacturer, based in Florida, uses advertising to urge commercial and sport fishing interests focus on management and conservation of fishery resources so that future generations can continue to utilize the resources. I personally favor the attitude of the latter manufacturer as they want to continue the concept of fishing and boating. As I see it, it's a question of large, short-term gain at the expense of the fish, versus smaller, long-term gain with some promise for the future in the latter case.

Getting back to the local charter fishing industry. There was once little or no value for a giant bluefin prior to the late 1970s, except at tournament time. As such, a few fish went home with the party on the roof of the car, tied in place and displayed much like a "buck" taken during hunting season. Other fish stowed in the trunk of car threatened to dislodge the exhaust system of the saging vehicle over bumpy roads. And in these cases, the odor of fish pervaded the car's interior for months to come, forcing the sale of a vehicle in one known instance.

In the late 1970s, if fish sale monies were earned, many boats had developed policies regarding distribution. These policies varied from boat to boat but I think it accurate to say most of the local boats allowed the party a substantial share in the earnings. Some of the boats advertised the day's fishing would be cost free if a giant tuna was boated but it seemed they rarely caught a fish.

Boat policies changed annually as the fish became increasingly valuable. Much of the VHF radio chit chat at times focused on this topic. Today, most boats keep giant bluefin, with each boat setting various limits on the monies a party would be entitled to should a fish be sold.

To me, it was surprising how many charter boat captains pushed their customers into a day of giant tuna fishing even though chances of success seemed very slim. I considered it poor business sense to come home at day's end with an alienated group following a no-bite day. In fact, some captains took their party fishing for giant bluefin tuna whether they wanted to or not, simply because of the potentially immediate financial reward. I can still vividly recall some of those early morning dockside conversations (arguments) between a boat's crew and party concerning the day's activities. Needless to say, certain businesses suffered badly with this attitude, although they managed to catch and sell a few fish.

Those captains assumed the attitude there would always be new customers to replace those taken advantage of, with only little thought toward their business reputation.

In the commercial as well as the private sector, many people believed the payments for their new boat could be achieved by the sale of giant bluefin tuna. In fact, I know a number of individuals who firmly believed this and today are either no longer in the charter business or no longer own their boat.

Like many other charter boat captains, if I had an unscheduled day, I too could be found on the grounds with a few friends looking for a bite from a giant in the hopes of supplementing charter fishing income. Some charter boats went so far as to chase after giant bluefin following the day's inshore fishing with tales of taking a fish after daylight ended. Fortunately for them, several fish buyers were still on the docks late into the evening processing fish taken earlier in the day.

Imagine, if you can, finding yourself on a charter boat you and several friends have hired for a day's outing. Having been talked into trying for a giant tuna, a strike comes, and it's our turn in the chair. Your dreams have suddenly come true and now it's you against the fish. Or so you thought. In the chair, harnessed to the rod, it's a situation new to you and you do your best to follow the inappropriate coaching offered. In short time you become exhausted and you find yourself being ordered out of the fighting chair by the captain. Quickly the mate is in the chair and his experience allows him to make rapid progress in the fight. A short time later this captain harpoons the fish and it is quickly tail roped. Little did you know this scenario had happened time and again on this boat and was planned by the crew in advance. As a result, you and your party are denied a portion of the fish sale monies. Thoroughly disgusted, you vow never to go fishing again.

Let me hasten to add that I do not wish to infer this was common practice among the charter fleet. The majority of captains I know demonstrated considerable integrity in the face of temptation and did their best to provide a positive, exciting and truly rewarding (no pun intended) fishing experience to their clients. Yet some boat captains, as previously explained, took advantage and wound up with a law suit on their hands. This has prompted many innocent boats to issue a printed boat contract to their parties requiring one's signature to cover the disposition of fish (tuna) boated in excess of stated weight. As I indicated earlier, some parties were taken advantage of and responded by taking legal action. Whether the contract issued would hold up in a court of law or not, it demonstrates the extent to which giant bluefin tuna fishing has gone in some areas.

Not too many years back, with a giant on and close to the transom, the fly gaffs were made ready by the crew. Not so today. Instead, the harpoon is made ready and used at the first opportunity. If chance allows, a fish may be taken earlier in the struggle lessening the change of fish loss due to frayed line or leader. In fact, a local welding company is well-known for its take-apart aluminum stick for in-boat storage with the forward section working very well as a cockpit harpoon. Bringing a fish close enough to gaff increases the chance of fish loss due to rudders, chines or propellers and is now done only when tournament rules mandate it.

As the number of giant tuna tournaments grew and with each year witnessing the fish becoming more and more valuable, it was not uncommon to hear of tournament rule infractions. The growing price paid for fish tempted some into ignoring the rules and regulations while others simply quit tournament fishing for the sake of the financial reward. It seemed the monies earned far out stripped any award given. In the late 1970s, tournament officials quickly realized that to prevent a boat from keeping a fish meant a severe reduction in the number of entrants. Today, most tournaments take a percentage of the fish sale monies earned (donated) with the remainder going to the boat. Monies accrued over and above that for operating expenses by the tournament are then donated to a charity of choice.

Being involved with several major tuna tournaments, I've heard dockside gossip of crews handlining a fish following rod breakage, double lines blatantly exceeding IGFA specifications, lines testing well in excess of 130 pound test, chumming well before the start of the day's fishing time, as well as harpoon use. One thing for sure, I would not want to be a member of the committee concerned with official protests. Validating a rule infraction, especially if it may disqualify one of only a few fish taken and thereby reduce the tournament success, would certainly create a furor of bad publicity within the aggregate of contestants, as well as the angling community. Some tournament officials might simply turn their heads rather than confront this difficult problem today. It's a sad situation, and one of the reasons I choose to no longer remain active on tuna tournament committees or fish for giant bluefin in the tournament arena.

Many times I've seen a boat arrive at the dock following a day's fishing with a giant in the cockpit obviously in very poor condition with numerous holes, torn flesh, bruised and soft sided, decorated with bottom paint from hanging tail roped off a side cleat. Obviously not export quality and what develops is an argument between buyer and crew as to offered sale price. What comes next is usually a threat to take the fish to another buyer with potential future boycott. Today's marketing by consignment has reduced this scenario and caused many fishermen to focus on the quality of their catch when brought dockside.

On the other hand, a tuna buyer might make a supply of fresh, choice hook bait available to a boat that consistently brings in a fish of good or high quality to ensure continued profit. Many would consider this to be good business strategy. In fact, many routine hook and line boats selling fish to a particular buyer go so far as to demand it on a regular basis.

Back in the "dark ages" of giant tuna fishing, if a boat fighting a fish neared another anchored boat, it was considered sportsmanlike to get off the ground tackle to give the fish-fighting boat all the room necessary. Today, that spirit of consideration is disdained as it disrupts fishing aboard the boat giving way. The loss of fishing time raises the fear of failure to get a strike with the potential loss of considerable sums of fish money. So, with a fish on, particularly in a fleet of boats, the chances of losing it on an anchor line of another

A poorly handled giant bluefin tuna taken from the Butterfish Hole in the early 1970s. Notice the torn flesh damage done by the flying gaff. This fish would not be considered prime export quality.

Medium bluefin tuna lying on the dock with gaff holes in their sides, bruised and soft sides and baking in direct sunlight. By the time the buyer arrives these fish will be almost worthless.

boat are high. Today, one must resign one's self to this situation.

A few years back fishing south of Nomans Island, at what is called The Claw, I had the opportunity to witness something I wasn't quite ready for. I had been trolling mackerel chains with only a bluefish bite for excitement. In among the finback whales a random trolling boat would get a strike or put a fish on but action was very limited for the number of boats assembled. Then it happened, a large pod of fish erupted, busting on the surface and the race was on. Boats converged en mass from all directions on this group of fish. To describe it mildly it was a "free-for-all." We were close enough to see outriggers clash, then bend, trolling daisy chains hastily deployed almost immediately cut clean off, harpoons launched as well as wheelhouse glass shatter with the affronting pulpit bent askew. Numerous threats of murder issued from the VHF radio with possibly two fish taken. Fortunately for some, those fish never showed again the rest of the day.

Today, vessels in the Harpoon and General Categories routinely contract with light spotter aircraft to locate pods of pushing giant bluefin, perhaps with several cooperating vessels splitting the hire of the aircraft as the potential earnings can more than easily cover the costs. Actively searching for fish now goes on daily from a vessels bridge or tower as well as from the air when conditions allow.

At times, one hears scuttlebutt about a boat suspected of boats taking a fish or two above the daily quota allowed by NMFS, rumors of a fish transferred from one boat to another, or of a second boat taking a stuck fish, or of a fish tied to a sea buoy and retrieved later by another boat. No doubt some of these stories might be accurate but strong enforcement and severe fines by NMFS in earlier years has dampened the enthusiasm of many for any such activities. As one local boat owner has stated, ''You stand to lose a heck of a lot more than you might gain.''

Earlier this year, over the VHF radio certain local giant tuna fishermen complained that the fisheries will soon come to an end if stronger conservation measures are not taken. They argued that spotter aircraft no longer be permitted in the fishery, and that the tuna seiners be prohibited from fishing Cape Cod Bay. They agreed such activities would interfere with, and reduce, their chances of catching and selling a fish in the coming season while fishing there. No doubt dollar signs have created their hypocritical reasoning.

This spring, early run giant bluefin had only little monetary value (compared to late season fish) on the export market. Fish buyers indicated these fish had little or no fat content and hence simply did not bring a high price. It was interesting to listen on the VHF radio to certain, obviously affluent, fishermen state their refusal to go fishing for them. Not in the name of conservation mind you, but simply because the fish paid so little it wasn't worthwhile. To them it seemed senseless to go fishing if they couldn't turn a profit in the sale of a fish.

Most of the attitudes commonly held by those fishing for giant bluefin today have resulted from the fish becoming quite valuable. Fishing techniques and state of the art equipment change, usually for the better. Attitudes change too, but not always for the better, particularly when large sums of money are involved. Today, more so than ever before, the ugly specter of greed and profit has come to strongly modify common attitudes as well as influence the future of the resource. How can there be any possible future for this resource when a single large fish is so valuable?

In the following parts of this chapter, let's take a journey back in time to some of the greats of bluefin tuna fishing.

2 SPORT FISHING FOR BLUEFIN TUNA

Captain Dick Lema: Tackle Innovations

When the idea of putting together a book on bluefin tuna fishing came to mind, Captain Dick Lema was high on the list of people to talk to for information that would blend the old traditions of yesterday with the new realities of today's fishing. As an active charter and private boat captain for many years, he was certainly qualified to comment on the changes that have occurred over the years near his home fishing grounds of Rhode Island. Today he is semi-retired but still sharp as ever. On the morning of our interview he was familiarizing himself with a new computer software program that allowed for the design of boat hulls. Dick was responsible for the development of several well known sport fishing boat designs such as Lema Boats, Bonito Boats and the famous Rampage Yachts.

Anderson: Over the years, you've been privy to progressive changes in tackle, techniques, electronic and other gear for tuna fishing. What was the first thing you felt greatly improved one's chances of catching a big fish?

Lema: One of the greatest things was good line. I say that because we used to fish with linen line. Boy, I tell you, the least little thing wrong, the line broke. When nylon came into play, that really helped, as it withstood the elements. Linen line was good when it was brand new but get freshwater on it and it just rotted. In my mind that was the first thing that helped a lot of people catch fish because before that they would get them on and then break them off. I did that myself lots of times.

Then, of course, was the use of lighter leaders. Back then, Murray Cianciolo was using 400 pound test aircraft cable with heavy sleeves and big swivels. He caught a lot of fish but then we started fishing lighter gear. For a number of years I had used 250 pound test Sevenstrand, and did well with that. Until one day on Nebraska Shoal the **Nika** out of Montauk came along and laid next to me, inside the buoy. Within a half hour they had a fish on, fought it and released it. They came back and a half hour later they're on again. Well, that's making me look bad so I call over and ask what they are using. The reply is #12 stainless wire (174 pound test).

Reluctantly I changed leaders and put number 12 wire on and five minutes later we're hooked up. From that day on I continued to use #12 wire and enjoyed quite a few hookups.

I recall that John Walton, who was very interested in tuna and doing a lot of sharking, was having trouble hooking up on a fish. He asked what I was using, as his #15 and #17 wasn't working. After that he started hooking fish like crazy but would then lose them. He'd hook up, be on for three of four minutes, then bam, the fish was gone. He would do this again and again. Finally I went over and asked him what the heck he was doing. He said he was using #10 wire (124 pound test).

"Boy, they sure hit on that," he told me. "Yeah, they hit on that, but what do you do about catching them?" I asked.

"I don't care, as long as I hook 'em," he replied. "I'm going to let 'em go anyway."

So you saw a progressive change from aircraft cable to single strand wire and then finally to mono for leader material. The first mono available to us for tuna fishing was 130 pound test. Got it from a friend in Lauderdale, and did we get strikes. Monofilament line was the greatest tool at that time, particularly straight to the hook. But, if the fish wasn't hooked in the corner, or hinge, you'd be out of business real quick, as that pound test didn't last too long in the fish's mouth.

When the heavier monos became available, some would have very strong memory and coil up like a big spring. We had to play tricks to get a bite on it, like using it after we dumped ground chum overboard, sort of hiding it.

Anderson: Correct me if I'm wrong, but it seems that back in the 1950s most people going out to catch tuna fish did so for the fun of it, instead of doing so for the money.

Lema: No one ever went tuna fishing (giant) before the time of the tournament. People didn't want to spend the money for bait, fuel, etc. The few that did, maybe did so to warm up on a fish or two. Those that *did went for the sport of it or the fun of it, or for the prestige. That was nice. Keep in mind the fish had little or no value. I'm not absolutely sure, but I think it was the 1956 United States Atlantic Tuna Tournament in Galilee where they had over 30 fish (giants) hanging from the fish stands, many fish being there for several days for photographic purposes. Imagine trying to do that these days?*

Anderson: What changes do you recall happening to the fisheries in the 1960s?

*Lema: I was the first one in Rhode Island to fish the draggers. I had a client from New Jersey named Andy Russo who loved giant tuna fishing and he wanted to start fishing in June. As far as I knew, we had fish in our area but just couldn't do anything with them. Come early August we started fishing Nebraska Shoals. One day, it was so calm, you could see a sardine if it jumped out of the water a mile away. We hadn't done anything, absolutely nothing, so I suggested to Andy that we go into the Sound to find Joe Whaley, who would typically be surrounded by a million and four birds, cutting the heads off whiting caught earlier that day on his dragger. After a short run we pull up along side the **Virginia Marise** and Joe is in the wheelhouse.*

"Hey Joe, seen any tuna lately?" I asked.

"Yeah, I sure did," he answered. "About two weeks ago one jumped right out of the water in front of me."

As I'm talking to him, sitting on the fly bridge which is about the same height as his deck house, I'm watching his son David cutting heads off the fish. A short while later he shovels them off the side of the dragger and I see a big boil next to the boat. I don't say anything, but then I see another boil, this time behind the boat.

"Hey Joe, does your wheel ever turn at idle?" I asked.

"What the heck's the matter with you, Dick?" he retorted. "I couldn't have a boat like that, the gear would get caught in the wheel."

"Ok, I just asked you, that's all," I muttered.

I jumped down off the bridge into the cockpit and hollered to Dave to throw me a whiting. That's all he had to hear. A barrage of whiting come flying at me, weighing a pound, pound and a half, thrown so hard they splattered. Got a real big whiting, hooked it on, told Andy to get into the chair and still ducking fish, slowly put the bait down. About the time the 15 foot leader was completely in the water, we're on.

I jumped up to the bridge and hollered to Joe: "Show you a tuna fish in a little while."

Then we took off after the fish that went right under his boat. But we got lucky and boated it about a half hour later; it weighed about 500 pounds.

Captain Dick Lema's Bonita, which he built by himself. He used it for harpooning and rod and reel fishing. Here Dick is hoisting a giant Atlantic bluefin tuna taken from Rhode Island Sound in 1963.

We came back to the dragger to show Joe the fish just as he was finishing up for the day. We laid to, cutting the extra whiting into little pieces but nothing happened. So we put a bait out, on a float, maybe forty or fifty feet from the boat. We might have chummed a total of twenty pieces, and we're on again. We promptly lost that fish.

The rest of that era, if someone wanted to tangle with a giant, as we were school tuna fishing almost daily, I'd come in early from offshore and try to find Joe Whaley. We'd wait until he pulled back on the net, take a couple of whiting, set 'em in, and just like that, we'd be on. Some of the other charter boats, after coming back to the dock from a day's school tuna fishing would ask: "Where did you catch that fish?" My reply was usually, "Well, you saw me out there." But I didn't want anyone to know about fishing behind a dragger, as I wanted to milk it for all I could, which I did.

That is until one foggy day. Having found Joe Whaley out of the four or five draggers fishing along the ninety foot bank to the west, we were just selling up when Bob Meloccaro comes out of the fog aboard his boat.

"Hey Dick, what are you doing?" he asked.

"Just getting some bait, that's all Bob," I answered.

*Well, I took off, 'cause I didn't want him to know what I'm doing. But I'm sure he already had a good idea of what was going on. Found another dragger, the **David D**, by shutting down and listening for the chain coming aboard as they were hauling back. I got in under the **David D**, got some bait quick and set two lines over. Here comes Bob Meloccaro again, and needless to say, I'm steaming mad. About three minutes later the **Joka** shows up with the Caturos aboard. So I picked up and took off, trying to find Joe Whaley and the **Virginia Marise** again. It was then I realized I couldn't play hide and seek with the first boats in our area with radar. That's when the word got out how I was catching my fish. When tournament time came, all the guys that had draggers cursed the heck out of it, because the tournament boats interfered with their fishing. The first day of the tournament I didn't go near a dragger, for that reason. That was great fishing, boy oh boy, never like that again.*

Anderson: You saw attitudes change in the 1970s when fish started to become valuable.

Lema: Sure. Many of us were fishing for the fun of it and enjoying the small reward in dollars and cents if we caught a fish. But it escalated and people were out there just for the money. The more I saw of that, the more I disliked it. Everybody and his brother who had a boat were going tuna fishing to make money. After a while it got to be that very prominent people, millionaires in fact, came down and asked what tuna were paying, as they were undecided about going fishing. That was the point in time I got very upset with the whole situation. Friends, people I've known for a long time, I'd tell 'em off. I'd ask them what difference does it make if they're paying 25 cents or two dollars? With all your money, what difference does it make? People's attitudes changed, and if they went fishing and didn't come back with a tuna, they were overly depressed.

It got so bad that the first year we built the 31-foot Rampage I didn't want to go out fishing. We had two boats in the water and Everett Pearson said let's go. My son Roger was with me and we both caught tuna. But that's the day I quit giant tuna fishing. It was such a hassle out there, people so hungry that sportsmanship simply didn't exist. If a boat had a fish on, the other boats could care less and simply wouldn't move out of the way. I guess that if they moved, they felt they'd lose their shot at making a thousand or fifteen hundred dollars. Not only were they not going to move, some people would maneuver along side and fish right on top of you. It was a shame, but that was it for me.

Anderson: What effect did the development of modern marine electronics have on our tuna fishing?

With Jerusalem, RI in the background, the Bonita is backing into the bulkhead in Galilee to weigh in a giant Atlantic bluefin tuna during the 1963 USATT.

Lema: Depth finders, or fish finders were a big, big help, along with Loran A and C. All the years I fished, I ran the sounder all the time. I could keep track of where I was by watching the depth of the water. Lots of times, however, I wasn't quite sure where I thought I was. And of course, it helped us to see bait and fish, especially when those bunches of fish years ago were south of Block Island. You would know immediately what depth they were at and you could get a bait to that depth. Then, it was only a matter of them deciding to eat.

Anderson: Do you feel modern day electronics helped spell the rapid decline of the resource?

Lema: No doubt in my mind it contributed greatly. Take Loran C, for example. With it everybody and their brother could find a spot easily. There was no need for that sixth sense, as we called it years ago. With today's equipment if so and so was on a fish, you got a set of numbers and could be on that spot sometime later in the day. With that piece of equipment you didn't have to be on the water every day to find the area the fish were.

A few years back smart guys, when chumming, would use a hand-held transducer, maybe out on a stick, to see fish on the machine, like how far down or behind the boat. He told them how far to put out the lines. That was a little trick I had for a few years, but before that I used a 'feeler line'. Real light mono, piece of bait on it. Get a strike, have a

Captain Dick Lema (L) and Frank Iadevaia (R) during the 1963 USATT. This 773 pound giant bluefin tuna was one of many hooked up that day. This year's tournament had a lot of large fish breaking lines and tackle.

good idea where in the chum slick the fish were swimming. No question, with the electronics we have today, the fish don't have a chance.

I used to have a saying, "Fish, women and horses. When they won't, they won't." But with the electronics we have today, the fish don't have a chance, as we can almost force them to bite. Finding the fish, getting chum to that level, offering a hook bait at their level, it's like creating a hatch. Sooner or later one fish will respond and you'll get a bite.

With the seiners, aircraft and electronics give them the upper hand, no doubt. No way a school of fish can get away. It's a matter of following the fish long enough until they are in the water depth that allows them to make a successful set.

Anderson: Do you think there were fish (giants) years ago in June, July and August?

Lema: When I first started working for Paul Leviten, who owned the **Little Pete**, a 53-foot Rybovich, we'd get back to Rhode Island from Florida in late May. He wanted swordfish, so some days we'd run along at 20 knots looking for a swordfish. Never slow the boat down, except when we couldn't tell if it was a shark or swordfish. If you can imagine, I had to wear a ski mobile suit in the tower, as it got so cold. Many times in early June, going to the Southeast (Dumping Grounds), we'd see giant tuna, sometimes one or two, other times big schools, underwater.

Paul was interested only in swordfish, so we never fished for them. This was in June, and all summer long we would see fish, until we quit in early September. The biggest majority of fish were from the Southeast corner of The Dump to the 25 Fathom Bank southeast of the Star. As I recall, it seemed there were always schools of fish in that area.

2 SPORT FISHING FOR BLUEFIN TUNA

Captain Bob Linton: Rhode Island Tuna History

Anyone who's spent time actively saltwater fishing in Rhode Island waters has either met or knows of Captain Bob Linton. He retired from active charter fishing aboard the **Mako II** in 1987. He's said many times, "I've seen it all," so naturally, if I wanted to profile the early days of rod and reel bluefin tuna fishing he was one person I had to talk to. A while back, I had the opportunity to sit with him and ask a few questions about years ago.

Anderson: When did you first start tuna fishing, Bob?

Linton: It was back in 1948. I was doing an awful lot of striped bass fishing and Frank Iadevaia was a regular customer. One day he said let's go over to Block Island and see if we can catch a few school tuna. We stayed overnight and the next morning headed for the old Fairway Buoy, southeast of Southeast Light. We didn't go too far and we had our first school bluefin tuna. I think we ended up with 15 fish that day. Imagine, the only gear I had was surf casting rods loaded with linen line, as nylon was still a few years away.

Surprisingly, offshore fishing then was pretty well developed, particularly out of Montauk and New London. A few charter boats and lots of private boats, some from Block Island. With quite a few school tuna around. All it took was for one boat to catch a fish and a sizable fleet would build up, maybe a total of 25 to 30 boats, particularly on weekends.

That first year, I didn't have a radio, so I couldn't talk with other boats.

"

Anderson: What did your customers do with the fish they caught?

Linton: Back then, people took them. It was rare when a few fish were left for the boat. There was really no strong market for the fish and the price paid was very, very low. Most of the time, if you tried to sell them, the markets didn't want any. For a good sized fish, you'd be lucky to get 11 cents, and that was a good price. With smaller fish, maybe 3 cents to 5 cents. And, that was after you headed and gutted them, sawed the fins off, washed them out, unloaded them and cleaned them. I didn't like to kill them but I certainly loved to catch them. If we took a lot of fish, it meant an extra two or three hours of work to unload them at the Pt. Judith Fisherman's Co-op and it meant a check for only $20 to $25. For that reason I was always undecided whether to catch them or not.

Anderson: How did people feel about tuna in those days?

Linton: I'm not sure about others but I felt those fish were worth more in the water alive than dead on the dock. Those fish promoted charter boat bookings, fuel sales, tackle sales and motel room rentals.

Anderson: How did you catch fish in those days?

Linton: Trolling. I commonly used feather jigs and cedar jigs.

In the early 1950s Captain Bob Linton found good numbers of school bluefin tuna off Block Island. These fish were taken on striped bass tackle while trolling feathers and cedar plugs.

Nothing fancy mind you, as there was not much in the way of terminal tackle available to us.

Anderson: When in season did you see those first fish?

Linton: The best school bluefin tuna fishing seemed to be in early July, which has changed completely with what goes on today. Nowadays, you're lucky to see school fish in late August or early September. I remember one year the first school tuna was caught the 17th of June.

I did a lot of offshore fishing, looking for swordfish **(Ed. note: Captain Linton has 54 ROD and REEL swordfish to his credit)**, *but basically we were tuna fishing, with swordfish a bonus.*

Anderson: Tell me a little about the tackle in those days.

Linton: Compared to today, it was crude. The first fiberglass rods were coming into use. We had a problem with some of them but not too much. Those fellows who came with bamboo rods frequently went home with the pieces. The most trouble I had with school tuna equipment was the mate would forget to ease up on the drag after we took a fish. Back into the holder with a tightened drag, the next fish, if sizable, would cause us to lose everything when the wooden butt broke. I remember one season I lost six or eight outfits that way. People would love to tighten the drags up on a fish, no matter what you told them. They simply hated to see a little line go off the reel.

Another charter captain, by the name of George Thompson, got Ocean City Reels to modify the star drags on his reels so people couldn't tighten them up. I think he used a special tool to adjust them. Back in those days, you've got to remember, people were not used to reels with drags, or fish taking line against a drag. They would get very nervous and excited if that happened.

To regress for a moment, the Montaukers commonly used the butterfish jig. At first, we used only the smaller type Jap feathers, but some days they just wouldn't catch well. After a while, we came around to using jigs. It is chrome plated, oval shaped and flattened, with a fixed hook and worked very well on some occasions.

Compared to today, you couldn't believe the number of fish we had. Then we went from day to night after the seiners came in during the sixties. I think it was 1963 and I heard Manny Philips on the radio, who ran the seiner **Silver Mink,** *tell me was going to try something new. He was going to try purse seining.*

Anderson: How did you react to that?

Linton: Well, I knew how successful the West Coast seiners were in the Pacific. That statement sent a chill up my spine. But he wasn't very successful. I remember what Captain Ralph Pitts, out of Montauk, said: ''They'll never catch these, they're too fast.'' I remember him saying that very well.

In 1953 Captain Bob Linton (L) and Dr. John Vallone (R) landed one of the first giant Atlantic bluefin tuna in Galilee, RI with an Ocean City ''cradle reel'' and Montague rod.

As I said, Manny made a few sets, but not much came of it. A short time later the **North Queen***, I think it was, showed up from the West Coast and they literally murdered the fish. Seems I recall a few sets with something like 250 tons and their calling our local seine boats in to help use all the fish. A number of other seiners showed up, maybe a total of 15 other boats, from the West Coast Pacific fleet and our rod and reel school tuna fishing collapsed after that.*

On an average day we might put 20 to 30 fish in the boat before that but the next after the purse seiners year we didn't catch twenty fish. That's how quick it went down and I just couldn't believe the serious affect it had on our fishing.

Anderson: Tell me a little about your involvement with giant tuna fishing. When did you start fishing for them?

Linton: Giant tuna fishing started here in the early 1950s, and I got my first one in 1953. I had fished the 952 USATT out of New London, but didn't do anything. I caught my first giant tuna at Nebraska Shoal the next year. In 1956, the USATT came to Rhode Island on the basis of the action at Nebraska Shoal. In the second year here, over 50 giant tuna were taken in the event. I recall that one day over thirty fish were taken. We had two of them, and surprisingly, most fish came from an area southeast of Block Island.

Back in 1958, we started out in June looking for school tuna but there was no good, early fishing. I had a dentist out on the 2nd of July and he brought a 9/0 Penn Senator reel filled wtih 39 thread (approx-

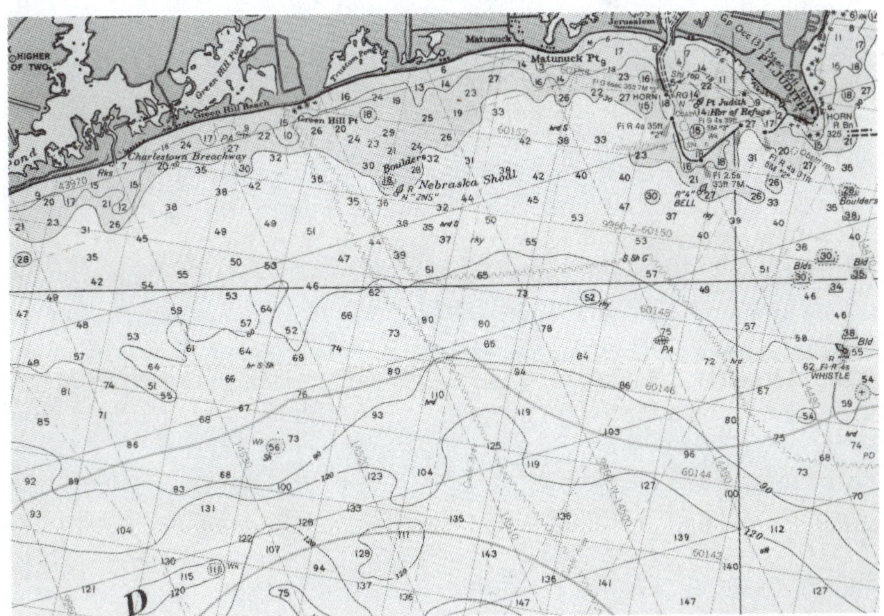

In the early 1950s the hot spot for giant bluefin tuna was Nebraska Shoal.

One day's catch during the 1956 USATT, 21 fish were over 400 pounds. Some of these fish were hanging from the previous day's fishing.

imately 117 pound test) line. That reel didn't hold much line of that pound test. It was intended for shark fishing and if we saw a shark, we'd bait it. There were an awful lot of mackerel around and we had several rigged up to use as shark bait.

Well, we were on our way back in from offshore and hadn't seen any sharks, but over the radio I hear of action to the southeast. So, we went that way. As we get closer, there was a fleet and I could see fellows running onto the pulpits with harpoon ready, but they wouldn't throw at anything. Saw that several times and getting closer a big fish broke right in front of the boat, a giant bluefin tuna. Then I realized giant tuna were all over the place. This dentist asked if he could throw out his mackerel and of course I said sure. We hadn't trolled for very long and sure enough a giant grabbed the bait. I had caught maybe a half dozen giants by then but I wasn't really good on them. Well, the next thing I did was look at the reel and it's darn near empty. Full spool, empty spool, back and forth for some time. Three hours later we finally lost it.

I had Dr. Vallone the next day; he fished with me a lot. It was the third of July and I had my own gear on which we caught a 600 pound fish that day. As you can imagine, the next day was the Fourth and there had to be 30 or 40 boats in the area. I trolled around watching the other boats, but I couldn't believe what I saw. Rods with Penn

Captain Bob Linton's Mako backing into the bulkhead at Galilee, RI to weigh in a fish during the 1956 USATT.

Squidders on them, bottom fishing outfits, and many of these boats were getting strikes but not many fish were landed. Bet you there were a hundred giants hooked but I know of only three fish landed. Not many people owned tackle in those days that could take a big fish.

In the late 1950s, Nebraska Shoal had lots of whiting and mackerel. Shoals and shoals of mackerel, the place was just alive with them. We only had to go three miles from the Harbor of Refuge breakwater and many days we'd have quite a few Montauk boats there.

Over the years, I've seen a lot of changes in the tuna fishery, particularly since the price increased on the fish. I'm sure the high price pulled a lot of people into fishing for giant tuna, as most people before that went fishing simply because of the fun and their interest in it. I saw how courtesy was quickly forgotten and people became overly aggressive. And, of course, technology has played a major role, especially with electronics, fiberglass boats and modern high horsepower engines. Attitudes have changed and there is definitely less respect for others. In fact, it got so bad a few years back, if someone saw you catch a fish, they would come right over next to you, and crowd you, thinking nothing of it.

*In my career, I've seen miracles. Early on, like knowing exactly where you were. I recall flasher type fathometers coming into use about 1956. That was a big help to us in catching fish, as well as helping us figure out where we were. In 1961, when I launched the **Mako II**, I was the first to have a paper recorder. It seemed a miracle to be able to see what was under you.*

Loran helped us find an area, regardless of the weather. You've got to remember, in the early days when I first started fishing, Lorans were war surplus. Not too many people could figure out how to work them or use them for navigation. Loran A was a little better, and Loran C really let the dumb ones find the spot.

Here's a funny story. The Woods Hole Oceanographic Institute (WHOI) began tagging bluefins and I thought it was a waste of time. I felt that all it was going to do was help the commercial fishermen find the catch tuna. I was probably the first to say that in our area. Then I talked with Frank Mather and the remark was made that the only way we were going to learn anything about the fish was through tagging. Well, that made a lot of sense to me and I started tagging bluefin. I was the first to do it, as we were offshore almost every day and school tuna fishing was my "bread and butter" in the late 1950s and early 1960s. Come Fall, I'd turn my attention to striped bass and bluefish.

2 SPORT FISHING FOR BLUEFIN TUNA

The DeNoia Brothers:
The Early Days

Some readers may have heard stories told back in the early 1970s of days with four or five giants in the slick almost immediately after the start of chumming. Mono, cable or wire leaders, it just simply didn't matter. Days with seven or eight strikes, maybe half as many or more fish in the cockpit. Exciting fishing, for sure, and on top of that, money could be made over and above the day's fishing expenses by the sale of the fish. A few people who did this on a routine basis began to develop a reputation, people who not only caught them chumming but trolling as well.

You have to be there to ease it, to witness the struggle in which only the angler's feet touched the chair while the weight of his body in the harness matched the drag setting on the reel with upwards of 90 pounds or more. In some cases, there were only two men in a boat measuring 35 to 40 feet in length, one in the chair and the other leaving the controls at the final moment to gaff the fish. Add to that the awesome sight of seeing a fish brought to the transom in under 30 minutes, fish weighing upwards of 700 or 800 pounds or more. In a fleet of boats, these same boats routinely hooked up and put fish into the cockpit.

One of these boats was the **White Stallion** run by John DeNoia (Jay) and the DeNoia Brothers in Rhode Island and Massachusetts waters. They soon became known as veteran, expert giant tuna fishermen. An aura grew about this developing rod and reel commercial fishery. Nothing quite like it had ever occurred before in New England. With the exception of an occasional giant bluefin taken in a trap net, this period saw the first, large-scale, season-long harvest of giant bluefin tuna.

Anderson: Tell me, Jay, what was the fishing like when you first started?

DeNoia: Tuna fishing was a gentleman's type of sport at the time. However, many people involved didn't have a lot of money. But back then we all respected one another's territory, so to speak, something which you don't find today. That spirit existed for most of the time I fished in Rhode Island and that included both the USATT and the Rhode Island Tuna Tournament. However, in the early 1970s we gave up on tournament fishing simply because it became a hassle, and we just weren't happy with it. We knew that rumors about some of the boats "pulling a fast one" were probably true.

Anderson: When did you see the fish start to become valuable?

DeNoia: It was back in 1973, I believe. We started fishing up north in Cape Cod Bay and things started to change. In particular, more and more people got into the fishing. In 1974, the price started to come into the picture and each year after that the price started out a little higher and fishing lasted a little longer. It was obvious to me, at least, that the fishing had become a completely different scene. The 1974 season was the first time, I think, we saw one dollar a pound; that was toward the end of the season. I remember that because it was the last year we had the Brownell built boat. That dollar a pound situation was almost similar to the one in which it went to ten dollars a pound this past year.

The DeNoia brothers put Ed Aronsen into this 720 pound giant bluefin tuna which took top honors at the 1971 Rhode Island Tuna Tournament.

Anderson: Did you see any attitude changes at this point in time?

DeNoia: The majority of people fishing then were still at it for recreational reasons. With the newer people, it seemed the price on the fish affected their attitude the most, as they didn't have a background of previous sportfishing experiences. No doubt in my mind, as soon as the price came up, attitudes changed, and giant tuna fishing turned into a cutthroat business. Each year as the price went up, the situation on the grounds got worse. As new people got into it, they looked for a role model. They wanted to know who was catching what, how they were doing it, and so on, so they could emulate them. As fewer of the original people were fishing each year and with more new people coming in as well, the attitudes got worse.

Moreover, the new people coming in emulated this changed attitude, as that was what they saw the most of. The first thing these newer people were into was the price and how much they could make, which was totally unlike that of earlier years. In the early days, people like John Walton and Ed Murray were seen as role models, as well as Captains Linton, Lema, Clark, the Catauros, Murray Cianciola and Don Slater as they were all fishing here in the late 1960s.

I don't know if you ever got to see it, but in the late sixties, Bob Meloccaro, John Walton and Hobie Westin would drop off their buoys down at Nebraska Shoals and run in for lunch, returning an hour or so later for the afternoon tide. Back in those days I was striped bass fishing and really didn't pay much attention to the tuna fishing.

That was a completely different style of fishing back then and today you wouldn't dare leave your spot. Just goes to show how much the fishing has changed since then, because there was no real value on the fish and it didn't control the behavior of people as much as it does today.

Anderson: When did people begin to realize that serious money could be made giant tuna fishing?

DeNoia: Probably in 1972, certainly in 1973, because people saw others actually making serious money, enough money that got them into thinking of buying their own boat. It seemed that the number of people getting into the fishing was doubling each year after that. Keep in mind that those asked to join in for a day's fishing, or those who volunteered to go along to help out, saw what was going on and decided this was the opportunity to buy their own boat as well as the necessary equipment.

Back in those days, being a little younger and more enthusiastic, we fished in some pretty awful conditions. Those days, before the money, the better equipped boats would stay at the docks during poor weather. After a while we realized it wasn't worth our time and effort to beat up the boat and gear, so we actually backed off on some

In the mid 1970s, this was a common sight. The White Stallion often had two giants a day to weigh in.

of the crazy things done in the past. Other people were hungrier to make money, maybe they had payments to make, and we watched them attempt and press things I would never dream of doing, not even in my wildest days. The fishery began to make a complete turnaround in terms of fishing effort under poor weather conditions, simply because of the increased value of the fish. If, for some reason, the price of the fish were to go down considerably, I feel we would lose a lot of fishermen from the grounds. Then we would go back to a lot fewer boats and people fishing because they enjoyed it, people who love the challenge and the whole pleasure of fishing.

Anderson: You've got a reputation for doing well but just how well?

*DeNoia: The first year we chartered the boat was 1975 and we went fourteen straight days catching 21 giant tuna and made some people nervous. It was very important to be out every day, because you never knew when the fishing would be good. The best year I had with the **White Stallion** was 67 fish, with the majority of those fish being caught in five days out of the entire season. That's why it was so important to get out every possible day. A lot of people simply don't see it but most days nothing was caught. Back then we didn't worry too much about days like that, because there was no competition. We were thinking of the good days when the conditions were just right and the fishing was good.*

Anderson: It seems to me that the mid 1970s was the transition era when commercial tuna fishing replaced sportfishing. How do you feel about that?

DeNoia: Absolutely, and today people have forgotten what the sport of fishing is really all about. Too many people see only the money side of it. There are some that have chosen to do this for a living. In the mid to late 1970s there was a developing attitude that fishing was something to make money. A few people would go out for several weeks, make a big hit, and it seemed the money was much more important to them than the challenge of landing a fish or the pleasure in doing it. During that period, I saw a number of boats purchased for the sole purpose of going out and making a fortune. I've been fishing for some time and I feel I know what's going on but I was surprised to see that some people didn't realize how difficult it really was to catch enough big fish to accomplish that. I compare giant tuna fishing to the lottery. Some people get lucky and make a few bucks, others keep trying and trying but just don't have any success.

Anderson: Can you make any money catching (rod and reel) tuna today?

DeNoia: Expenses today are extreme and if you're going to make it worthwhile you can't just look at how many dollars you can generate.

You have to look at what those figures represent in terms of the overall financial picture. If you don't, you can end up losing an awful lot of money. You have to look at your fuel costs, bait costs, how many days the conditions will be right for fishing, where the fishing might be, what you might be able to catch, dockside expenses and the price for the fish must also be considered. The list goes on and on.

There has been a lot written lately about catching and selling the fish for a profit. Especially about the very high prices the fish bring, and glamorizing it to the point where people read this and say to themselves, "Look at all the money this guy is making." Before too long, they too want to get in on the action, I personally think they write too much and cause some of the attitudes that exist today. Some things would be better if left alone. When people read about fish that are worth thousands and thousands of dollars, it's pretty spectacular. I feel these things have done much to expand the number of people in the giant tuna fishery. As a result, more and more inexperienced people out there take unnecessary risks with the weather. There are just too many inexperienced people out there some days all trying to catch the same bunch of fish. It seems no one has any courtesy for another anymore, which can affect the safety of those involved.

One of my biggest objections is the use of the airplane. If you're working on a bunch of fish, the last thing you need is for a plane to come along and put another boat on them. And besides, a circling plane attracts more boats to the area. The boats follow the planes and this tends to concentrate the boats in one area. This puts a lot of pressure on the fish and they never get a rest. I think this has caused the fish to stay further offshore, not coming inshore as in the past.

Anderson: What's your opinion on the health of the fish stocks?

DeNoia: I think it would make things easier if we could have some confidence in the data that we are being supplied with. A lot of people don't want to believe there are a reduced number of fish, although it's hard to say for sure. I've seen an increase in the amount of fish myself but they seem to be biting less.

2 SPORT FISHING FOR BLUEFIN TUNA

The Murray Brothers:
First Family Of Giant Tuna Fishing

Though there were many great anglers and captains who preceded them, the Murray brothers, Ed and Frank, have established a record of family accomplishments in the world of giant tuna fishing that probably can't be challenged or duplicated.

Ed Murray practically grew up in boats during his childhood on Long Island. His grandfather ran a charter boat out of Fire Island and his uncle had a charterboat at Woodcleft Canal in Freeport. Ed fished with them as a child and later mated for his relatives and other skippers. He wasn't even a teenager when his rod bent to the power of bluefins exceeding 100 pounds at the Mud Hole and off Fire Island.

Ed's first boat was the **Wanderer**, a 28-foot Verity skiff he used to catch both the first tuna of the season out of Fire Island and the first swordfish ever caught on rod-and-reel from that inlet.

The family woodworking business enabled Ed to build a 34-footer for the 1959 season. That boat was removed from the shop just a day before the business burned to the ground and was named **Cookie**, in honor of Ed's first son, who was born "Edward", but has ever since been known by his infant nickname.

The first **Cookie** broke the ice on the bluefin season three years in a row and also recorded an amazing three rod-and-reel swordfish trolled in 1959. After that it was on to bigger boats—a 41-foot Carolina in 1961, a 41 Hatteras in 1964, a 37 Cubavitch in 1974, a 44 Rybovitch in 1978 and a 43 Merritt in 1981. The Hatteras was named **Cookie II**, but all the others have been known as **Cookie Too**. Many of these boats were co-owned with New York angler Don Stott. A new super-fast Renegade of over 50 feet will be the latest **Cookie Too** in 1991.

Ed (R) and Ed ''Cookie'' (L) Murray in Montauk, NY, in the fall of 1966 with one of their many giants weighed there.

The Murrays soon expanded their area of operations from New York Bight to Montauk and points north. They also traveled to Newfoundland for the great fishing of the mid-1960s and showed the locals how to catch the super-giants when the fishing at Canso Causeway, Nova Scotia was tough.

Ed was a pioneer in the Stellwagen Bank, Massachusetts fishery which exploded in 1971. With Stott, brother Frank, Uncle Tony Menella or various friends in the chair, Eddie recorded hundreds of giants from that area, most of which were released before the Japanese started paying big money for them. Ed developed a bad back decades ago and has left the pulling to others while he runs the boat and does the brainwork. The **Cookie Too** is now run by Cookie and another son, Paulie, who have become probably the top giant tuna crew in the world. They start with the waters off Cat Cay, Bahamas trolling in May and then head north wherever the fish are from New Jersey to Maine.

Ed figures that between his earlier days and what the kids are doing, the family has caught between 1,500 and 2,000 gaints over the years, most of which have been released. The largest they weighed in was a 1,256-pounder caught by Don Stott at Canso Causeway. Ed says an even bigger one was released in the same area, as have other "granders" from both Canada and Massachusetts.

However, this is only part of the Murray Brothers story. Their grandfather made fighting chairs and built fishing rods decades ago and the Murray brothers eventually started doing the same thing. Ed started building basic fighting chairs in 1964. A decade later I installed his original chair in the bow of my Mako 22. At first he used forged components purchased from other manufacturers. When such components couldn't be obtained in 1972, he started having the parts forged on his own and from that point the famous Murray Brothers chair took off. Jeffrey, Eddie's only son who's not crazy about fishing, ran the factory before moving on to his own projects.

A move from Long Island to Riviera Beach, Florida in 1976 permitted expansion of the business into a full-line tackle shop with an emphasis on big game gear. Very shortly, Murray Brothers, under Frank's watchful eye, became one of the premier tackle stores in the country. Many innovations in tackle and lures were introduced there or through their catalogs.

Murray Brothers was also a pioneer in saltwater video productions, and that field has so fascinated Ed that he sold the business in 1988 in order to concentrate on making the finest fishing videos around the world.

Al Ristori, noted writer and tuna fisherman himself, gave us some insight into Ed Murray. "Though I've only fished with Ed Murray a few times, I can certainly testify to his fishing genius. The first time was a casual morning trip at Chub Cay, Bahamas which quickly produced my first blue marlin after not even seeing one while fishing with another skipper all week. Several years later I drove to Gloucester and was promptly rewarded with a doubleheader of giant tuna in one day.

However, even the greatest of fishermen have days when nothing goes right. In 1972, Ed towed famous artist Stanley Meltzoff and I out to the A Buoy off Boston in Cookie's 16-foot Boston Whaler. We weren't there to catch giants, but simply to chum them to the boat so Meltzoff could get in the water and observe their movements before doing a series of paintings for Sports Illustrated. That day I ended up hand-feeding several giants until we ran out of chum, not even the casually-feeding giants were hard to photograph underwater—and Meltzoff decided I should hook one the next day so he could study it while tethered to the boat."

"Everything worked just as planned until the gimble on the portable fighting chair (definitely not a Murray Brothers creation) fell apart with the swivel at the rod tip. Meltzoff fixed it once but the same thing happened again as I worked the giant to the small boat—at which point we suddenly realized that we were alone in fog and rain with an outboard which wouldn't start and a tuna that was towing us around in circles—plus no means of communication with the fleet."

Fortunately, a dragger headed back to Boston appeared out of the fog and we asked them to call the **Cookie II**. Half-an-hour later I climbed aboard the Hatteras and started the fight all over again with a rejuvenated giant—only to have the old wooden rod butt break. It had been perhaps the worst tuna fishing day of Ed Murrays life—five giants hooked and all lost for one reason or another. Bad back and all, Ed jumped down from the bridge and with fire in his eyes started handlining the 130 pound test Dacron. With "give no quarter" brute force, he was moving the giant close to the boat when the clasp on his watchband popped open and sliced the taut Dacron as neatly as a knife!"

There may be more knowledgeable tuna fishermen in the world, but Eddie Murray would be hard to beat as an individual—and it's hard to believe that any family could outdo the continuing accomplishments of the Murray clan!

2 SPORT FISHING FOR BLUEFIN TUNA

New York Bight Bluefins

The origins of tuna fishing along the East Coast of the United States can be traced to the North Jersey coast, where the sport has grown to be one of the most popular aspects of our fishery. Now that we enjoy fine results with modern tackle and accessories while fishing on fast, seaworthy boats, consider for a moment how it was in the "good old days".

The late, great fishing writer, Van Campen Heilner, spoke of those early fishing days in his classic Salt Water Fishing (Alfred A. Knopf, N.Y. 1937). As Van Heilner states, "It was impossible for us to do anything with them, because we weren't properly equipped I suppose. But we tried awfully hard. There was Zane Grey, Bob Davis, Fred Alexander, William Scheer, Jake Wertheim, Chris Feigenspan, Joe Cawthorn and the writer. Later there were others and there may have been one or two I've forgotten.

We fished off Sea Bright out of bank skiffs, sitting on campstools and we gave those giant horse-mackerel some of the finest collection of hooks and lines you ever saw. The rest was fun for the horse-mackerel. Scheer even had a special wire line constructed and a rubber-lined crotch to put his rod in, but reels weren't large enough in those days and he couldn't even hold them with that.

We had an arrangement with the bluefishermen that when they got horse-mackerel in their chum slick they'd raise an oar in signal and we'd run over and start in on them.

Sometimes they'd take the bunkers we threw over; sometimes they wouldn't. They looked as big as hogsheads there under the sterns of our dories and some of them ran over a thousand pounds. I saw a fish there one day so big it scared me. I was afraid to put a bait over for fear he'd take it.''

Hoffman's Anchorage in Brielle, NJ has weighed in many giant bluefin tuna. This 800 pound class fish is awaiting pick up from the local buyer.

That's the way it was off what is now known as Sea Bright, New Jersey between 1912 and 1916. Real big game tackle and harnesses hadn't been developed as yet. Heilner noted that ''Grey had the best tackle there was then, but even his, coupled with his great skill and knowledge, was insufficient for the job.

It was Jake Wertheim (using one of the first harnesses that Heilner had ever seen) who finally succeeded in catching the first New York Bight horse mackerel—a 286 pounder on September 13, 1915. Though only a ''medium'' by today's standards, that fish broke the great Pacific Ocean record of 251 pounds set in 1899 by Col. C.P. Moorehouse off Catalina Island, California.

Wertheim's bluefin remained the American record until Christian W. Feigenspan caught a true giant—a 407 pounder, also off Sea Bright, on September 1, 1923. The latter catch stood as the United States record for just over 10 years before Francis Low started the dramatic move up in giant tuna sizes with a 705 pounder from the same area on September 11, 1933. Though larger tuna had already been taken in Nova Scotia and Great Britain, New Jersey didn't lose the American mark until B. Davis Crowninshield edged Low by five pounds with a giant from Ipswich Bay, Massachusetts on August 8, 1938.

Heilner remarked that ''Twenty-five years after our first efforts the fish were still there in the same place as they always have been and probably always will be, but this time anglers were equipped and started catching them.''

Unfortunately, the bluefish fleet off Sea Bright is no longer the place to go for giant tuna—though it's not inconceivable that one might wander in there. Modern giant tuna fishing in New York Bight requires a good deal more running. While the relatively nearby Mud Hole provides the usual fall fishery, the only spring action ever recorded (except for an odd fish taken by sharkers) has been around such far offshore areas as the Bacardi and Texas Tower wrecks.

The spring fishery for giant and medium bluefins is a very recent development, having been opened up by Captain Bob Pisano on his **Tuna Hunter** from Brielle Yacht Club in June, 1987. Though he lost a giant near the boat that year, Pisano succeeded in catching one the next June and that fishery broke wide open in 1989 after Pisano caught the first giant on June 5.

When the giants first appear, they are feeding actively on huge schools of herring, squid and sand eels. Trolling with spreader bars or daisy chains of mackerel or squid seems to be the only method of catching them during the early fishery, but they tend to settle down after a few weeks of rising water temperatures and can then be chunked. During the 1989 season , chunking started toward the end

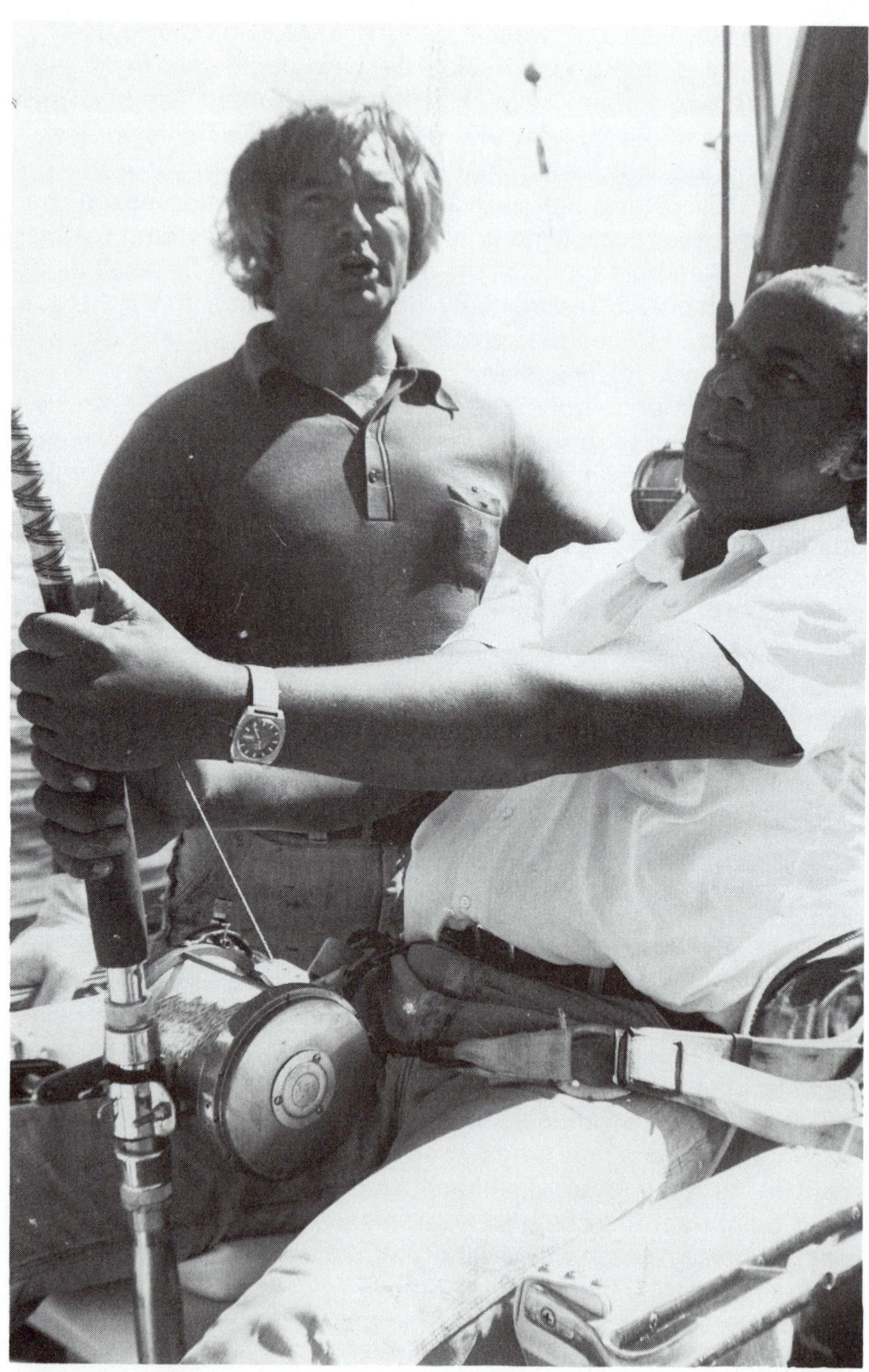

Captain Bob Pisano watches the last minutes of the late Roy Parson's New Jersey State Record bluefin. Parson's 1,030½ pound bluefin of 1981 has not seen a challenger throughout the eighties and should be standing well into the nineties.

of June. Though the giants responded to water temperatures in the seventies by heading east, great numbers of medium and large school bluefins were chunked right into the fall. Yellowfin tuna were also abundant on the same grounds during the summer.

The Bacardi and Texas Tower areas on the 30 fathom curve (about 65 miles ESE of Manasquan and Shark River Inlets) have long been fall hot spots for school bluefins. Great fishing for bluefins was encountered around the Bacardi from October through early-November during the early 1980s, but it wasn't until unseasonably cold water ruined the inshore fishery during mid-August 1988 that significant numbers of anglers started chunking that offshore area during the summer. There was literally no end to the tuna action on the 30-fathom line in 1989, since NMFS prohibited the retention of all but giants in mid-October. The few boats which fished the Bacardi for tag-and-release fishing after that experienced incredible action with bluefins up to 250 pounds.

School bluefin tuna fishing used to be a standard summer sport in the Metropolitan area. Boats from New Jersey and western Long Island ports would start trolling schoolies in late-June or early-July, and they'd then catch them regularly throughout the season. The slow charter boats of that era rarely had to run much more than 20 miles for the school tuna, and they'd return with boxes full of the hard-fighting (but then worthless) fish.

Chunking for school tuna was also often a late summer attraction in the Mud Hole area, and a huge fleet gathered in that area during the 1960s, especially when tinker mackerel were available for a deadly live bait.

Unfortunately, that consistent inshore sport, based on a virtually virgin bluefin tuna population, was ripped apart when the West Coast tuna seiners arrived with their massive boats and spotter planes. The bluefin population was severely depleted in just a few years during the late 1960s, and the few East Coast tuna seiners prevented any rebuilding by continuing to massacre the remaining schools of tuna as they came up the coast each spring.

As is well-documented in this book, the entire nature of tuna fishing changed during the 1970s, and has never been the same since. Though it's unlikely that we'll ever again see the consistent close-to-shore fishing provided by the virgin populations of bluefins prior to the arrival of the purse seinsers, the restrictions on bluefin fishing did help improve action during the 1980s—and there's no forecasting what these unpredictable oceanic game fish will do.

Giant bluefins traditionally provided a late-summer to early-fall Mud Hole fishery. Indeed, that consistent action was the basis for the beginning of the United States Atlantic Tuna Tournament

Captain Al Ristori with his 1980 New Jersey State Record of 1,022 pounds stood for only one year. About the same time in September of the next year, Roy Parson's fish edged out Al's record by only 8½ pounds.

(USATT) at Brielle, New Jersey in 1939. The USATT stayed in New York Bight ports until the Rhode Island fishery broke open.

Giants were so abundant in previous decades that some were even caught by party boat anglers. Captain Les Baletti of the **Palace II** made a specialty of party boat tuna fishing at such areas as 17 Fathoms and The Farms in the fifties and sixties, and customers, sailing from Hoboken and Manhattan, caught great numbers of mediums and large schoolies plus some giants despite having to use tackle which would today seem relatively crude. Baletti remembers one giant being subdued by a disabled tavern owner who fought it from a wheelchair. Captain Freddy Moore was another who specialized in that party boat tuna sport with his **Teal** from Staten Island.

Party boat tuna fishing is one of the relatively unique fisheries in New York Bight. A great many party boats engaged in that fishery when school tuna could be chunked in quantity during the 1960s. Since this fishing tends to be best in the evening, after the mob had left, some even scheduled mid-afternoon departures. Party boats from such ports as Sheepshead Bay, Belmar, Brielle and Point Pleasant continue to schedule tuna trips whenever the fish are in the Mud Hole area—and many run overnighters to the Bacardi when that fishing is hot.

Giant tuna fishing in the Mud Hole area used to start in August, and could last well into the fall. However, it virtually died out in the 1970s when population levels dropped to only about 10 percent of what they had been. Fortunately, restrictions imposed by NMFS brought about some improvement—and a mixture of large schoolies, mediums and giants suddenly reappeared in the Mud Hole during the fall of 1979.

Every year since then, giants have shown in the Mud Hole area some time after Labor Day. This fishing varies greatly from year-to-year, with anything from only a few giants to several dozen being boated in September and October. Some years there are also lots of schoolies and mediums, but those smaller bluefins are virtually absent other years.

The Mud Hole features a complete mix of sizes and in the early 1980s it appeared there could be giants in local waters which would rival those of Canadian waters. In 1981, Al Ristori was fishing in mid-September with Captain Bob Pisano on the **Runaway 36** from Manasquan when the late Roy Parsons caught a 963 pounder that would have broken the previous state record set on Pisano's boat except that Al caught a 1,022 pounder just a couple of hours later!

At about the same time the next year, Pisano and Parsons teamed up to push the mark up a tad to 1,030½ pounds but there wasn't a challenger throughout the rest of the eighties. For instance, though 1989 may have been the best giant tuna year for Metropolitan anglers in decades (due to the combination of spring Bacardi fish and those from the Mud Hole later in the season), the largest New Jersey giants were an 850 pounder on Captain Doug Lombardi's **Calculated Risk** from Hoffman's Marina in Brielle and an 833 pounder by high-liner Captain Nick Cicero on the **Sandy** from Manasquan.

The Mud Hole giant tuna area stretches from the BA Buoy off Sea Bright to the southeast off Manasquan. It's actually a trench leading from outside New York Harbor to the Hudson Canyon. The most popular areas are along the edges of the Hole near the Oil Wreck, Arundo Wreck and Monster Ledge. However, giants can show up in unexpected areas. During the fall of 1987 many were encountered in depths of less than 100 feet at the Slough, off Seaside Heights. A major, unprecedented run of giants developed about 10 miles east of Manasquan Inlet from late-July into early-August of 1988 when the fish were discovered there feeding on vast quantities of sand eels.

Chunking for giants in the Metropolitan area is similar to that practiced in other areas, though local anglers have long deemed it necessary to use mono leaders rather than wire. However, Captain Oscar Amoruso of the Atlantic Beach-based **Marlin** insists on using the same #18 wire leaders he's been so successful with in New England waters. I was with him when he put Mary Barnett into her 100th giant tuna while fishing in the Mud Hole on a picky day with that heavy wire.

Metropolitan skippers traditionally utilized ground bunker chum as well as bunker chunks but that practice has been virtually discontinued during the 1980s. Though mossbunker is still the normal chunking material, butterfish is also used, while ling and whiting obtained from draggers make even better chum. Bunkers are the most common bait and it's often possible to obtain them alive in the rivers before going offshore. Live ling and whiting caught off the bottom while chunking make excellent baits. Other standards include squid, butterfish and small, live bluefish.

The Metropolitan New York area can definitely claim to be the cradle of giant tuna fishing on the Atlantic Coast. Though it's long taken a back seat to other areas, the unpredictable nature of the giant tuna can change that overnight, just as was the case during the mid-summer run off Manasquan Inlet in 1988 and the June, 1989 fishery at the Bacardi which drew tuna specialists from as far as Massachusetts.

2 SPORT FISHING FOR BLUEFIN TUNA

Canadian Bluefin Fishing

Canadian tuna fishing is very basically different from that found along the East Coast of the United States. School bluefins don't come inshore north of Cape Cod and even mediums aren't often encountered to the north. However, Canada plays host to great numbers of mature tuna, including most of the super-giants.

The earliest sportfishing for giant tuna may have taken place off Liverpool, Nova Scotia in 1871. Edward C. Migdalski, in his classic Angler's Guide to Salt Water Game Fishes (The Ronald Press, N.Y. 1958), describes the capture of a 600 pound horse-mackerel on a handline by a schoolmaster named Tom Patillo. However, Canadian rod-and-reel tuna fishing appears to have begun with Commander J.K.L. Ross. After losing 22 bluefins in 1908, Ross returned to Nova Scotia to lose another 19 before catching a 680 pounder.

Captain Laurie D. Mitchell came over from England to push the tuna mark up to 710 pounds. While working at Abercrombie and Fitch, the great sporting goods store of that era in New York, Mitchell was introduced to Zane Grey. The famous author and sportsman talked Mitchell into a tuna fishing expedition in Nova Scotia which resulted in the capture of many giants up to Grey's record 758 pounder. The latter stood as the North American record (an 851 pounder was caught off Great Britain in 1933) until Dr. John R. (Goat Gland) Brinkley of Del Rio, Texas boated a 788 pound giant in Nova Scotia during August, 1936. A new world record was established in 1938 when Nova Scotia produced an 864 pounder for F.A. Kenney.

Nova Scotia tuna fishing reached a peak in 1950, when Commander Duncan Hodgson (son-in-law of Commander Ross) boated a 977 pound bluefin. The international team competition for the Sharp Cup originated in Wedgeport, where giant tuna fed on vast schools of herring in Soldier's Rip. The local lobster dories were turned into very basic sportfishing boats, and the tuna were chummed to the boats. The post-World War II fishing was so good that over 800 tuna were taken in 1948. Some of those fish were only mediums, but (according to S. Kip Farrington in his Fishing The Atlantic, Coward-McCann, Inc., N.Y. 1949) the 1947 catch averaged over 500 pounds.

Yet, as great as the tuna fishing at Wedgeport was, it died out completely over the years and has never come back. During the 1960s, the Canadian giant tuna fishery shifted far north to Newfoundland. The revered American angler, author and cinemaphotographer Lee Wulff, had caught giants there prior to the war. However, the huge schools of squid which drew the bluefins disappeared in 1941 and the fish didn't return until 1957. The Newfoundland fishing was entirely different from that of Nova Scotia. Boats trolled through schools of giants rather than chunking them in a rip. Great numbers of bluefins were trolled in Conception Bay and other areas, and multiple catches were very common. Eddie Murray remembers dozens of tuna carcases floating in the water by the pier in St. Johns as there was no market for the fish—until a German started buying them for $15 a piece.

Murray released most of the many fish he caught up there, and noted that they only trolled one line into schools of the 500 to 600 pound giants in order to avoid double hook-ups. The vast schools of squid would change the color of the water and the giants often jumped in the air to stun them before picking the squid up at their leisure. Capelin were another abundant forage fish and the giants would also chase schools of mackerel right into the rocks.

Just as the Newfoundland and fishery was dying out, there were rumors of super-giants being spotted at Prince Edward Island. At first, the local lobster and cod fishermen thought the huge fish were sharks. However, tuna fishing started in the late 1960s. The big breakthrough occurred in 1970 when Mel Immergut of Brooklyn boated a 1,040 pounder on one of the local lobster boats to finally break the thousand-pound barrier on bluefin tuna.

Prince Edward quickly turned into a tuna fisherman's Mecca in the seventies, as ''granders'' became reasonably common in the period from September to mid-October. 800 pound bluefins were routinely caught off the main port at North Lake. Many days were

A typical fleet of Canadian lobster dories turned into basic sportfishing boats.

lost to bad weather but no other area offered such an opportunity to break all-tackle and line class records.

After the first few years, the Canadian government reserved the fishery for local lobstermen who equipped their boats with home-made fighting chairs of every description and earned a good income in the off-season, particularly as the giants started bringing big money from the Japanese.

The next discovery was back in Nova Scotia but on the opposite side of that province from the fishing of earlier decades. The greatest giants of all were located in the Canso Causeway area, where they would corner schools of herring and mackerel from late-October into early-November and feed heavily before starting their journey to the Gulf of Mexico for the winter spawning season.

The Canso giants actually averaged over 1,000 pounds and the peak was reached when Ken Fraser boated a 1,496 pound bluefin at Aulds Cove on October 26, 1979. Though many granders have been caught since then, no one came close to Fraser's mark during the next decade.

Unfortunately, the Canso fishery declined to little or nothing during the eighties, and the Prince Edward fishing also became spotty, though Dr. J.M. Steffey set an 80 pound line class record of 1,116 pounds at North Lake on September 26, 1985.

Canadian waters are truly the home for huge bluefin. The All-Tackle World Record belongs to Ken Fraser's 1,496 pounder caught October 26, 1979 in Nova Scotia.

While the super-giants of the seventies seem to have passed from the scene, some more moderate-sized giants have been showing up in the waters of Prince Edward Island, Nova Scotia and New Brunswick leading to the hope that there will be another surge of record tuna in the future. However, where those fish will be located is anyone's guess.

As noted in this chapter, the sportfishing areas have changed greatly over the years. The great trap fishery at St. Margaret's Bay in Nova Scotia also died out during the eighties. The latter operation involved trapping skinny giants when they arrived to feed on the mackerel schools in May, and then fattening them in pens all summer until they were ready for the high-priced Japanese market in the fall.

Sportfishing in Canadian waters seems to have been restricted to trolling with daisy chains of mackerel during the past few decades. Nothing comparable to the chunking in Soldier's Rip has been developed, though American restaurant owner Jack Baker did try chunking off Prince Edward Island. Don Merten fished there out of Souris in 1971 on his **Valient Lady** from Montauk, and caught a giant by drifting a bait around a herring boat. However, in most cases it seems that there are too many schools of bait swimming in the area for the giants to settle down in a chum line.

Canadian tuna fishing provides a real contrast to the American sport in many ways. One of the most significant differences involves the lack of running time. In virtually all cases, trolling starts almost immediately after clearing the dock or harbor. Unlike American sportsmen, Canadians haven't gotten into the long runs to distant grounds which have often saved stateside seasons. Perhaps the development of faster boats and exploration in areas far removed from convenient ports may result in Canadian tuna fisheries not even dreamed about at this time.

Though chances of catching a tuna in Canada are fewer and many days may be lost to bad weather, there is that shot at a super-giant. The rates charged by the lobstermen are ridiculously low by American standards. To top it off, everyone enjoys meeting the down-to-earth folks who live in the rural areas of the Canadian Provinces.

WELCOME TO RHODE ISLAND
DEPARTMENT of PUBLIC WORKS, DIVISION of HARBORS & RIVERS
UNITED STATES ATLANTIC TUNA TOURNAMENT
TWENTY SECOND ANNUAL CONTEST
SEPT. - 9th. - 10th. - 11th. - 1964
NARRAGANSETT, R.I.
POINT JUDITH

3 BLUEFIN TUNA TOURNAMENTS

United States Atlantic Tuna Tournament

In August 1989, the best known bluefin tuna tournament on the East Coast was held out of Block Island, Rhode Island. The 44th U.S. Atlantic Tuna Tournament (USATT) was run with more than 40 Eastern fishing clubs competing during the August 22nd to 24th event. According to Harold D. Schaefer of Brooklyn, New York, who has been a member of the tournament for 49 years , the first USATT was held in 1938 in Forked River, New Jersey when Walter O'Malley, owner of the Brooklyn Dodgers, challenged another angler to a fishing contest. During World War II the tournament was suspended and again in 1974 and 1975 when fuel was in short supply in Gloucester, Massachusetts. The tournament moved to Provincetown, Massachusetts for four years and returned to Block Island, Rhode Island, in September 1981.

The USATT is a club event and although individual anglers can win separate trophies, the fisherman who catches the largest tuna doesn't necessarily win the USATT trophy. Instead, teams receive points for the largest and most giant bluefin caught. In 1988, no club member landed a bluefin weighing more than the 310 pound qualifying weight. Back in 1981, early on the first day of that tournament Jack Dempsey was fishing for the Galilee Tuna Club aboard Captain Don Slater's **Invader**. He caught a 1,140¾ pound giant bluefin tuna, which stands today as the largest world record tournament bluefin. On the cod fishing grounds this spring, I got a hold of Captain Don Slater on the VHF radio and asked if he would be willing to get together some evening to tell me about the fish. Here's his story.

Captain Don Slater (R) and angler Jack Dempsey (L) who was fishing for the Galilee Tuna Club combined to catch this 1,140¾ pound giant bluefin in the 1981 USATT. To this day it's the largest bluefin tuna landed in United States waters.

Slater: We had marked a couple of fish 80 feet down, so we put out live whiting, one at 75, another at 85 feet and another 45 feet behind the boat. I was tending the lines and I saw the float go under. I hollered to Jim, "Strike," and the next moment he set the hook. Fishing in a fleet, the fish took off right under the anchor line of a New York boat and was soon wrapped around it. As I backed down to the anchor ball, I hollered to him to let go, which he did quickly. Now, this fish had been in the anchor line for at least five minutes but we had a very light drag setting so the line didn't break. When we got to the ball the mate could see the direction of the twist, and with a couple of flips we got the line free. Now we could put some pressure on the fish.

Anderson: What kind of equipment were you using?

Slater: The rod was a 100 pound class Shakespeare built in Rhode Island by Ericksons. Rather 'soft' as we say. The reel was a 130H Penn International loaded with Trilene 130 pound test mono with a 300 pound test Ande leader. I think the hook was an 11/0 Mustad offset #7698B, and the bait was a live whiting.

I personally like a softer rod for tournament fishing, as they are a little forgiving. What I mean is, you can make a mistake and sometimes get away with it. Not so with an unlimited stick. With a heavy rod, you can put the pressure to the fish but you can also pop 'em off easier.

Anderson: Did you know right away you were hooked to a good fish?

Slater: When this fish hit, he just kept going off, going and going and going. I told Jim we had a real heavy weight here and shortly the spool was three-quarters of the way down. Lucky for us, with the line around the anchor line and ball, the fish didn't do much. He seemed to be lazy and didn't pull hard. Once we put some pressure to him though, he moved off to the SE. Now, I had a good angler in Jim Dempsey as he's caught over 50 giants to date. I cautioned him not to move the drag lever, particularly with a spool only a quarter full. I usually don't put a lot of drag on a fish right off and in this case I backed the boat down for quite a while. Not getting any line back, I turned the boat and ran up toward the fish. We had a lot of line in the water and I'm sure that created a lot of drag and tired the fish. Once we got ahead of the fish, and with the spool looking a lot better, I suggested to Jim he move the drag lever up above the strike position.

With that, Jim began to rock the fish and then he said he could feel the hook coming loose, like it was tearing out. Well, I thought we'd hooked the fish in either the gut or its gills, so I suggested we take it easy. So Jim eased off a bit and surprisingly, the fish didn't fight hard.

A little while later, with the fish straight down, we might have had 45 pounds of drag on. Every time Jim lifted him a foot, we got a foot of line in the reel. Then we started to see those figure eight movements

Frank J. Mather, III in the chair fighting a bluefin tuna during the 1978 USATT.

from the fish and both Jim and I knew the fish was tiring. I felt the fish was gut hooked and hurting. But this fish didn't quit as they sometimes do. We were fighting this fish's weight and its circling swimming motion. Finally the fish came up maybe 60 to 70 feet behind the boat and his head came out of the water all the way back to the end of its gill plate. I said to Jim, "My gosh, we've got a fish over 1,000 pounds." As you might imagine, we got a little nervous but Jim kept up with the pressure on the fish.

Anderson: When you decided the fish was beat, how did it go at the transom? Any problems?

Slater: *After we saw the fish, it made some short spurts and then finally came up again behind the boat. When it did, I was on the leader and this fish came right across the back of the boat, parallel to the transom. The mate, who I called "Smoking Joe," as he always had a cigarette in his mouth, was responsible for gaffing the fish. Well, as I pulled, he gaffed the fish lightly, maybe down an inch or so from the top of his back. I hollered, "You don't have him, you don't have him! Give me the gaff, give me the gaff!" Leader in one hand, gaff handle in the other. Well, here I am, trying to push the gaff out of the fish, so that the gaff head can come down its full eight inches. With all that, the fish takes off. Good thing for us the hook doesn't come out. About 8 to 10 minutes later the fish is at the transom again, and the gaff goes into the fish real good. No question we have this fish. Tail roped and head pulled up along side the boat, I had a chance to look the fish over real good and I knew it was over 1,000 pounds. I can judge pretty good as I've put 288 fish in the boat over 310 pounds and I've got three fish over 1,000 pounds to my credit in my 38 years of charter fishing.*

Well, we called tournament headquarters and told them we had a fish and everybody asked how big. I didn't want to say much over the radio so I said a respectable fish, one that would qualify.

Anderson: How long was Jim on the fish?

Slater: Funny thing, we hooked up five minutes after the tournament officially started and we had the fish alongside at 8:35 a.m. So a total of 30 minutes on the fish. Should have done it quicker if we took the fish clean the first time we had it at the transom.

Anderson: Have any trouble getting the fish into the boat?

*Slater: Are you kidding? We couldn't do it. There were only three of us in the boat. We could only get the fish up so far but we couldn't get his head up to the level of the covering boards. I had to call the tournament headquarters at Block Island on the VHF and request permission to take another person from our club aboard to help us boat the fish. I explained it was gaffed, tail roped and secure. After several minutes of conversation, Mr. Schaefer gave me permission to let another person come aboard to help out. Bobby Audet, who was on the **Nina Marie**, gave us a hand and we finally got the fish into the cockpit. But not before our block and tackle jammed and pulled apart. Took us a while to get the tail down and the fish fully into the cockpit. Looking at the fish then left no doubt in anyone's mind as to its potential weight.*

At this point in time nearby boats kept asking how big it was over the radio but I was busy in the cockpit. With a tape measure, the fish proved to be 121 inches long with a 96 inch girth.

Anderson: Any chance you recall what was going through your mind at this point in time?

Slater: We looked at our options and decided to take the fish in to Block Island. So off we go and wouldn't you know it, tournament officials can't get the fish out of the boat. The equipment only allows them to get the fish up three or four feet off the cockpit deck, which makes me very nervous. Well, it hung there for quite a while and in the meantime photographers are taking pictures and we've got a hose on the fish to help keep it from drying out. Finally, a boom type tow truck is eased to the edge of the dock and the fish is lifted up and off the boat onto the dock. Now, with the fish out of the boat they can't weigh it as the scale only goes to 1,000 pounds and the fish frame isn't high enough.

After a long day of fishing, these boats are returning to Galilee, RI after participating in the 1963 USATT.

Anderson: What happened then?

Slater: Paul Fillipi, who runs Ballards Inn, had a state certified platform scale. Ed Fisher, the weighmaster, tells me the big problem is getting the whole fish onto the scale. So, a 4' × 8' sheet of plywood was cut in half and laid on the scale with the fish on it. That's how it was weighed and not until late in the afternoon. Certainly the fish lost weight out of water, in the sun, although we wet it down as often as we could, but I'd be willing to bet it lost up to 20 pounds or 2% of its weight.

Anderson: How much did the fish pay?

Slater: That fish was sold right there on the Island and brought $4,000. Back in 1986 I had the only fish in that year's tournament, a much smaller fish, and it paid almost the same amount even though it was five years later. Last fall, the prices paid to the boats were pushing $13 to $15 a pound. I wish the fish money wasn't quite so high. That's what ruined the fishery.

Anderson: Tell me a little about fishing for bluefin when you first started.

*Slater: Around 1970, I started fishing Gloucester with John Walton, who owned the **Chief Joseph Brant**. The first day I fished with him we hooked up on three giants, just like nothing. The next day we caught one fish but that started it for me. The next year I took my boat*

The 1962 USATT saw some good action. Here a few fish are hanging after weigh in. These fish were taken on wire and cable leaders which were commonly used during this period.

up and fished clients for three weeks. Back then I was married, five kids, working three jobs and money was tight. All I had were 10/0 Penn Senators, which were too small and sometimes blew right apart from the extreme fishing pressure. I finally got a pair of 14/0s, used, on sale from Ashaway Line and Twine. They held up fine.

The mono line we had then wasn't anywhere as good as what we have today. Back then, put a little pressure on it, with a chafed spot and it would let go. I think it was in 1971, I caught nineteen fish, mostly due to the fact I was fishing monofilament line.

Anderson: What do you remember about selling tuna years ago?

Slater: Tuna fish were paying nothing in those days, maybe 2 or 3 cents a pound, and the reason people went out tuna fishing was for the fun of it. Years back, we let a lot of fish go, especially school fish. We tagged fish for Frank Mather at Woods Hole, as it was no big deal to catch 15 to 25 fish a day in the early 1960s. We only had to go to the A Buoy or the old Fairway Buoy and if you went down to Cox's Ledge, you'd catch fish all the way. I remember looking down from the tower, and with a fish on, see unbelievable numbers swimming along with it. And schools on the surface. Didn't always catch 'em but if we got one, you could coax a few strikes with the diamond jigs.

I'll never forget once when I took a load of school tuna to the Point Judith Fishermen's Co-op. They gave me a slip on the weight and they were shipped off to the Fulton Fish market in New York. I didn't really expect much and I certainly didn't expect to see what I did when I opened the envelope a week or so later. It was a bill for $25 for the shipping costs. Imagine, the fish simply weren't worth enough to cover the cost of freight charges!

The worst thing that ever happened was the high price that developed for the fish. I believe it caused everybody who was on the water, who liked to fish, to chase the tuna to make a buck. I remember the first year NMFS put the quota system into effect. I was fishing out of Cape Ann Marina in Gloucester and the day before there were 40 to 50 boats fishing along with me on the Northwest corner of Stellwagon Bank. The fishing closed at midnight and the next day there was me, with a party, and only one other boat simply because you couldn't keep the fish. With the fishing closed, we either let the fish go or tagged them and then let them go. After that, we were the only boat for the rest of the week. I was there with my party fishing for sport. That showed me there were a lot of meat fishermen fishing for money to pay bills. Hard to imagine with the style and class of boats they owned. Without the lure of making a few bucks, these same fellows simply quit fishing.

3 BLUEFIN TUNA TOURNAMENTS

Rhode Island Tuna Tournament

Back in 1958, a group of local big game fishermen, recognizing that Rhode Island waters offered some fo the finest giant bluefin tuna fishing on the East Coast, and wishing to establish Rhode Island as the "Tuna Capital of the World," organized and incorporated the Rhode Island Tuna Tournament. The port of Galilee was selected as the permanent base of operations because of its close proximity to well known and highly productive giant bluefin fishing areas. The long Labor Day weekend was selected as the permanent tournament date.

Since 1958, hundreds of giant bluefins have come to the dock with a total of 24 tournament winning fish. However, no qualifying tuna were taken in 1958, 1966, 1975, 1976, 1986, 1987, 1988 and 1989. Since 1971, the Tournament Committee has recommended the tag and release of fish under 310 pounds. Tuna taken by the Tournament are sold and the proceeds are given to the Hodges-Lawton Unit for Crippled Children at Rhode Island Hospital, a charity strongly supported by the Palestine Shriners.

In the late 1960s and 1970s the RITT grew to be the largest tournament of its kind in the world. Contestants annually number over 300—some years over 400—and boats enter from an eight state area. With the return of the fleet in the late afternoon, thousands of spectators would jam the bulkheads and docks hoping for a glimpse of a giant bluefin and a very large crowd would gather around the scale. In 1965, angler Jim Cullen from New York weighed in an 804 pound bluefin tuna, at that time the largest bluefin ever landed in a tournament thus setting the World Tournament Record for that species. In 1977, angler Tom Crafford of Narragansett, Rhode Island, broke that record when the scales pushed to 990 pounds, the largest fish ever entered in the RITT. Since then that record has not been surpassed in this tournament.

In 1977 Tom Crafford (L) and his Sandipeg went into the record books. This 990 pound giant broke all previous records in the RITT. Since that day this record has not been surpassed.

Only a few years back, Tom Crafford was a very active angler and well known by the Rhode Island angling fraternity. Having known him for over twenty years, I asked him to tell me about his fish.

*Crafford: We were fishing out of my boat, the **Sandipeg**, this second day of the tournament over the Labor Day weekend. As I recall, we anchored up in the middle of the fleet right on the west bank of the Mudhole. The weather was ideal, only little wind, and we were chumming with small butterfish and using a cut butterfish for bait. We had marked a few fish at the 70 foot level and that's where we had the bait.*

(Author's note: Along with Tom, Tom Wyss acted as captain and ran the boat while Murray Cianciola and his son Don worked the cockpit. These individuals had been fishing as a team for three years prior to this day.)

Crafford: The bite came at 11:12 a.m. and I was in the chair, having been decided earlier by means of drawing straws. Strike drag was only 35 pounds with full drag approximately 75 to 80 pounds. The outfit was a bent butt rod with a 12/0 Fin Nor reel holding 130 pound test Ashaway Greenspot Dacron with a single strand wire leader and a 10/0 Mustad hook. Once hooked, this fish took off and it took a while for me to get settled in the chair. Then, I put the pressure to the fish.

(Author's note: Tom remarked that quite a few times his backside came right off the seat of the Pompanette Big Game chair when he put the reel to full drag.)

Crafford: The only problem we had was with a boat on our port side. Our line attached to the fish swimming off picked up one of the baits of the adjoining boat and they thought they had a fish on as well. In a while, with my fish surfacing, we all could see the other line and hook running along ours. What seemed like forever, we finally managed to pull that hook off the line by hand.

(Author's note: Tom went along to tell the fish was very strong, but expert boat handling kept the fish just off the transom.)

Crafford: It took me 33 minutes to bring the fish up to the transom. Don leadered the fish and Murray gaffed it. We tailed roped the fish and then proceeded to get it through the tuna door, which was barely large enough. Once in the cockpit, moments later, it decided it didn't like the boat and it went wild. Bouncing and thrashing, I thought we were going to have a serious problem but of course we hastily fled to the bridge of the boat. Back at the dock Ed Fisher was the official weighmaster, and he informed us we had no 750 pounder as we reported. He guessed the fish to be very close to 1,000 pounds. Well, he was off by 10 pounds and I had to hand it to him, he could judge the weight of a fish pretty good.

(Author's note: Ed Fisher was the state weighmaster and involved with many a tournament. No doubt he developed a very keen eye).

Crafford: I'll say this, one man doesn't catch a fish, the credit has to go to the whole crew. My friend Murray knew just what to do as he had many giant tuna to his credit. And another thing, I always made it clear to the crew that regardless of how many we caught or how much they were paying, the money was going to the Shriners and in this case the Hodges-Lawton Unit for Crippled Children at Rhode Island Hospital. No one on the boat needed the money.

Never did I dream it was going to be a record fish, but we all knew we had a good one. I had caught a few fish in the 300 to 400 pound range but naturally they had nowhere the stamina of this brute. The fish brought approximately $1,100 and was donated to charity. Today, with fish worth up to $17 a pound, it would have been worth close to $13,000.

Well, I've seen what it's done to some of the fellows. Years back, a boat coming into the fleet never compromised another by anchoring too close. That's all changed today because the fish are worth so much.

Captain Al Anderson (L) put Jack Oakley (R) into this 348 pound bluefin which took the Bacardi Cup for the first fish boated during the 1984 RITT.

Another story, another day. This time involving the Bacardi Cup awarded for First Tuna Boated in the 1984 RITT. John Oakley chartered my boat for the first day of fishing in the RITT. Jack, as he's called, has participated in many tournaments and felt he might have a chance to boat a fish with me as the previous year the **Prowler** had taken 38 fish. This particular morning we left Snug Harbor Marina at the usual sailing time of 5:00 a.m. with a crew consisting of Jack, his nephew David, and Steve Tombs as a mate. What action had occurred the day before was in the area I call Haab's Ledge, in tribute to the late Captain Walter Haab, who ran the **Seacon** out of Montauk. Everyone in the Connecticut, Montauk, and Rhode Island charter fleet respected and admired him greatly. This area is on the west bank of the Butterfish Hole and for us it was a three-hour steam at 13 knots with fair tide from Point Judith.

We arrived in the area to see a fleet of nearly 100 boats, most of which home ported out of Connecticut or New York with a few RITT boats. As we arrived, boats in the tournament had already begun to fish as it was past the 8:00 a.m. starting time. Instead of just finding an open area to anchor, I took the time to scout around to see what was happening. A good tuna fisherman takes the time to look things over for a "bite" going on. A number of boats in the southern part of the fleet were experiencing action and a number of fish were being fought. Fighting the urge to speed the boat up, we finally reached an area where there was plenty of freeway between us and other boats and the anchor was put overboard.

As we were coming tight on the anchor rode, Steve readied a 130 pound class bent butt outfit in the aft port side rod holder. I was watching the Furuno Color Scope and saw a few fish at the fifty-foot depth. Steve then taped a 12 ounce flat black, spray painted sinker to the 130 pound test clear Ande Mono a few feet above the snap swivel. While he was doing that, I took a hook bait (butterfish) from the cooler, hook inserted and leader already set to go and tied it on. A moment later the bait was fishing at approximately 50 feet, with the PENN 130H International set on strike. I went back to the center console to look at the color machine once again, and I heard the reel go off singing. All this happened so fast I never shut the engine down or had time to jot down the Loran numbers of our position on the console. As I had done many times, I reached over to the quick release on the port side and let go from the anchor line ball.

The current was moderately strong running to the WSW, and the bitter end of the anchor rode slithered overboard quickly. Putting the boat into gear, I backed down away from the anchor rode as Jack came off the seat to go for the rod. The abrupt momentum of the boat caused Jack to lose his balance. Anyone else would not have gotten up as quickly but Jack was at the rod a moment later.

With luck, this fish angled away from the fleet, going off to the SW in the tide set. I hollered to Jack to slowly ease back on the drag to prevent an overrun because with approximately 40 pounds of drag, it's very difficult to get the rod butt out of the holder and carry the outfit to the chair. We had taken the time to set up the harness in the chair seat so Jack got into it and we snapped him to the reel. I was then advised to radio the judge's boat and inform them we had a fish on the time of hookup (8:30 a.m.).

Everything happened so fast, we never even started chumming, although a good amount of bait had been cut up on the way out. With no other lines to retrieve, we could focus our attention quickly on fighting the fish. Jack is a good angler and with gloved hand he laid line evenly back on the reel, knowing when to lift and reel and when to sit back and relax as the fish spurted off. Approximately 25 minutes later I leadered the fish and Steven gaffed it. Jack cautioned me several times about forcing the fish at leader time, afraid we might pull the hook or pop it off, as we were using 250 pound test mono leader. To make a long story short, the fish was hooked in the hinge of the jaw, the leader was fresh, and if need be, we could have fought that fish all day long with little threat to the integrity of the leader.

A short time later, reporting our catch, the judge's boat informed us we had the first fish of the tournament. Jack decided we should quit for the day and get it back to the weigh-in scale. He was hoping to weigh in the first fish of the tournament, and we had a three-hour run back to Pt. Judith with a fair tide.

Moving back to the general area we had been fishing, we recognized a few boats and there was our ball. A short time later, once on the anchor, we block and tackled the fish into the boat. As it turned out, we had to buck the ebb tide as we approached Block Island and several times changed our ETA with tournament headquarters. Little did I know Dan Head, Tournament Director, had plans for us as we came through the Galilee-Jerusalem breachway. Escorted by the USCG, sirens blaring, fire fighting hoses spraying, we made our way up to the bulkhead at tournament headquarters and scale. On the way in, as we had plenty of time to clean up, stow gear, etc., we put the tape measure on the fish and plugged the length and girth figures into the formula. It suggested a weight of approximately 350 pounds. On the scale the fish had an official weight of 348 pounds and Jack Oakley took the Bacardi Cup for the first fish boated in the 1984 RITT.

3 BLUEFIN TUNA TOURNAMENTS

Atlantic Tuna Club

I'm sure the founders of the Atlantic Tuna Club never envisioned the sad state of affairs of the bluefin tuna as it exists today. Not only had the resource declined to a point in which fishing is being allowed only under a moratorium as a result of this fish having tremendous market value but the commonly held attitudes and ethics of their time are struggling for existence in today's angling community.

Let's take a quick look at a club now celebrating its 75th anniversary. The club was incorporated in 1914 at the time World War I broke out in Europe and today is the oldest tuna fishing club on the Atlantic Coast. I believe the first, and hence oldest tuna club in the country was established at Avalon on Catalina Island, California, and was incorporated thirteen years prior.

The development and formation of ocean rod and reel fishing in America started with the establishment of the New England striped bass clubs in the 1840s and no doubt their activities precipitated formation of the Atlantic Tuna Club. The founders of the club espoused the ideals of "Fostering and protecting the game fishes of the waters of the Atlantic Coast of the United States of America, to promote and encourage rod and reel sea angling with lightest possible tackle, to diffuse information and promote social intercourse among the members of the Club." There must have been considerable interest in fishing those days as the list of club members in its first year of existence totals 140 individuals, well-to-do gentlemen, mostly businessmen from New York, Boston and Providence areas, with interest in deep sea angling.

The Atlantic Tuna Club had its roots at Block Island, Rhode Island, with its club house located there until 1952 (except for one year, 1947, at Christies Restaurant in Newport). Since then, meeting sites and activities have been held in Galilee and Providence, and its new club house site is now in Snug Harbor at Wakefield, Rhode Island.

To give you a flavor of the goings-on back in those days, one of the incorporators of the club, Dr. Charles K. Stillman, recorded the following, "The Club started off splendidly as regards personnel. A small but neat and attractive cottage was rented on the island and the steward engaged, but the following season proved to be one of the worst on record for fishing.

"1915 was a poor year, but it was nevertheless the first year that any considerable number of orthodox anglers visited the island," wrote Stillman.

"1916 was considered a successful season. Records of the club show that members took 297 tuna in August, 169 in September—a total of 466 tuna. The actual number was doubtless greater due to the failure of some members to register catches. It is safe to say that approximately a thousand tuna were taken on rod and reel that season." (Some false albacore or little tunny may have found their way into that count.)

Stillman went on to say: "1917 had splendid fishing through August but the fun ended on September 3rd, as a result of severe northwest storms. 1918 saw almost identical conditions, the fishing being phenomenal until early in September, etc. Fishing in 1919 started well but was broken up by a northeaster about the third week in August.

"The past season, 1920, has fulfilled every expectation. The fun started on July 21st. Within a couple of days the sea was alive with them (tuna)...The number caught limited only by physical endurance. The club record for 1920 was 483, but according to the steward, Mr. Nute, not more than half the catches were registered.

"The amateur who runs his own boat also will never do as well as the sportsman who goes out with Elmer Allen, Edwin Dodge, Elmer or Norman Dodge, Jason Mott, W. Conley, Kit Littlefield, C.W. Rose, Harry Smith, W.D. Havens, Ev Hoxie or any other registered boatmen."

Club history goes on to record portions of a letter written by Mr. Andrew Gray Weeks in 1920, painting a picture of the tuna fishing at Block Island back then.

"They (tuna) usually reach our waters the last of July remaining into October in numerous schools of fish weighing from twenty pounds up to their limit of growth, one thousand pounds and over.

The (local) market fishermen troll with four lines, two on outriggers, two men to a boat, using wooden squid, silvered, and only thirty to forty feet of very heavy line.

"The smaller fish, twenty to sixty pounds, are hauled in hand over hand; the larger ones may be secured but almost invariably part the line. Heavy gloves, it is needless to say, are a part of the outfit.

"To give you some idea of the numbers taken I will mention the record of boatman Harry L. Smith. From July 27 to September 24 he took 18,925 pounds of dressed tuna. His largest day was 1,600 pounds, but over 3,000 pounds have been brought in by other single boats. He also took 3,065 pounds of bonita.

"There are about ten boats that take out rod fishers and others that confine themselves to market fishing. From dealers records it seems that 25,000 pounds have been landed in one day. It is hard to estimate accurately the weight of a season's catch, but it must be around 300,000 pounds.

"Members have taken 483 tuna this season, a goodly portion on light tackle. Two of our members, using heavy tackle, caught eighteen and twenty-four respectively in one day.

"The occasional schools of enormous fish have played havoc with even heavy tackle and the numerous schools of 75 to 100 pound fish make light tackle somewhat of a gamble."

In the early 1920s, Captain H.K. (Kit) Littlefield's Lelia D often put together fine catches of school bluefin tuna, false albacore and bluefish.

In a November 5, 1920 letter, Mr. Julian T. Crandall of Ashaway Line and Twine wrote to Mr. Weeks. He stated: "A picture of a 900 pound tuna which was harpooned off Block Island. This same captain had caught many of these large tuna and states that there are quantities of these big fish in these waters."

Much of the information available regarding the early activities of the club was lost in the Wednesday, September 21, 1938, hurricane that swept over Block Island. At that time the Club occupied a room at Ballard's Inn, which was partially destroyed but the club register, some trophies and the majority of the furniture were saved. As a result, Mr. Paul C. Nicholson was able, as Chairman of a historical committee, to prepare and have published a book entitled, "Atlantic Tuna Club, THEN and NOW," dated 1954. On its seventy-fifth anniversary, a newly compiled and updated history of the club will be available, written by local sportswriter and photojournalist Thomas Meade, bringing the last twenty-five years of club history into focus.

Unlike earlier times when the club members actively competed for established trophies at the expense of the resource, the philosophy of the Atlantic Tuna Club is considerably different today. In its 1984 Statement of Policy, the clubs states: "The Atlantic Tuna Club, the second oldest fishing club in America, was founded for the purpose of bringing principles of sportsmanship to the catching

The founders and Charter members of the Atlantic Tuna Club (L to R) A.J. Crandall, Zenas W. Bliss, L. Dana Chapman and Edmond E. Hills.

of tuna and other oceanic gamefish for pleasure. In view of the mounting evidence that a severe depletion of the world's population of Atlantic bluefin tuna has occurred, it is the opinion of the Board of Directors of the Club that the catching and killing of bluefin tuna is inconsistent with the principles upon which the Club was founded and members are strongly urged to tag and release all tuna brought to the boat."

Along with this, a policy change occurred in 1984 regarding the Ralph Hammond Koelb Memorial Trophy in which the award was changed from boating the largest giant bluefin anytime and anywhere, to the largest giant bluefin boated in a recognized tuna tournament not exceeding five days duration. To further encourage conservation, the Club established the Frank J. Mather, III Trophy to be awarded to the member tagging and releasing the most giant bluefin tuna in any one year. And along this vein, the Foster Cup and the Charles W. Willard Trophy was changed to recognize the tagging and releasing of the most school tuna.

A while back I had the opportunity to sit with Mr. Webster Goodwin, secretary-treasurer of the Club, who has been an active angler and Club member for many years. He was gracious enough to steer me toward the necessary information needed to profile some of the Club's history, its activities, and to give personal opinion on several topics.

Anderson: I'm on the water everyday and I'm there because I have to make a living. I no longer see the respect that boat crews used to show to others in the attempt to make large sums by tuna fishing. The Club stands out as one of the few groups that continues to uphold traditional sportfishing ethics.

Goodwin: Well, that may be true and there's no question that the value of the fish today has warped the ethics of tuna anglers. The dollar bill has seemingly taken precedence over anything else and it's unfortunate in some ways. It's hard to believe that people go out just to catch a fish with rod and reel for the money involved in it. It never was that way, the club frowns on it; we can't do anything about it except talk and do our best to urge members to tag and release and be sportsmen about it. In other words, not to be money-grubbers. Don't misunderstand me, with a 500 pound tuna on the end of the line, a good many of our members, I think, would probably bring it to the dock and sell it. And some wouldn't, simply on principle.

A few years back, it was my observation that a giant tuna on the end of the line that didn't have the value it does today was tagged and released. In fact, I believe there was ardent competition by some club members in this regard. There weren't many in the sportfishing community who knew just why this was going on.

Webster Goodwin weighed in this 760 pound giant bluefin for the Atlantic Tuna Club during the 1977 RITT.

I think Frank Mather probably inspired tagging in the club, as well as the club tag and release program (other species). As a highly respected man regarding bluefin tuna, his ideas were supported by the club. The eventual demise of this species seems to be true. He's told the truth all the way along and fought the battle but he's been licked. I think the Club has supported his efforts from the very beginning, when he was at Woods Hole, Massachusetts.

Anderson: Looking at the Club handbooks, I've seen no recipient for the F.J. Mather, III Award for 1986, 1987, or 1988, by Club members for the tagging of a giant tuna.

Goodwin: No affidavit had been submitted and as a matter of fact no club member caught a giant tuna last year. There were one or two caught in 1989 that I'm aware of. What I'm saying is our members are out trying but they're not tagging the giant fish because they're not catching. It seems the resource simply isn't there for our Club members to catch.

This story really doesn't end there, however. Giant tuna fishing is an expensive pastime today. Could it be that many members of the club, now totaling eighty-nine in number, no longer choose to catch a fish, tag it, release it, knowing full well the frustration and expenses incurred without compensation? In light of the fishery's situation today, not very many people could afford the time or cost to do so in the name of conservation.

Thumbing through the 1989 Club Handbook, it became apparent that a number of long-time club trophies had no recipient in recent years. Mr. Web Goodwin again indicated fish were not being caught and hence catch affidavits not submitted. In the last six years, the Lloyd Robert Crandall Memorial Trophy, awarded for the largest broadbill swordfish rod and reel, had no recipient. Since 1985, the Frank J. Mather, III Trophy for tagging giant bluefin tuna has had no recipient. The Ralph Hammond Koelb Memorial Trophy for the largest bluefin tuna boated in a recognized tournament in all waters without territorial restrictions was last awarded in 1984 to Jack Oakley, who chartered my boat the first day of the Rhode Island Tuna Tournament and received the Bacardi Cup for the first giant bluefin tuna boated.

What does the future hold in store for the Atlantic Tuna Club? Looking back in time for a moment at the club history, one sees a tremendous list of angling achievements, not simply because many of its members had the wherewithal, outstanding angling skills or modern equipment but also as a result of a healthy tuna fishery resource. I'm sure many Club members in the 1920s thru 1960s envisioned continued tackle improvements, larger and faster boats, more active angling competition, with larger and tougher fish to catch. It is doubtful, though, anyone envisioned the severe decline of one of the fish its members sought and for which the Club was named. The decline of the bluefin would have seemed impossible to Club founders.

With today's Atlantic Coast fisheries situation and continuing trends a number of Atlantic Tuna Club trophies may well be retired with new awards established to take their place. No doubt the future is dim concerning angling for tuna and billfishes but other gamefish species may be substituted for angling competition. One thing is for sure, the Club has come to the end of an era and the start of another.

3 BLUEFIN TUNA TOURNAMENTS

Point Judith Masters Invitational

In early 1980 a group of sport fishermen decided to create a small invitation-only tournament to pursue giant bluefin tuna. This even was fueled by long-term unofficial competition by these same fishermen on the offshore grounds. It was called the Point Judith Masters Invitational Tuna Tournament with weigh-ins at Galilee.

The first year saw 26 boats competing with 83 registered anglers. Of these, three were women; one of whom was my wife, Daryl, who the previous year had allowed me to register her in the eleventh Annual Block Island Invitational Billfish Tournament. She would come along for a week's vacation stay on the Island but if the weather was sour, would elect to stay on the Island rather than join me and the mate for her routine day of seasickness. To make a long story short, she won the Heaviest White Marlin trophy for a female angler in that 1979 tournament. Heretofore, she had tangled with only bluefish but with a fish on, her instructions were to consider this leaping white marlin as just another bluefish and not to get nervous. On 30 pound class tackle she subdued a 59 pound ''Skilly'' to be the second woman ever to boat a white in this prestigious tournament. So began her short career as a tournament anglerette.

In the first Pt. Judith Masters, I had three Connecticut anglers entered who had never tangled with a giant bluefin tuna. But that didn't seem to matter too much. The first several days of the tournament were forecast to be rough and Daryl elected to stay home in Narragansett as she knew she would run the risk of mal de mer. Actually, the weather was beautiful offshore those two days and angler Stu Purvis took a fish weighing 408 pounds the first day while angler Greg Montana landed a 493 pound bluefin the second day. We had another fish on that day but it was lost in the anchor line of another boat. Combined, the two fish had us in contention for first place in the tournament.

On the last day, only little wind was forecast by the National Weather Bureau and Daryl consented to come along. This third day, September 1, 1980, dawned clear and cool with winds predicted to be variable. Well, so much for the forecast. It blew northeast and since we were fishing approximately 24 miles off the beach, seas built to 4 to 6 feet. Early on, it was decided that if we got a bite, Daryl would go into the chair. Come mid morning, sea conditions got to her and if looks could kill I was really going to pay for this adventure. As the day wore on a few fish were taken in the fleet and prospects of getting a bite looked good. I had managed to jig a few live whiting off the bottom and one of them was swimming around just above the bottom attached to one of the 130 pound class outfits we had fishing. In a short while, we marked our first fish of the day down deep near the bottom. Well, our turn came.

We were fishing out of my bonito and bass boat. A 26 footer with an aluminum tournament big game chair mounted forward on the raised casting platform. The **Prowler** was the smallest boat entered in the Masters Tournament and I believe it signaled the start of small boats and big game fishing in Rhode Island waters. When it came to fighting a giant tuna, we had a distinct advantage as it was very easy to go ahead and turn on a fish. With a small tower from which I could run the boat, I could easily watch angler, rod tip and line all at the same time. Fighting a fish from up forward, we had no restrictions with the line as the underwater gear was at the other end of the boat. But our problems developed when it came time to leader and gaff a fish, because in this boat one was high off the water standing in front of the chair. We were forced to wire and gaff a fish on the side of the boat, well away from the rod tip. With a little practice, I'd leave the tower toward the end of the battle and run the boat from the center console below. That put me in a position to leader, or gaff or tail rope a fish readily.

Getting back to my wife, she was sleeping as her bout with mal de mer left her feeling miserable. I'm sure the excitement of the hookup awakened her and if not, certainly the shouting involved with getting the other lines in and getting off the anchor line ball did. Knowing she had to fight a giant tuna in that condition resulted in a horrified look on her face. Realizing she wasn't doing well, both Stu and Greg bodily lifted her, carried her forward and put her into the chair. Moments later we got a pair of wet cotton gloves on her and she moved forward to get the outfit out of the bow mounted rod holder. It seemed like it took forever to get the outfit free of the holder and put the rod butt in the gimbal of the chair. Shortly we had her in the harness and she kept telling us she wasn't sure she could do this.

Fortunately, this bluefin elected to swim away from most of the boats in the fleet. It didn't look too bad if we could get a little line back, which I directed her to do as soon as possible. I'm afraid the editor wouldn't allow printing her reply to me. After that episode, I used the word "Honey" quite a bit. We notified the judges promptly, and then she put as much pressure as possible on the fish. Only problem was, her behind came off the chair seat everytime she did and that scared her to death. The drag pressure may have gone as high as 45 to 50 pounds, I can't remember. Well, the excitement finally got to her and she hollered for a bucket. I told her it was not a good time to get seasick. Again an unprintable reply. Now, well away from the fleet , I could chase the fish down a little to help her along. But we heard some bad language when the fish took line against the drag.

All this time, Greg and Stu were giving her encouragement from behind the chair. With the line marked at 50-foot intervals, she could see she was making progress and it helped her spirits. As usually happens, the fish came up to the surface and I was directed by her to move the boat ahead to help get some line back. I'm sure that at this point in time, in her mind, she was convinced we were going to get her fish. I'll never forget watching her toward the end of the struggle. She would stand on the footrest sitting back in the harness but always with one hand on the chair arm. Having a safety line to the outfit gave her little or no comfort or security. I've got to give her a lot of credit in reading the behavior of the fish during the battle. This was the very first time she had been out giant tuna fishing, and she was quick to see changes in the fish's behavior during the battle. Quick to take line when the fish eased up, leaning back and relaxing as the fish took line against the drag.

It was then the steering on the boat quit. Seems like the oil cooler for the power-assisted Mercruiser steering had developed an internal leak and all the power steering fluid had gone out in the raw water exhaust. Carrying spare oil, we managed to get back in business shortly. Doing circles, we realized this fish was tiring quickly, and being straight down, on its side, meant the battle would be over soon. I explained to Daryl what to do in the closing moments and she performed flawlessly. As the fish came up this final time, Greg leadered it, Stu gaffed it, and moments later I had a tail rope on it.

Daryl got kisses from all the crew for a job well done, and considerable congratulations over the VHF as I radioed the judge's boat we had taken a fish. Back into the fleet towing the fish, we got back on the ball and then put the fish into the boat with a block and tackle

Captain Al Anderson (L) teamed up with his wife Daryl (R) during the First Annual Point Judith Masters Invitational Tuna Tournament to land her first bluefin. This 307 pound bluefin missed the minimum qualifying weight by three pounds.

hung from the tower. It was quickly decided we would end fishing for the day at that time. During this period, Daryl never moved from the chair. On the way in we put the tape measure on the fish and plugged the numbers into a formula I have for estimating a tuna's weight. The figures said approximately 300 pounds. If so, the fish would not qualify, as a minimum of 310 pounds had been established by the tournament for eligibility.

Well about the time we get to the Fairway buoy southeast of Block Island, the power steering quits again. With no spare oil left, it's almost impossible to steer the boat. Lucky for us, the **Joka** came by and Billy Catauro gave us some oil. Without their help, I'm not sure we could have made it safely in.

The weigh-in scale was located in Galilee and tournament officials had arranged for the crane belonging to Rhode Island Engine Co., Inc. to take fish out of the boats. At the bulkhead the fish was quickly plucked out of the boat and put on the scale as the fog closed in. What we had already guessed was now history; the fish did not qualify as it weighed only 307 pounds. My wife accepted that in a sporting manner but naturally I was very disappointed, although very proud of her achievement. It just was not meant for us to win the Tournament. As it turned out, we took second place with a combined total of 901 points, a point per pound for fish boated.

A few days later I'm shown the black and blue marks around her lower back from where the harness rode up, not to mention a few other bruises. In case you're wondering, the fish were sold and monies were shared by anglers and boat.

This is probably as good an opportunity as there is to mention how grateful I am for the good nature and support I've gotten from my wife over the years. She has always been supportive of my charter fishing endeavors. When I decided to leave a teaching career a number of years back and go into a full-time charter operation using our savings to build a new boat, she gave me loads of confidence by being supportive. Getting up with me at 4 o'clock in the morning day after day to prepare breakfast and make a lunch prior to going to work as Office Manager at Ram Point Marina, has certainly demonstrated a willing spirit. I owe her a great deal for my success.

4 TACKLE AND TECHNIQUES

Tackle Choices From Ed & Frank Murray Brothers

I think it's safe to say that the growth of giant bluefin tuna fishing precipitated a minor revolution in the big game tackle industry from New Jersey to New England. Far and above anyone else, it was Ed and Frank Murray who popularized fishing for giants from New York's Mud Hole to Montauk and on up to New England. For many years they were recognized as the top rod and reel giant tuna specialists and they plied the waters from the Bahamas to Montauk to the Canadian Maritimes chasing giant bluefin. The names giant tuna and the Murray brothers became synonymous, and they began developing tackle and equipment which took them to the very pinnacle of the sport.

In the mid 1970s, as the price of the fish came into the picture, and with most giant tuna being landed by the rod and reel fisheries, there began to develop a tremendous demand for specialized tackle and equipment, in particular the Murray Bros. big game chair. In 1972, the Murray Bros. fishing tackle business was started and in 1975 they sold their cabinet making business in Long Island, New York.

Thus began a full-time tackle manufacturing business relocated to West Palm Beach, Florida; a good move since much of their product line was in demand by other blue water fishermen on an international level. But before any product became available, it was tested extensively, particularly aboard the **Cookie Too** operated by Ed "Cookie" Murray and his brother, Paul, both licensed captains. Their other brother Jeff ran the Murray Bros. woodworking factory where the chairs are built. Today, Frank's son Vinnie, handles the daily operations of the factory. Cookie Boats, Inc. is a charter fishing business for owners Donald Stott and the Murrays. One year the **Cookie Too** took 92 giant tuna, including 16 in one day.

Ed (L) and Frank (R) Murray have come a long way since 1972. Today the Murray Brothers feel at home in West Palm Beach, FL.

Let's take a look at some of the changes in tackle that occurred in the giant tuna fisheries and the reasons behind them. For many years bluefin tuna tackle fell into either one of two categories: expensively exclusive or run of the mill.

REELS: For those who could afford it, the Tycoon FIN-NOR reel, size 9/0 and 12/0, were top of the line on the tuna grounds in the late 1960s. Less expensive reels were manufactured by Ocean City and Penn Fishing Tackle Mfg. Co., with the latter's Senator series being the most commonly seen in the fleet. In the late 1960s, the International series from Penn appeared and became immediately popular due to their look, design and comparatively lower cost. Superior to the Senator series, their lever drag design allowed pre-set drag tension, much like that of the FIN-NOR, far superior to the previous star drag system. Along with this was a much larger drag washer surface which dissipated the heat from greater drag friction. The Penn 130 and 130H, along with the 80 and 80W models, began to see longer factory production runs in the early 1970s. These hefty reels were a mile stone in giant bluefin tackle development.

RODS: The rods commonly used in the late 1960s were quite unlike those of today but as the fisheries heated up in the early 1970s, rapid changes occurred. The first fiberglass blanks were made in the 1950s by Conolon, followed by Harnell, then

Shakespeare, Fenwick and a host of others. Wooden straight butts, very common in the early 1970s, simply couldn't take the strain produced by battles with giants and a number of small machine shops, like Frank's Butts, began producing straight, as well as bent butts. AFTCO was the first to commercially produce inexpensive, hollow aluminum bent butts for the giant tuna tackle industry. Bent butts took a while to catch on, as this created problems in the chair, which will be discussed later. Many rods sported Mildrum roller guides, an absolute necessity with the popular lines being employed and some rod makers chose the more expensive Tycoon FIN-NOR series guides. To meet demand for a more streamlined guide, AFTCO introduced its roller guide series, appealing to those with a smaller pocketbook. Today the AFTCO Big Foot series leads the industry in terms of cost and performance.

LINES: Certainly the most critical element in a giant tuna outfit, lines had progressed from the dark ages of linen to braided nylon to braided Dacron, with monofilament enjoying limited popularity in the early 1970s. Ande soon replaced Platyl monofilament. Ashaway Line & Twine began producing a high quality Dacron line in the 1950s that was favored by many. Unlike mono, Dacron had little stretch properties but could be readily spliced. Prior to this time, lines tested no more than 130 pounds. As the fear of losing a

The 80 and 130 pound level drag reels with AFTCO aluminum bent butts are the standard equipment used by most giant bluefin fishermen today.

During the mid 1950s, the Hardy rod with a Penn Senator 16/0 and braided dacron line was the best available equipment at that time. The only problem with this combination was the straight wooden butt. Aluminum butts were not available till the 1970s.

valuable fish increased, a demand soon developed for even heavier test lines and 150 pound, 180 pound, and 200 pound test became available. This, in turn, created problems at tournament time, as most events were conducted in accordance with International Game Fish Association (IGFA) rules and regulations.

As time progressed, angler preference turned to the black-colored Dacron line, with Gudebrod being the first to provide anglers this option. Today Cortland line is popular. It has a soft weave providing an expandable inner core. Murray Bros. Tournament Dacron enjoys considerable popularity as well.

A while back I had the chance to talk to Ed Murray Sr. about this development. According to Murray, the concept of black line started when they fished south of Block Island using a spotter plane. As he recalled, "We were on a school of giants and the pilot along with Captain Jimmy Donovan, also in the aircraft, told us our double line looked like an anchor rope. At first we used those broad felt tip pen black ink markers but then we went to India ink applied with a small terry cloth rag. We only darkened the first 50 feet or so but to others back at the dock with the line on the reel it appeared that we used all black line. As a result of a growing demand, line companies began to produce black-dyed Dacron line. Interestingly enough, one line manufacturer advises us that dying the Dacron reduces its strength test considerably. An all black line can be difficult for captain and crew to see early mornings, late afternoons and on dark days, so it's still best to darken only the end.

LEADERS: In the early 1970s with good numbers of fish around at times, braided cable was used while chumming and it enjoyed some success. It rarely failed but it soon became apparent it did not catch as well as stainless steel piano wire. As tuna prices climbed, IGFA regulation length leaders and double lines were soon forgotten, as this jeopardized taking a valuable fish. As heavier pound test monofilament became available, it replaced #15 wire (240 pound test was most common) on the chumming grounds. Trollers continued with the stainless steel #18 and #19 wire testing 325 pounds and 360 pounds respectively. The heavy monos brought slightly more success but could be chaffed through by sharp teeth. This lead to the development of "mouse trap rigs."

Talking with Ed Murray about this development, he said: "I was probably one of the first to successfully use a short piece of cable that was coiled and then taped to the hook. Concealed inside the bait, it opened on the strike. I gave one of the first to Jim Cullen, owner of the **Patricia**, captained by Frank Hammer, the night they left to fish the Rhode Island Tuna Tournament in 1965. He went on to win it with an 800 pound plus fish."

Tube And Sinker Rig

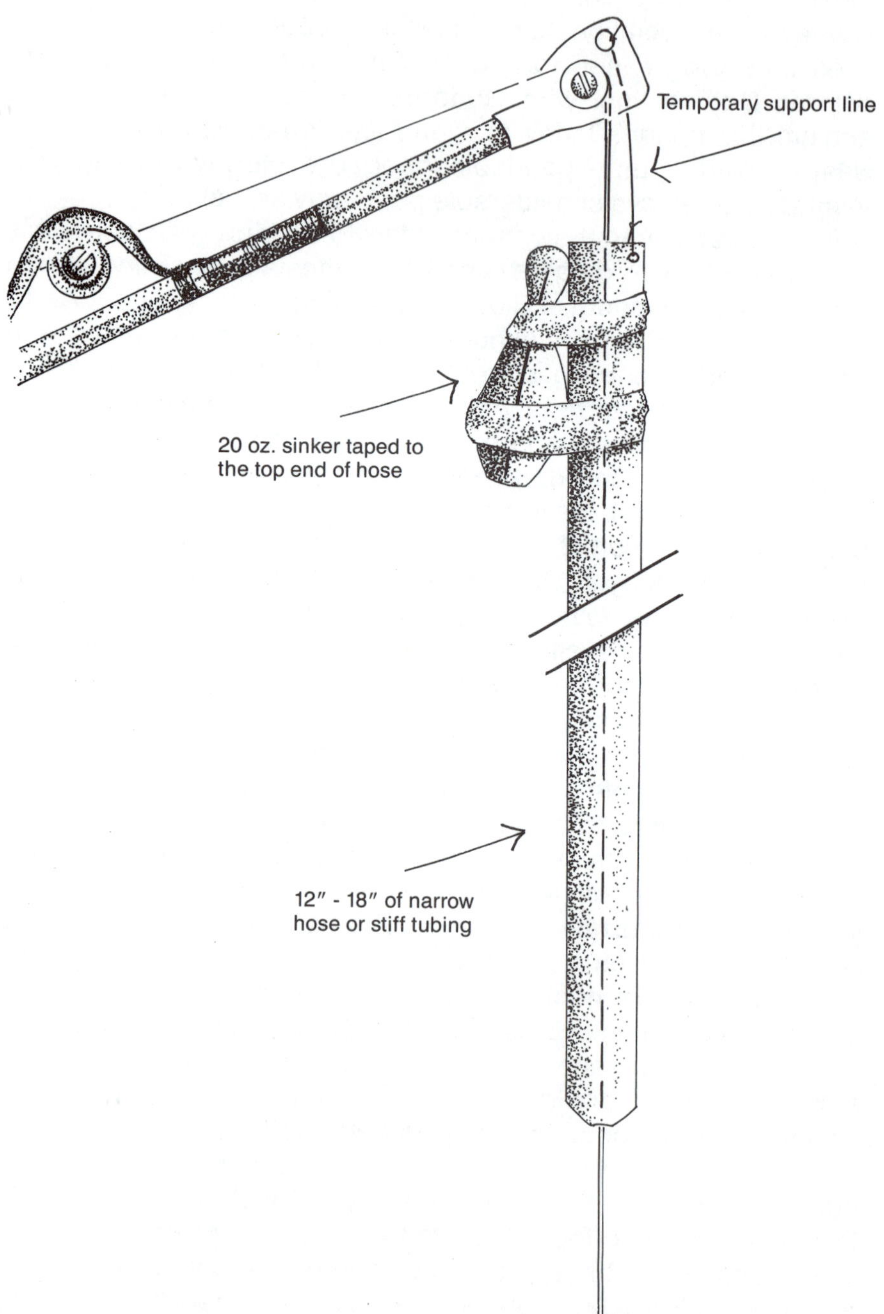

Later on, the "tube and sinker" developed, in another attempt to prevent the loss of an exceedingly valuable fish as anglers turned to fishing their mono filled reels "straight to the hook." Many felt the chances of losing a fish due to chaffed or cut line was offset by the increased hook-up rate.

HOOKS: No doubt about it, the hooks most commonly relied on were Mustad with the #7734 knife edge point, triple strength, forged eye tuna hook favored by those using stainless steel wire leader and the #7698C knife edge, long point, triple strength Mustad Sea Mate, ring eye by those using mono leaders. For some reason this hook was discontinued but Murray Bros. placed a special order for this hook and now has them in stock. The models #7690 and #7699 run a close second, with all models being forged. As the fish became more valuable, there was a trend toward using the 2 and 3 extra strong hooks.

I believe most would agree that there was a trend toward smaller sized hooks as it became harder to get a strike on the chumming grounds. Mustad had established itself as the premier hook company and the models and sizes available met the demands of most anglers seeking giants. In fact, it was taken for granted that when the time came the hook could be counted on to do its job, assuming of course, the right model and size had been chosen. Pulled hooks, those tearing out of the fish's mouth, increased in frequency as anglers applied more drag pressure in crowded situations while trying to take a fish quickly.

GAFFS: Early on in this growing commercial fisheries, we heard the horror stories of flying gaff heads falling off the pole just as the fish was leadered into range with the consequent loss of a fish. Or, we were shown the straightened head of a straight gaff or badly bent or broken gaff pole from an attempt to take a "green" fish. Inexperienced and unskilled hands at gaffing time resulted in not only ruined gear but a lot of badly damaged fish, which reduced the size of the payment check. The first backbanded gaffs came into use aboard the **Cookie Too** as a result of straightening out an 8-inch Pompanette gaff on a 900 pound fish. Bud Hudnall, ex-president of Pompanette was aboard, and two days later we sported backbanded gaffs.

Harpoons, which previously had been used in New England only at the pointy-end of the boat, began to see use from the cockpit. By the mid to late 1970s, cockpit harpoons, cut down to be more wieldy, were common except at tournament time. Their use allowed a fish to be taken sooner, with less chance of fish loss as the catch did not have to be brought quite as close to chines, rudders, propellers, etc. In addition, greater attention was paid to sticking a fish in a way to avoid drastically reducing its value. Gaffs were reserved for use at tail roping time, which is the basic scenario today.

HARNESSES: As the use of straight butt rods vanished from the giant tuna fishing scene, so did the shoulder and kidney harness. Bent butt rods necessitated a bucket harness and for a awhile only the FIN-NOR was in wide use. It got the job done but the Murray Bros. bucket harness was considerably better. With fiberglass reinforcement to reduce pinching and readily adjustable buckles, it did not tend to ride up on an angler's back. Today, there are several brands to choose from.

DAISY CHAINS and SPREADER BARS: Some might argue that daisy chains and spreader bars fall under the realm of bait but when urethane and PVC replicas of mackerel and squid sit next to hooks and line on the tackle counter, I can't agree. No doubt these rubber life-like artificial baits originated to supplement the fresh, or brined, natural baits being employed by trollers. Confessing to have only rudimentary knowledge of the origin of trolling baits in bluefin tuna waters, it appears the rubber baits were first employed by those who had spent time fishing for giants north of Cape Cod.

The introduction of daisy chain trolling with natural baits was first successfully attempted by Captain Ellis Hodkins on the charter boat **Cape Ann**, out of Gloucester, Massachusetts. Their use signaled a higher sophistication to the fishery. The Moldcraft squid basically had the market all to itself at that time. M & M Tackle was the first to offer rigged artificial lure chains and bars to the giant tuna angler but many were rigging their own well before then.

ACCESSORIES: With increased sophistication of the fisheries in the late 1970s and early 1980s, cockpit rigging tools and materials began to play an important role in the day's success. Whether kept in a large tackle box for easy storage and quick access or in a tackle locker, most boats had several pairs of fishing pliers made by Stanley or Manley, spools of waxed nylon line, dental tape, large size de-boxes, numerous knives, rigging needles, balloons, styrofoam "peanuts", corks, cans of flat-black spray paint, folded newspaper, sinkers, files, black plastic tape, rubber bands and much, much more.

Many tuna tackle advances over the years have necessitated improvements in various pieces of equipment. Bent butt rods required dropped gimbals in the fighting chairs or readily adjusted gimbal positions. With improved tackle and advanced techniques, greater numbers of giant tuna came boatside. The standard gin-pole gave way to the transom door. No doubt the advances will continue.

4 TACKLE AND TECHNIQUES

Gear For The Boat

As we idled along toward our anchor ball at the edge of the fleet, and with the fish now in the cockpit, we began the routine of heading back to port.

My charter customer was relaxing as we cleaned the boat and stowed our gear. "Boy, I still can't believe how easy we got this fish into the boat. The hardest part, of course, was bringing the fish to the boat."

With a laugh at that statement, I climbed partially up the tower and began taking the pin out of the shackle that held the upper end of the block and tackle in the welded gussett of the tower leg. This triple block set up, with ball bearing sheaves and braided, hollow dacron line, made the job of hoisting a giant tuna aboard relatively easy. Now that its job was done, I was removing it to stow it in a safe place.

"A while back, hoping we'd land this giant, I wondered how we'd ever get it into the boat. Now I know," the customer said.

A moment later I explained that when the tower of the boat was being designed, I specified the use of materials (aluminum) allowing fish weighing up to 1,000 pounds to be boated (should we ever be so lucky). Marine Machinery Service of Providence, Rhode Island (Dante Towers) used Schedule 80 aluminum for the rear tower legs.

The block and tackle is an effective method to haul big tuna aboard but on many boats it's a thing of the past. Most boat builders today offer the perspective owner the option for a transom door, albeit a bit more money. Originating with custom boat builders, particularly down south in Florida, stock boats today commonly have them. As a result, we don't see too many fish being towed home today.

The gin pole with a block and tackle makes hauling a large bluefin aboard easy.

Anchoring tackle is essential to bluefin tuna fishing and so is the gear needed to retrieve the anchor with the least amount of effort. A popular system uses a large red Norwegian style float ball and a stainless steel ring to retrieve the anchor and rode. After fishing and as you get ready to bring in the anchor, the captain makes mental note of the compass heading the bow is pointing towards. The ball has a short length of line and large brass or stainless snap at the end. The stainless steel ring is placed over the anchor line, then the brass snap is clipped in place trapping the anchor line inside the ring. The captain eases ahead to the ball at a slight angle. Coming up to the ball, one of the crew extends a gaff from the cockpit to pick up a short length of tag line with a spliced loop at the end. Run through the stern hawsepipe, the loop is quickly secured to the inside cleat. With that, the throttle is eased up and the bow of the **Prowler** is turned into the current set.

Now trailing behind, the ball begins to run down the anchor rode hesitates momentarily as it settles deeper into the water and then pops up as the anchor flukes break free from the bottom. Several moments later the large diameter 6 inch stainless ring runs over the neat line splice onto the anchor chain. With a splash, the ball twists one way, then another, signaling the end of its run to the anchor. As the boat is slowed, the chain settles deeper, locking the ball and ring at the fluke end of the Danforth anchor, now bobbing on the ocean surface.

In addition to the block and tackle, sportfishing boat builders will add a transom door, which makes getting a large fish aboard very easy.

''Now that's slick. Sure beats going up on the bow and hauling in the line,'' is heard from a member of the party.

Backing towards the ball, the ½ inch nylon is casually pulled into the cockpit as we idle along. Coming to the ball, the chain is carefully retrieved and finally both anchor and ball are lifted aboard.

''These days, anchors are set, as well as retrieved, from the cockpit,'' I explained. ''In my opinion, anyone up on the bow fooling with the anchor line simply doesn't know what they are doing. I suppose some guys are afraid they'll suck the bitter end of the line into the wheel if they come up along side. Guess they figure it's cheaper to pull the mate out of the water than pull a strut, wheel and shaft or rudder out of the bottom of the boat.''

With that comment I get raised eyebrows and a sideward look from the mate and we both break into a short laugh.

''Be sure to get that 'quick release' in before I hook 'er up.''

Reaching to the side cleat, the quick release and tag line is given a quick freshwater rinse ready for trouble-free use next time at anchor.

Like the unique shape of each piece of a puzzle, the block and tackle, ring and ball as well as the quick release, all fit into their respective spaces of the picture.

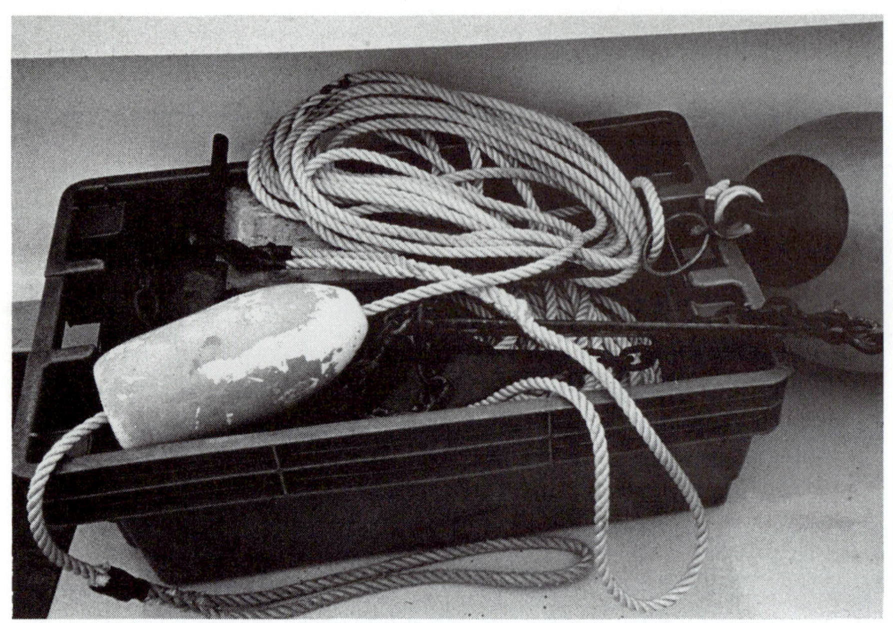

The standard ground tackle for anchoring in a tuna fleet is a large Danforth anchor, chain, Norwegian style float ball, tag lines, anchor ring and fish tote.

Over the VHF radio one of the local captains is heard to ask about the fog conditions outside the wall, or Pt. Judith Harbor of Refuge. No improvement is reported and the fog is still as thick as ever. Seeing that there were no targets on our heading line within the mile and half range of the radar, I reached up and grabbed the log book and pencil. A moment later I was recording the loran numbers of the spot where we had the strike, written earlier on the Formica top on the console so I woudn't forget it.

Bumping the throttle up and switching to the three-mile range, it took only a few minutes for the Northstar to update our speed, course and time to go to the West Gap. With the autopilot engaged, my attention again turns to scribbling additional notes in my daily Log Book.

Checking the cockpit, clean-up chores were progressing smoothly; in fact nearly completed. The 4-foot by 8-foot piece of white tarplin, now water logged, covered the fish. Bleeding had almost ceased, and the tail and meat hook ropes were soaking in soapy bleach water. At speed, the 1¼ inch washdown pump and deck hose made short work of the job.

"Well, I've got to hand it to you captain, no sooner had you adjusted the depth of those baits than we got a bite. In fact, just before we got the strike, I thought I saw several fish again at the ninety foot level. That color video sounder tells you right where the fish are."

"You're right," I replied, "and most boat owners go so far as to have two fathometers on the boat. Usually a color machine on the bridge and a somewhat less expensive paper machine for the cockpit. The fellows in the cockpit need to know not only when the fish are under the boat, but at what depth. Without a fathometer, or sounder, it becomes a guessing game, and in our industry these days it simply puts you out of the competition."

Modern day electronics have become an intricate part of tuna fishing, particularly under poor weather conditions. There are times, however, under ideal weather conditions when fish can be taken without the aid of any electronics.

I once saw gigantic clouds of sand eels being pursued by a number of finback whales about eight miles southeast of Block Island. The gulls and shearwaters, along with the columns of expelled air and water vapor from the whales, easily identified the area of action. Among these animals were giant bluefin tuna, a number of which could be clearly seen as they pushed along. Others swam among the whales, picking off injured sand eels as they settled in the wake of their feeding.

Somewhat clear from the whales, we had a boil, then another, followed by a moderate splash behind the daisy chain. With that, almost as if in slow motion, the starboard rigger bent backward further and further and then suddenly rebounded in a forward motion. The noise of all the aluminum surging forward was masked somewhat by the sound of the reel clicker, even with over 40 pounds of preset drag, as line raced off the reel following this fish. Release pressure of these outrigger clips were set to maximum, something necessary for trolling the weight of a spreader bar or daisy chain. A far cry from those days of a clothes pin with a rubber band looped several times at its end! And, I was grateful for those solid cast, bronze and chrome plated rod holders holding each bent butt outfit in place, which could easily withstand the load pressure of a strike.

Quickly the two other lines were retrieved and shortly after the angler was in the chair, the safety line from the fighting chair was snapped to the ringed rod clamp. This chair manufacturer provided a massive, cast bronze gimbal, one I felt would take the abuse of everyday charter fishing. Although not quite as fancy and smart looking as a Murray Bros. chair, and considerably less expensive, its ruggedness and side arm rod holders were proving it to be a good choice for me. At the time I was building the boat in 1980, the Murray fighting chair ranked number one, but my budget simply disallowed the cost of purchasing the best.

A while back I had the chance to sit and talk with Ed Murray about his involvement with giant bluefin tuna fishing. He is undoubtedly

Captain Joe Eldridge's (far right) Striper had the state-of-the-art in fighting chairs. In 1959, he used this Rockaway chair to fish the USATT that year.

one of the best qualified today to profile and explain the tackle and equipment developments of recent bluefin angling. Not only as a result of a long family history involvement, but also his forty years of tuna fishing experience starting at the age of twelve.

"The modern day fighting chair, as we know it, was developed by Rybovich." Murray stated. "Ironically, my father built one like it years ago when I was a youngster. Our product today represents a lot of refinements which began as an attempt to improve the existing gear. Lots of testing goes on before we make a certain component available. I tell you, some guys could break anything."

Years back, he used his craftsmanship talents in cabinet making to build a fighting chair for his boat. Contemporary chairs were crude, had little or no eye appeal, and frequently let go under the strain of giant tuna fishing. He wanted a better built chair to handle any giant, so he figured he could build a better one for less than he could buy. Friends who saw the finished product liked it so much they started asking him to build them chairs.

Asked about that, Murray said, "We were building a top-of-the-line, high quality fighting chair that lasted, and by word of mouth it got around and people started calling, wanting to buy them."

In the early 1970s, Frank J. Mather, III fished aboard Captain C. Mayo's Chanty III. In one day he caught three giant bluefin in the 500 pound range successfully using the fighting chair and a leather kidney harness.

As the development of the industry continued, the leather kidney harness was replaced with the bucket harness.

The early chairs sold for $1,350. Today, the best Murray chair costs more than $6,000. If you think that's costly, consider the English made Hardy Reel, model 12/0 Zane Gray model, slightly under $4,000. Or, a custom built sportfisherman by Rybovich, Merritt, Monterey, Garlington or Knowles can be well into the six figures, or better.

In a recent article for a major boating publication, a list of ten well-known people in the sportfishing industry were asked their opinion as to what one piece of equipment contributed most to their angling success. Ed Murray was the top name on this list and his reply to the question was the fishing log book.

"Knowing under what conditions (the moon, time of year, and locations) we caught fish helps me to catch even more fish. I used to keep records in a book but now all that stuff is on computer. How's that for progress? The log helps to keep track of things and works as a great reminder."

Now shaping up is a tackle mosaic with the dockside sale of a giant tuna as the overall picture; the money as the incentive to assemble it. Many of the pieces already in place represent the once abundant resource. Other pieces represent the Japanese export market, located almost in the center of the picture. Clustered around them are pieces representing the long line, seine, harpoon handline and rod and reel fisheries industries. Most of the tackle and equipment pieces have been pressed into their respective places.

A few remaining spaces await those pieces representing even newer equipment, with continuing refinements still to come. For some reason, a number of pieces representing conservation and domestic management are missing but hopefully only temporarily. Perhaps most striking are those pieces representing the sportfishing ethic and conservation activities of a seemingly by-gone tuna fishing era.

4 TACKLE AND TECHNIQUES

Tackle And Techniques

In front of the boat now, little gulls and terns flutter, gather and then break away. Again, gathering, one suddenly swoops and picks, and then breaks away. Several groups of mixed birds are working along this particular tide rip. Down wind are streaks or slicks, and the stormy petrels or "chickens," as we call them, are dancing over them. Watching the way the gulls and terns work, it's obvious to me they are flying over individual feeding fish; tuna fish-school bluefin tuna fish. The birds easily see these fish and their prey, looking for that opportunity when an injured morsel writhes close to the surface. What it must be like to be able to hover over these lit-up, excited fish, watching their every move, outlined against the blue-green depths of the ocean, adjusting their wing beat to the tail beat of the fish. What it must...

"Fish on!" startles me back to reality, and then "I've got one too!" is heard next. Both fellows hanging on the arched 20 pound class rods on opposite sides of the boat at the transom. Now for the third time this morning, with three almost similar sets of Loran numbers written on the console surface. No doubt in anyone's mind we had found a willing school of two-year-old bluefin ravaging pods of late season squid not very far southeast of Block Island, with its southern facade bearly discernible through the morning haze. In fact, we were just outside the twenty fathom edge known as Sharks Ledge, about a mile and a half west of the Fairway buoy. For many years as I can remember, this has been a good location for all sizes of tuna, from schoolies to giants.

Regular daily visitors to the marina docks in the late afternoon, local people and attending tourists, would peer into the cockpit for a glimpse of the day's catch. One retired gentleman would frequently comment on the consistent success of the boat. Little did he know that a little experience allowed one to easily spot the road signs that exist on and above the ocean's surface that frequently point to the presence of fish. In fact, these signs at time scream in one's face, saying, ''Here's where they are.''

Assuming other factors, which I'll discuss shortly, are suitable, I call these road signs **Biological Indicators**. Keep in mind that many animals constantly search the near offshore waters during the summer for food. Over the years, many, many days stand apart from most others as examples of what I mean. For instance, getting back to the opening of the story, we were experiencing action in an area considerably removed from that of the previous day, well inside the area referred to as the Tuna Bank. On the previous morning while in this area trolling for school fish, we saw pods of bait, ''raining bait'', I call it, as the calm surface appears to have rain falling on it, although it's actually disturbed by sand eels.

We also saw birds, such as little gulls, terns, shearwaters, and petrels; whales and slicks, oily looking water, caused by feeding fish and having a watermelon smell.

Trolling offshore structure breaks and working slicks created by feeding fish with small lures will often produce school bluefin in good numbers.

Later in the day, trolling southeast down to the Tuna Bank, we experienced similar action to that just described. Why didn't I go right back to the Tuna Bank where we had all the action the previous day? Common sense would indicate that as the place to start, right? Maybe, but when the obvious **Biological Indicators** point to fish, it's best to give it a try at that spot.

There was another reason I decided to slow it down and begin trolling. That reason was based on my experiences of observing how rapidly tuna can push in from offshore, as well as the fact that many times these animals come inshore in what I call waves. Not all at once but in massed arrangements or ranks like a phalanx. Assuming, of course, **Physical Factors** allow for it such as water temperature, water clarity, presence of bait, etc.

It is common to see and hear of boats that have "over-run" the fish and then have to come back inshore. With a paying party, this is somewhat embarrassing. It constantly amuses me to see how many fishermen think that the farther offshore they go, the more and bigger the fish will be. On the contrary, and again depending on conditions, there can develop a relatively narrow band or zone over contour lines that hold fish.

So to summarize some of the commonly made mistakes:

> 1-ignoring the obvious signs,
> 2-overrunning the fish,
> 3-not realizing how fast these fish can move.

Recent research on bluefin indicate they may swim at sustained speeds of 5 to 6 knots when searching for or digesting food. Whether you have fished for bluefin in the New York Bight area, southern New England, Cape Cod Bay or Gulf of Maine, there have been traditional "hot spots" time and again. And I'd be willing to bet the reason has been the presence of bait, such as mackerel, herring, squid and sand eels along a major contour line. Typically in this area during the decade of the 1980s, this has been between the 20 to 40 fathom lines. Prior to that, in the 1970s, many fish were taken inside the 15 fathom curve, and it's my opinion this was a result of a much healthier resource. With greater numbers of fish back then, competition for food may have forced them to come closer to the beach.

While speaking with many people in the fishery today, I frequently heard the story, "Oh sure, lots of fish around again this year, but they didn't come in close to shore. Just spooky, I guess, from all the boats after them." Maybe so, but my experience indicates otherwise.

Of course the absence of fish from traditional areas could be due to unfavorable conditions (physical) such as water temperature, water clarity and salinity as well as the absence of bait. Fish "worked on" during 1989 in our area were well offshore in 40 to 50 fathoms and remained there for sometime. Years back, it would not have been necessary to go so far to find fish. We knew mediums and giants were there from the stories brought back by the commercial draggermen. Stories about laying to and shoveling back overboard literally tons of immature butterfish, not even large enough to quality as super-small, in which the Japanese buyers had recently begun to show interest. Stories about watching fish surge through the discaded catch with handlines overboard and large butters as hook bait. Stories about making more money handlining giant tuna than dragging.

In the offshore bluefin tuna fishery over the years, I've come to learn not only where to look for fish, but when, or what time of the season, under what conditions. Let me use a few examples to illustrate this point. Traditionally, school tuna of one to five years of age would show up in the late summer months, typically August or early September, unlike that of years ago when they usually made their appearance in early July or even June. It was a troll fishery using cedar or chrome jigs, as well as Jap feathers, typically best over major contours, but not always. Find the bait, you find the fish; frequently inside 25 fathoms and not far from either Montauk Pt. or Block Island.

Unlike the school fish, the giants were the first to arrive, typically mid to late June, and many times in those same areas later visited by school fish. Apparently this class of fish wasted little or no time getting to the food-rich waters of southern New England. From the early 1970s through the mid 1980s, our waters swarmed with tremendous numbers of sand eels on the offshore grounds.

I can recall witnessing the explosions of medium and giant tuna busting in this bait from miles away. It reminded me of those early days in my striped bass fishing adventures. Leaving the Pt. Judith Harbor of Refuge, I would run to the west in my skiff looking for shoaling mackerel on Nebraska Shoals. With six or eight live mackerel racing dizzily round in a trash barrel for a live well, I'd then scoot down to Green Hill or Charlestown and live line them for stripers. But many early mornings saw giant bluefin after the same quarry, with eruptions and hurtling bodies only a few yards away from my position. Many mornings I would simply put away any intention of live-lining, and just watch the giant bluefin tuna harass the mackerel. What a show they would put on!

A common tool used today to aid in finding fish is the sea surface temperature chart based on infra-red satellite imagery. When clear skies allow, sea surface temperatures can be delineated to within tenths of a degree Fahrenhite. These pictures can be in your hands within hours of the satellite fly-by, and can be invaluable, not only in search of bluefin, but other tuna species as well.

Captain Len Belcaro, of Offshore Services, plots these temperature changes and he agreed to let us reproduce a portion of THE EDGE, June 12, 1989, Vol. 4, issue 1, to demonstrate the information that can be obtained in plotting sea temperatures and thereby the location of fish.

Long Island - New England

SEA SURFACE TEMPERATURE CHARTS
Two Degree Thermal Contouring

DATE: 6-12-89   NOAA 11   TIME: 4:01 AM
                       Satellite

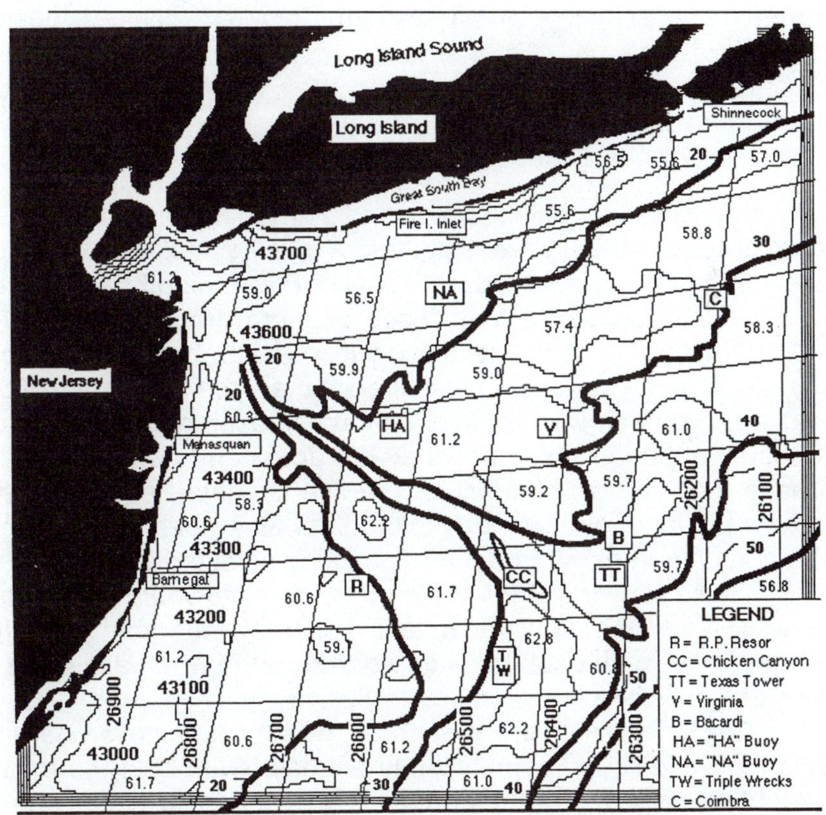

This body of 61 degree water located near the Bacardi wreck produced good early season action on medium and giant bluefin tuna that year.

PLACES TO ACCESS SEA SURFACE TEMPERATURE CHARTS AND OCEANOGRAPHIC FISHING ANALYSIS

ROFFER'S OCEAN FISHING FORECASTING SERVICE
8542 S.W. 102nd Street
Miami, Florida 33156

OFFSHORE SERVICES
2679 Route 70
Manasquan, NJ 08736

NOAA/NEDSDIS/DNDC (subscription)
Satellite Date Service Division
Att: Gulf Stream Subscription
Room 100
World Weather Building
5200 Auth Road
Washington, D.C. 20233

NOAA/NWS/FO (Telecopier Information)
Room 302
5200 Auth Road
Washington, D.C. 20233

Another way to find big fish is to find a dragger, particularly an inshore dragger working over soft bottom for silver hake and whiting. Late summer finds our Mud Hole east of Block Island being towed over, with upwards of a half dozen or more draggers out of Pt. Judith. Hauling back, the net spills out good numbers of small fish, which float to the surface. These floaters mark the towing line of the boat and I've been witness to giant tuna smashing and feeding on the surface behind these boats as the doors and net come to the surface. And again when culled over fish are shoveled overboard, early in the next tow. The idea is to follow along behind a dragger with a very long-handled dip net, plucking selected baits from the water. Those showing signs of life go quickly into your well-aerated live well. When fish show, you race to that area, preferably with a live bait ready to go on each hook and drift through with baits close to the surface.

The first time I did this, lobing fresh, dead, cut bait overboard as we drifted, I watched some sizable animals swim past the boat. I thought to myself, "My goodness, we're trying to catch one of those!" Several fish taken later that day, back on the scales at Montauk, weighed in at just over 1,000 pounds.

Enough of those earlier memories for now. Back to our opening action; we didn't have long to wait as moments later we hooked up. In the bow-mounted chair, my experienced angler put it to the fish. Tail roped about 40 minutes later, the three of us realized we would never get the fish in the boat. Towed back to Snug Harbor Marina, the groaning scale pushed to 900 pounds and it was that same year Tom Crafford took the largest fish ever entered, a 990 pounder, in the Rhode Island Tuna Tournament in September of 1977 and another fish from the Mud Hole.

As the fishery accelerated from recreational to commercial in our area, we began to see individuals relying less on experience and more on underhanded methods to locate fish. Some people getting into the fishery had no choice because they had little or no experience. So what did they do? Why follow the highline boats, of course, like the **Cookie Too**, run by Ed and Paul Murray, or the **Tally VII**, run by Sal and Joe Bellavia, but that usually required an awful lot of horsepower, and a boat capable in rough sea conditions. Many didn't have those kind of boats, so they simply ventured to the general area and if these highliners couldn't be visually spotted in the haze, the "detectives" used radar. Racing from target to target, they eventually found them; sometimes. As you might well imagine, this got to be very expensive on some days, so we then heard about a few getting together to hire an aircraft. Not to spot the fish, but to look for the highliners to get the loran numbers. These same individuals, if they didn't have a plane flying for them, would cruise at high speed looking for circling aircraft, many times aircraft employed by others for this same reason.

And the radios some of the boats soon had! Scanning VHF radios and their directional antennas blossomed on the towers and bridges of some boats, along with radio scramblers. Sure this was costly, but the money spent didn't disappear out the exhaust or down the wake of the boat.

But don't be so naive as to think those were the only ways to find them. When it came to the chum fishery later in the season, the problem of locating the fish diminished considerably. Now, all that was required was to decide which of the "fleets" was most likely to experience action. Like circling buzzards, should a boat or two hook-up, there was a rush by certain boats to get to the vacated ball. You knew what boats would attempt this, boats whose owners wouldn't let something like tradition, courtesy, proper manners, common place ethics, etc., stand in the way of their getting a fish. Things like that simply didn't matter anymore and it became a situation whereby some took advantage of others, and thought nothing of it. In fact, some called over the VHF radio, bragging about how fast they got to a vacated ball and hooked a fish. They bragged about how little time and effort was spent in taking a fish.

Setting up and chumming with other boats years ago was thought to increase one's chances of success, as it was commonly believed it kept the fish in a general area and gave all the boats a good shot of having a few fish swim under it. You found and hooked a fish because it was swimming in your chum slick, and not someone else's.

In summary of this section, the full list of **Biological Indicators** would include:

1-Bait fish, i.e., sand eels, butterfish, mackerel, halfbeaks.
2-Birds, such as little gulls, shearwaters, terns, stormey petrels.
3-Whales, such as finback, sei, humpback.
4-Slicks caused by deep feeding fish.
5-Sargasso Weed.
6-Portuguese Man O War (jellyfish).

The list of Physical Factors includes:

1-Sea water color.
2-Sea water clarity.
3-Sea water temperature (surface).
4-Light intensity.
5-Salinity.
6-Sea state (rough or calm).
7-Wind direction and velocity.
8-Current direction and velocity.
9-Water depth.
10-Bottom configuration.
11-Bottom composition (mud, sand, etc.).
12-Thermocline.
13-Lunar phase.
14-Barometric Pressure.

4 TACKLE AND TECHNIQUES

Jigging And Chunking Techniques

Picture this scene: birds watching fish and their prey as they fly over them, and us with our third double-header of the morning. There's little doubt in anyone's mind about having found the fish. Having the rod nearly torn from one's hands, or pumping up a fish, is the thrill and excitement members of the charter party are looking for. Putting fish on the hooks and watching facial expressions and listening to shouts and directives, is the thrill and satisfaction I anticipate every day. There are many ways to catch bluefin tuna on rod and reel and I consider myself to be very fortunate to have tried most of them.

One of the most enjoyable ways is by jigging. During a third pass both of the outboard rods are firmly held as anglers stand facing aft and leaning against the coaming. Their rod tips are pointed slightly back and down toward the ocean surface. Rods are not just held, but are jigged in a special fashion that enables the rod tip to move about 18 to 24 inches forward with every sweep. A forceful forward motion sweep, with line and lure coming tight again before the next sweep, averaging 2 seconds for the sweep, with a two-second interval. This sweeping tempo, typically has to be demonstrated several times before each member of the party picks it up. It's a motion that many clients over the years learned was necessary to imitate or copy closely. A motion they soon realized brought strikes and if not done properly, usually brought the wrath of the captain down upon them. This is jigging motion not made obvious when close to other boats in the fleet and sometimes done for only short periods of time. Its jigging motion done discreetly and at times only when the bow of the boat was pointed at another boat nearby to hide what was going on. But with fish on, rod tip held high, no urging was needed to get some clients to perform for those luckless anglers in other boats as they passed near. Oh, how I shamelessly loved that part of it.

Jigging Actions

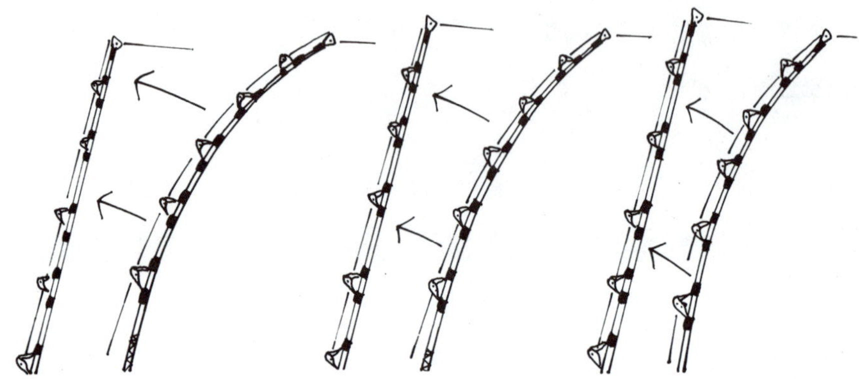

Regular jigging motion of the rod tip.

Actions of various lures through the water.

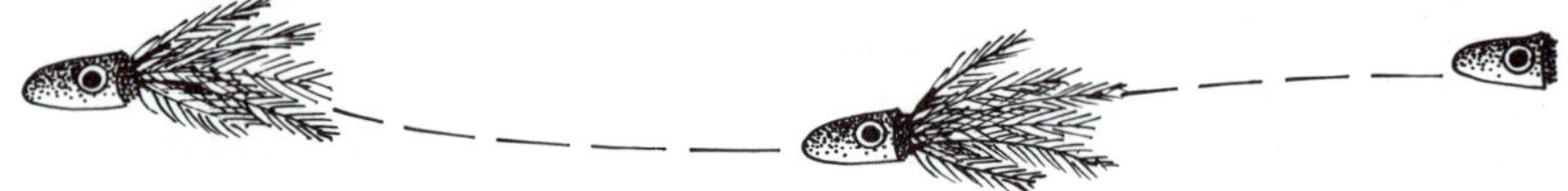

Jigging a feather.

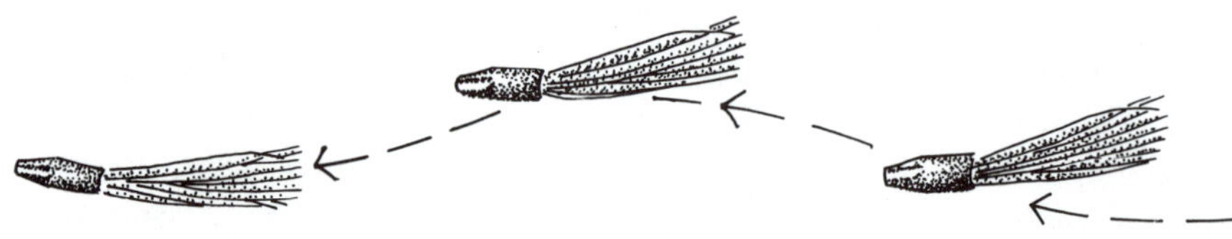

Jigging a Hex-Head lure.

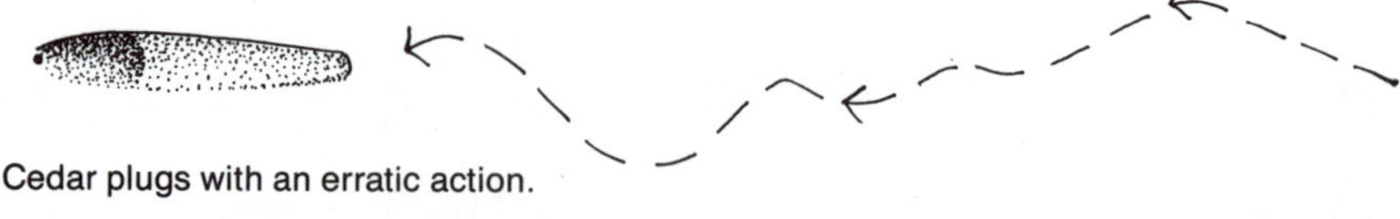

Cedar plugs with an erratic action.

Straight running unjigged lure.

With two stationary lines and two jigging lines, it was the jigging lines that consistently had strikes and fish on. It usually didn't take much urging early in the day to have members of the party pick up these stationary rods and jig as well. These rods required a slightly different technique and it too had to be demonstrated a few times before everyone caught on. Holding the rod upside down, with rod tip down and pointed slightly aft, it's jigged so that the rod tip nearly touches the transom, occasionally entering the water.

Many were the days I told the customers it was all right to get the rod tip wet. To hold the rod tip upright was a waste of time and on occasion I would take the time to demonstrate why. Class would be in session and for most it was quickly obvious why that didn't work. With a strike or two the boat was slowed slightly and directives were given to increase the jigging tempo (shorter, faster sweeps). With all lines loaded, the boat was slowed to idle speed but still in gear and anglers were told to follow their fish, passing rod and reel over or under other lines as necessary.

It was during this action that the greatest moments of cockpit confusion reigned and at times brought tears of laughter. But not always, like those times when anglers, seeing line peel off the reel and assuming it had somehow gotten into free spool, pushed the lever the other way. Instantaneous bird nests were followed by loud expletives from the captain. Or when an angler with thoughts frozen in time forgot to level wind the line evenly back onto the spool and consequently had it jam up under a post frame. Or when an angler who simply failed to move, as if his deck shoes were nailed in place, precipitated a threatening tangle. Or when an individual with limited rod handling talents flopped into the fighting chair with the rod and reel upside down in the gimbal and was forced to turn the reel handle backwards.

Perhaps best of all was the fellow whose head and shoulders grew so close to the reel that he wound the draw strings of his hooded sweatshirt into the line on the spool. With his face and chin locked to the reel the handle would not turn since the spool was jammed by the cotton draw strings. Fortunately the draw strings were cut and the angler was rescued from near strangulation but not before he surely had thoughts of the fish winning this confrontation.

Back to the jigging and the question in the back of your mind as to why it's so effective. Injured squid, for example, do not swim in a straight line at a constant speed. In fact, neither do other prey that tuna feed on. My guess is these school bluefin are quick to visually spot a feather, Hex-Head or Cedar Jig moving erratically in the wake, suggesting an injured animal and an easy prey, which then prompts the bite.

Let's turn our attention to another day on anchor and chumming. Fluttering down, a dropping AVA diamond jig simply does not come tight when it should, and I immediately turn the reel handle of the Penn 6/0 (114HL) Senator II and lean overboard with the outfit outstretched. Hollering, "Fish on!" I focus everyone's attention on the bent rod and reel spool turning rapidly against a moderately tight drag. As the line pours off the reel, I'm moving to avoid an horrendous tangle with those fishing in the chum slick behind the boat. That's right, I said fishing in the chum slick behind the boat. A moment later the alerted crew begins to carefully retrieve both deep baited lines but chumming continues with a distant near-surface bait remaining in place. Passing this loaded rod to waiting hands, the remaining baited line, well back in the slick, poses no immediate threat of entanglement.

I see fish marked at 50 feet on the scope and the next readied rod and reel with attached jig is pressed into action. Watching fish mark at the fifty-foot level, one of the party simply states the depth and the jig is soon working there. A bump, then slack line and then another "Fish on!" is heard. This bluefin, like the previous one, melts line off the reel but only after a series of headshakes and short dashes back and forth. Finally realizing it was in trouble, it took off in high gear. With two fish now hooked on light tackle, it takes anglers with some dexterity to keep lines apart.

Keeping a close eye on the recorder you can mark fish at mid-depths which are not responding to the chunk baits. Drop a diamond or butterfish jig down and you'll be surprised at the results. This 70 pound bluefin couldn't pass up a jig.

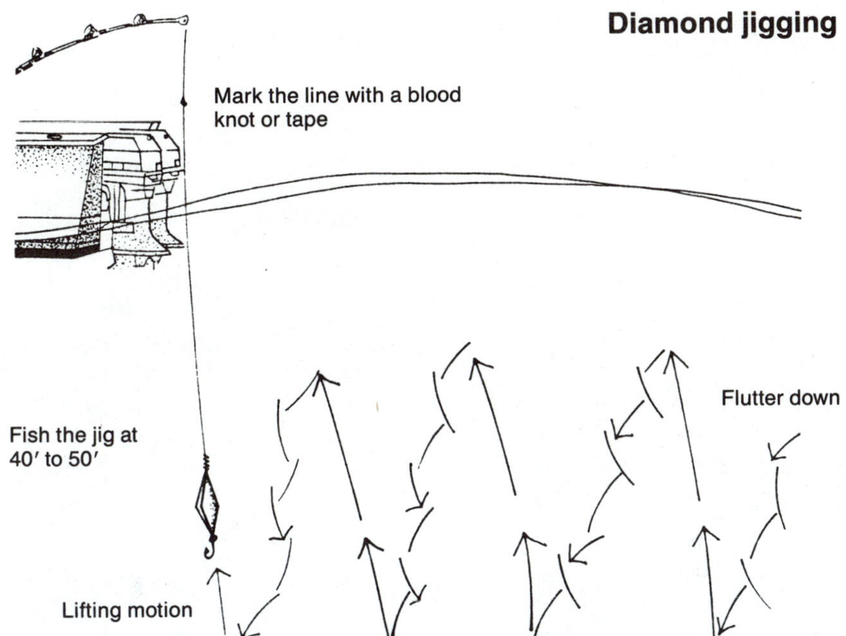

Lifting the rod tip about 6 feet, then quickly dropping it will result in slack line. This allows the diamond jig to flutter down. This type of action will draw the attention of bluefin.

Sitting on the anchor all day while larger fish ignore baited offerings is not conducive to the business of charter fishing. School sized fish, though not exactly what the party wanted (at least they thought so until they were hanging on to one), were providing exciting action. With the proper tackle and technique, these fish have saved the day more times than I care to recall.

Fish busted off in the anchor warp can be avoided by taking the outfit up to the foredeck and passing it around the anchor line. This is easily done under calm conditions but prohibited when seas roughen.

Curious about the outfit? A seven-foot rod, light tip, but with growing backbone, sporting a 6/0 Senator II loaded with 50 pound mono straight to the 4- or 6-ounce diamond jig. A swivel holds the 6/0 or 7/0 Siwash hook in place. Line capacity is close to 500 yards of 50-pound mono. The gear ratio, just under 3:1, is nearly ideal.

What, no leader? you ask. That's right, these fish can be taken without a leader. In fact, leaders reduce the number of strikes. Tuna have sharp eyes. There have been plenty of days with one, two or even three fish busted off but many days we left the grounds with a fish or two in the boat. Better to have some action and break off a fish or two than to have no action at all because the fish are leader shy.

Paying close attention to the chum slick and the baits will result in more hookups and boated fish like this.

On another occasion while chumming, the following conversation took place.

"Are you watching the chum slick?"

"Yeah, but I haven't seen anything."

"Watch these next couple of pieces real close, these four pieces going down right now. Keep watching. All four of them. Keep looking. How many do you see, still four? How about now?"

"I see four, I think. No, no, only three now."

"Where did that fourth piece go? I count only three now."

"Yeah, but I didn't see any fish."

"Well, there's a fish or two back there in the slick, and looking down into the depths you usually won't see one unless it turns and flashes. With their dark colored back and the darkness of the depths, they are almost impossible to see from here in the boat. What you can easily see are the cut pieces of chum. These cut butterfish shine like a new silver dollar and are easy to follow as they settle in the slick. When a piece disappears, it's because it was eaten and taken from your view."

"These fish are about 25 to 30 feet below the surface. Throw those cut pieces up current toward the bow of the boat so that by the time they pass the transom they've settled a bit. Before they disap-

Working the lines

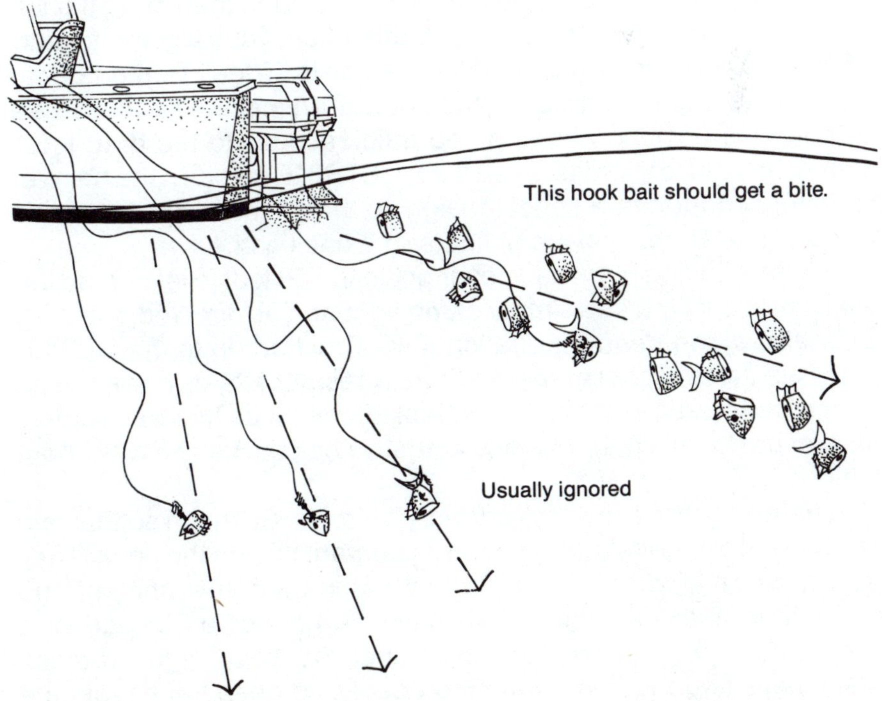

pear in the current, you want to give yoursef the chance to watch them as far down as possible to see if there's a fish in 'em. Keep your eye on the hook bait and tell me what you see."

"Looks OK to me and I can just barely see it. Nope, the leader's gone. Can't see the leader any more."

"Fine, but look where the hook bait is in relation to the chum pieces as they settle away. Can you see that it's a lot deeper than the other pieces and closer to the boat?"

"Yeah, how come? You pulled line off the reel fast enough to give plenty of slack, so it could settle away with little or no resistance, right?"

"That's not the problem. With this bait the weight of the hook is enough to cause it to settle faster than the cut pieces, taking it out of the mainstream of the cut chum."

Reaching for the bag of styrofoam peanuts, as the small packing sized pieces are called, a small one is inserted into the mouth and body cavity of this bait. Inserted so that the narrow body cavity simply holds it in place. Carefully, back into the water, several more thrown cut chum pieces accompany it as it settles. Watching very carefully, it is seen to settle away slower but still sinks at a rate faster than other pieces. Back in the boat, a larger peanut is pushed into place in the body cavity and the bait again carefully allowed to settle away with several more accompanying pieces.

"Looks good, let it go to the fourth or fifth mark, then bring it back and do it again. If you're going to catch a fish, you're going to start off by hooking it first. Each mark on the line is 50 feet. Remember to stand on the right hand side of the outfit. Turn the reel handle so it's in the down position allowing you quick access to the drag lever arm. At any hint of a strike, push it up to STRIKE and turn the handle. Keep just enough free spool tension so that in the event of a strike you don't have an over-run of line and a backlash."

The free sinking hook bait never got to the 30 foot level behind the boat. Suddenly the line simply came tight and as directed, the drag lever arm of the Penn International was pushed up to the STRIKE pin. This fish simply set the hook as a result of its own swimming momentum. Little did this angler think he might be lucky enough to have a turn in the chair, let alone actually hook the fish he was about to fight.

At times, bluefin tuna are very wary animals. So much so that one has to keep this constantly in mind if you want one on the hook. They appear to be alert to anything unnatural in their environment and suspicious about anything that might be connected to part of a meal; things like leaders and fishing lines that could signal danger. Many days find the fish swimming deeply, so deep in fact that the

Rigging a hook bait

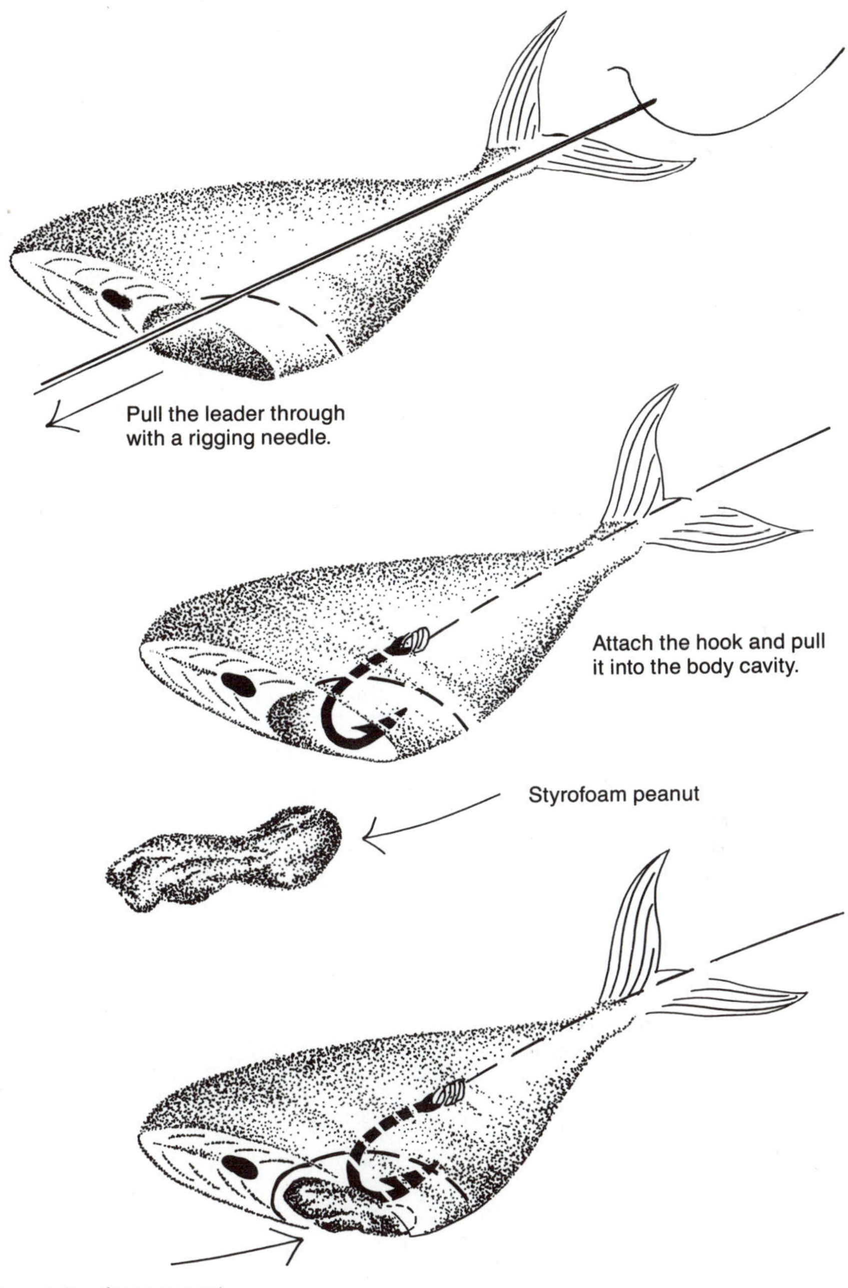

Use a large butterfish cut in half with the viscera removed from the body cavity.

Cross section view of a bait deployment scheme that may result in an "Avoidance response" on the shallow and mid-level baits by the fish.

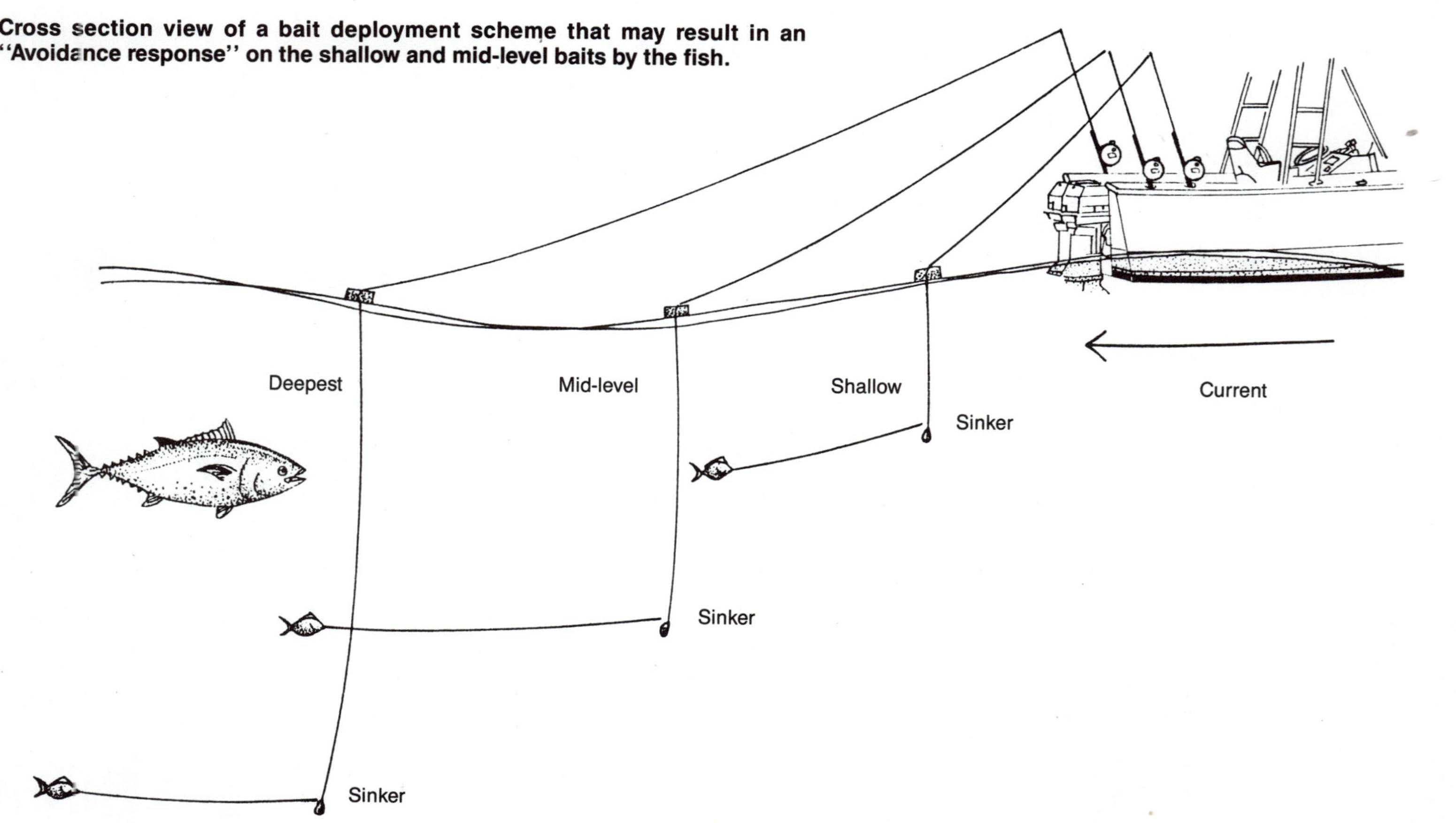

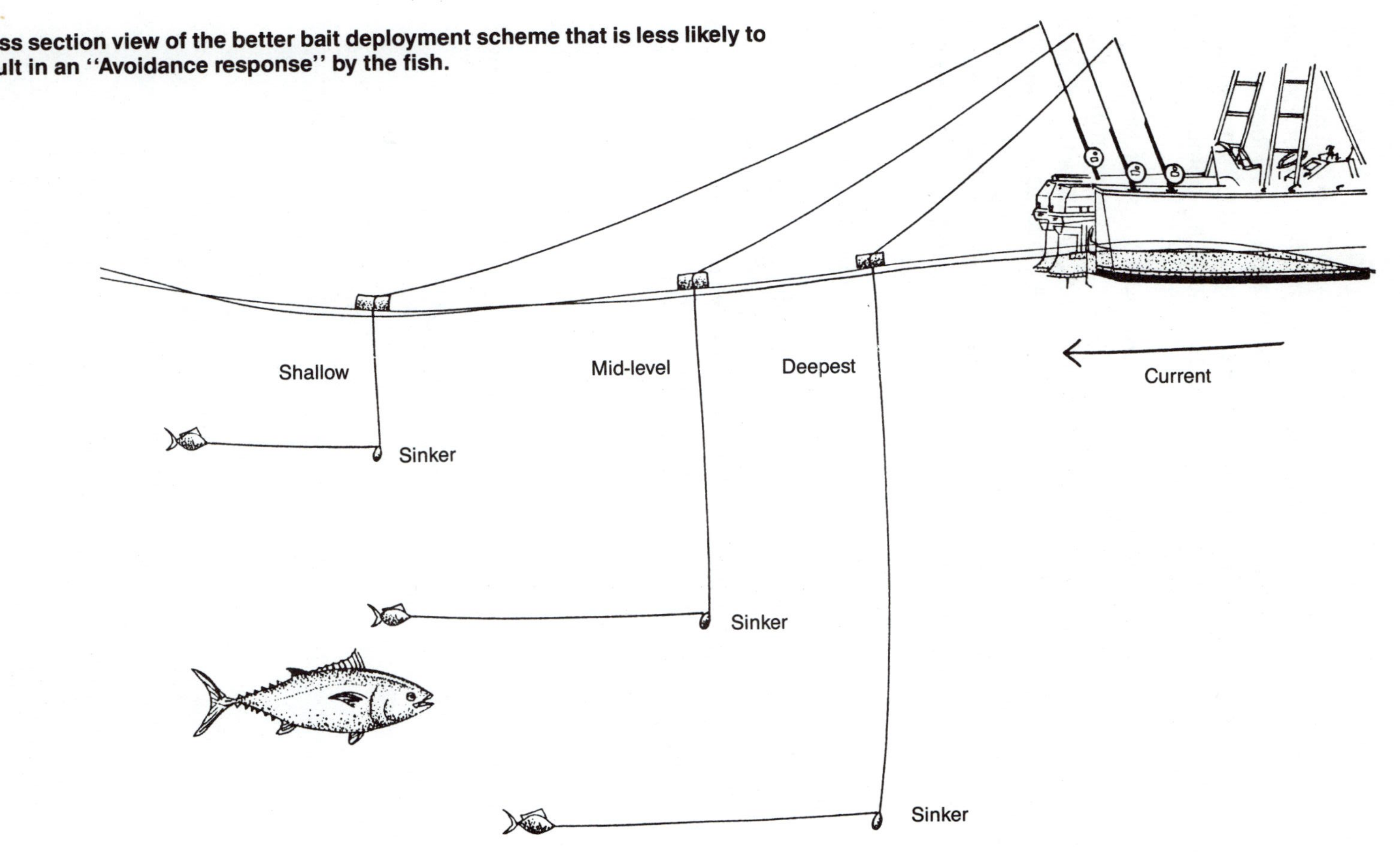

Cross section view of the better bait deployment scheme that is less likely to result in an "Avoidance response" by the fish.
Current
Shallow
Mid-level
Deepest
Sinker
Sinker
Sinker

free-sinking baits would never reach them. The only option is to put out a stationary bait with a sinker and float to hold the bait at a constant level. Obviously, if you're marking fish 100 feet under the boat, that's where the baits should be. Maybe one bait at 90 feet, one at 100 feet and a third at 110 feet. Simple enough, or it is? The location of the "up and down" lines are as important, in my opinion, as the levels of the baits themselves.

The most common method used by most anglers to put out stationary lines often causes a avoidance behavior in the fish. The "up and down" or vertical lines interfere visually with adjacent hook baits. That is, a fish may avoid a bait due to presence of nearby lines.

However, this avoidance behavior is somewhat reduced, depending on the swimming disposition of the fish, thereby increasing the chances for a strike. How the baits are deployed influences the chances for a strike. In the current behind the boat, baited lines tend to line up, one nearly behind the other, with much less distance between the vertical lines than the rods are separated in their rod holders. This crowding of lines can, in my opinion, reduce the chances for a bite, particularly when improperly deployed.

Tuna fishing is sometimes dependant upon paying attention to many little details while jigging or chunking.

4 TACKLE AND TECHNIQUES

Tips And Tricks For Bluefin

"Fish on, get those other lines in as quick as you can." With that, the 80-pound bent butt outfit in the port side of the rocket launcher began to bounce vigorously. The braided Dacron spurted off, reel clicker singing, following this hooked bluefin tuna.

Fishing southeast of Block Island this particular day, in an area that would become known as the Gully, we were fast to our sixth bluefin tuna. Overcast skies, dead calm seas and unlimted visibility accompanied about a dozen private and charter boats drifting and anchored, chumming for tuna.

"Get him snapped to the reel on that side and swing the chair. Wring those gloves out again and get them on him. For crying out loud, stand that bent butt outfit upright in that rod holder so it's out of the way." With those directives attention could then be focused on the angler in the chair; an angler who wanted to tussle with a giant bluefin tuna in the worst way. An angler who, by his own count, had been giant tuna fishing nearly a dozen times without so much as a bite. He fished for giant tuna up on the Cape as well as in Rhode Island, going where he thought he might have a shot at a fish and on this particular day bringing five other fellows with him.

Friends, business associates and a relative who had each taken their turn in the chair before he agreed to try it next. Earlier in the day he confessed only hopes of being lucky enough to get a bite. Polite enough to let each of his guests proceed him in what he secretly thought would surely be the last fish on. He thought to himself, "No way in the world was this captain going to catch a fish for all of his clients this day."

Mouse Trap Rig

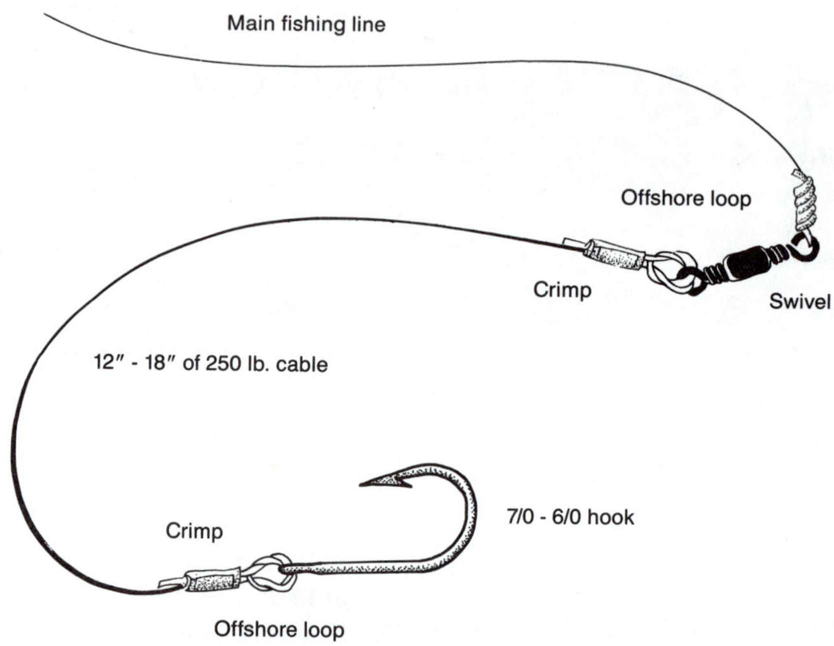

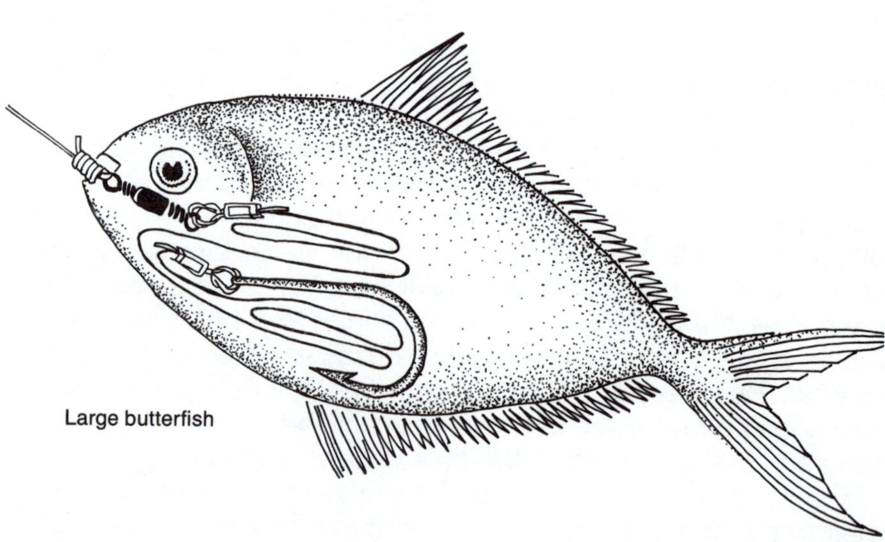

Fine scissors and tweezers should be used to remove the gills and abdominal contents of the butterfish. The rig should then be passed through the gill plates and into stomach. After the rig is in place dental floss should be used to tie shut the mouth and gill plates.

"OK, Frank, you've watched everyone else do it today, so you've got no excuse for screwing things up." Frank Hodges, the soon to retire President of H & H Screw Products of Ashton, Rhode Island went to work on his fish. Later in the day on the way back to Pt. Judith, he said it was obvious our success went way beyond the bounds of luck and we talked about a number of things which I felt contributed greatly to our accomplishment that day.

I explained that leader material, like the Ande clear color was very important. Using a can of flat black spray paint to darken and hide the sinker was important, as well as the use of black plastic electrical tape for securing the sinker on the line well away from the hook bait. I also indicated the reasons for these techniques coming into play. Years back, when there were plenty of giant tuna around, competition among the fish for food eliminated the need to hide a hook, color a line or paint a sinker. As a few well-experienced tuna fishermen have said, "There were plenty of dumb ones around willing to bite."

When the money factor came into the picture, things began to change. The monetary value of dockside fish initiated ardent competition on the fishing grounds by those looking to make some money to pay their expenses. The spawning of these sophisticated tricks would probably never have been developed as quickly otherwise. Tricks like the "mouse trap," the spray painting, the darkened lines and mono straight to the hook. Not only the techniques, but tackle and equipment saw rapid changes and improvements as well, with the cost of these refinements offset by the sale of fish. Simply put, the rapid advances made in techniques, tackle and equipment for giant bluefin tuna never would have happened were it not for the development of the Japanese export market.

Keep in mind that no matter how fast a boat you had, or how skilled a crew, or what level of the state of the art electronics you had aboard, you first had to get them on the hook. A few years back, little or no attention was paid to the fact that fish could see. Little or no attention, that is, until the guy next to you constantly outfished you. We had been lulled into an attitude by tradition, a tradition of spending as little as possible to catch a fish. Heavy, tarred line tied straight to the hook for codfish; heavy cable leader for swordfish, tuna and sharks; lighter plastic coated wire leader for bluefish. Keen eyesight by the fish mattered little in those earlier days and the terminal tackle employed was very crude by today's standards, except during tuna tournaments.

Angling competition, particularly in the late 1950s, began to develop a slow but steadily growing list of tricks employed for hooking a fish on the chumming grounds. Heavy cable gave way to coffee-colored stainless steel wire. Clouds of ground chum hid a heavy mono leader and live bait came into the picture. In this case, terminal gear could still be rough and crude, obviously easily seen by the bluefin but mattering little as the live bait was quickly taken. But without a live bait you had your work cut out for you and finesse was needed to get a bite.

Those who routinely fish for bluefin tuna are aware of this fish's ability to see well. Sharp, keen vision is typical of all tuna and though it may surprise some, they also have the ability to focus on objects both near and far. In the offshore environment, waters are relatively clear but the total amount of light available decreases rapidly with depth. In deep swimming fish like the tuna, the lens of the eye functions for both light gathering and focusing. With their nearly spherical lens, tuna have the advantage of being able to nearsightedly examine objects close to their snout while still retaining the ability for lateral far-sighted acuity. Their large eyes adapted to feeding in the depths and they have larger and greater numbers of retinal light receptors than other fish. In addition, these fish have blood vessels carrying blood at a temperature well above that of the colder water to actively warm tissues like the retinal layer of the eyes and vision centers of the brain. With a metabolic level far above that of strictly cold-blooded fish, their vision is much more superior than we might otherwise anticipated. For years those physiological abilities gave anglers fits of frustration.

Coming tight on the anchor line, previously thawed and cut chum now slowly, but steadily, goes overboard. Bent butt outfits, previously readied, await attachment of a leader and hook bait. Reaching into the large Igloo cooler, a large butterfish hook bait and a leader, also previously readied on the morning run to the grounds, is attached to the swivel. All of the hook baits in the cooler are nearly identical, except for the pound test mono leader diameter and strength. Setting the shallow and furthest bait, I told one of the crew this was the lightest leader, testing at 200 pounds. The bait at mid level was connected to a larger diameter and stronger 250 pound test leader. The deep bait, set perhaps eight to ten feet off the bottom, was going to have the heaviest leader material at 300 pound test. The reason is that the deeper a bait goes, the more difficult it is for the tuna to see due to diminished light levels. In other words, a less easily seen leader in the shallow depths and a heavier leader in the darkened depths just above the bottom, which in this case was 150 feet away.

I also went on to explain that we were taking a chance with the lighter leader on the shallow bait. It might easily fray and be broken by a tuna's sharp teeth. However, if a few fish came by at that level,

This bluefin was taken in the early 1970s when the trend was to use wire leaders. Today monofilament leaders are the ticket, especially the thinner diameter lines.

we stood a good chance of getting a bite. Chancing a bite where the fish is hooked at the jaw hinge, we could go home with a fish while others stared in bordem at their heavily leadered outfits. I also explained that the spray painted, flat black sinkers attached to the lines were also progressively staged. The furthest was the sinker from the bait set in the upper levels of the water column 50 feet down. The sinkers got closer to the hook bait as depths increased. Again, the concept of increased light intensity in the shallow depths assisting vision in a very wary fish.

Frequently checking the baits to see if they were fishing properly, checking sinkers, leaders, baits and hooks helps pass the time. But more importantly, the action reinforces the concept of working at it and giving it a good try. On most, if not all days, I wanted a fish on worse than members of the party. And for good reason, as I took it personally when the fish ignored my offerings—a matter of professional pride or something like that. With the price on the fish, it made it even worse when I failed to get a bite; kind of like rubbing salt in an open wound, so to speak.

Let's go back to the flat black spray painted sinkers. This situation is similar to one in which a magician mysteriouly suspends some beautiful girl on stage in front of a black curtain. The audience is fooled into believing hokus pokus but actually thin, black wires cannot be discerned against the background color of the curtain. At depths, looking ahead at a given level, the background is dark. Perhaps spray painting the sinkers flat black in color results in their blending into the background, making them harder to see. The darkened Dacron line probably also blends in with its background and the mono, at depths with much less light, has nowhere near the refracting qualities. Over the years I've learned to be very careful handling a mono leader as mono can be scratched and roughened. Salt from evaporated sea water is hard enough to actually scratch a leader if improperly handled. Abrasion can create an opaque leader the fish can easily see. You may not be able to feel the scratches but you now have a multi-faceted surface that refracts light which the fish may see and shy away from. Not much different than the annoying scratch on your car's windshield.

Back around 1980 I had the good fortune to have a high liner anchored and chumming not too distant from us. Fortunate for me in that it got me to thinking about ways to increase the chances of getting a strike. But on that particular day, I got a lesson. Boy, did I ever get a lesson; in more ways than one! For example, every half hour or so they either had a strike or were fighting a fish. I had the glasses on every move they made and saw some things quite new to me.

A few days later, after considerable pondering, I figured a few more things out as well. Did my party give it to me! I've had to swallow my pride on many occasion and this day I was belly full. Not catching a fish is bad enough but to be next to a boat catching them with my party watching is a fate worse than death. Others would have been unable to stand it and would have quickly pulled the anchor, fishing elsewhere. Even though my pride was taking a severe beating, I stayed and kept at it. Moving would have been an admission to my giving up. I kept watching.

One of the secrets to being a good, really good, tuna fisherman is the ability to observe and to see things when they are happening. Perhaps a better word to use is perceive which means to see and understand. Before I get back to explaining the lesson, there's something else I had the dubious good fortune to experience. This good fortune seemed to follow wherever I moved. I occupied two different spots at Snug Harbor Marina in the 1970s and 1980s, both of which were immediately adjacent to the fish weighing scale and fish cleaning section of the main dock. If someone in Rhode Island had a good fish, chances were it was going to wind up on the dock next

Fishing In The Shadow

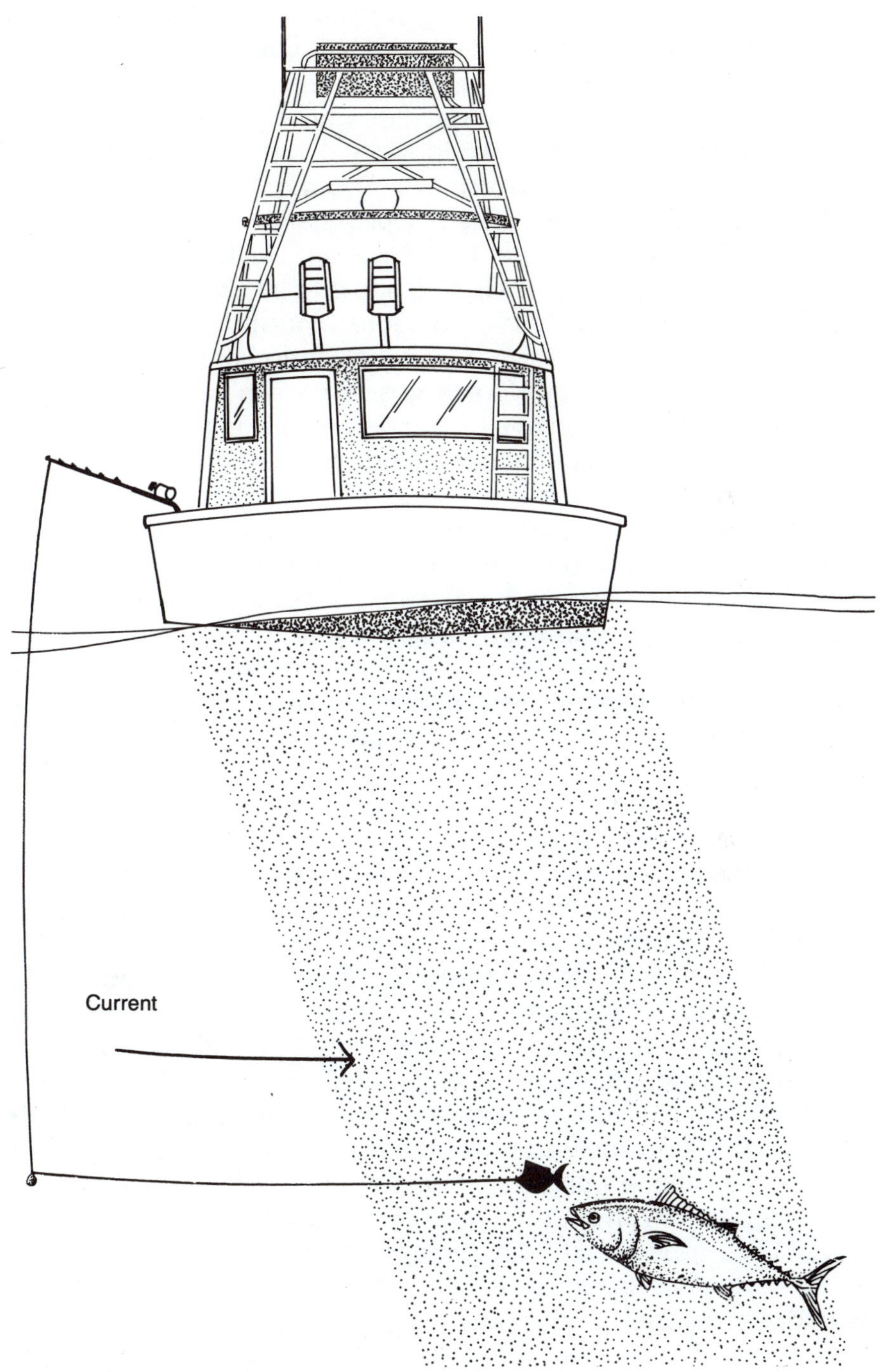

Presenting a bait in the shadow of your boat may provide a hook-up when others are not catching.

to my boat. Since Snug Harbor Marina was a major sportfishing center offering fuel, bait, tackle, groceries, ice, as well as being a major tuna buyer. A lot of fish came to their docks.

Beginning in the mid-1970s, anyone in their right mind would have relocated their charter boat. My parties were exposed daily to what seemed like what the whole world was catching. But not me, I was too dumb and too stubborn to move. The way I figured it, the only chance I had to survive was to get a lot better at catching them and I was constantly reminded of that decision. Unlike the majority of other skippers constantly hounding one another for tips, tricks and information, I watched and tried to figure things out for myself. I persisted and it eventually paid off. But that's another story.

Getting back to the day I took a lesson, it wasn't much later that I pulled the same thing on one of my competitors. Let it suffice to say we simply didn't get along very well and his anchoring nearby was strictly coincidental. Imagine, if you will, the **Prowler** at anchor measuring 35 feet by 12 feet with the sun climbing toward its summertime zenith. Well beneath the boat a shadow area of similar dimensions extending into the darkening depths. Perhaps you may recall walking into a darkened movie theater from the bright light of the street? Or searching for a pair of black shoes at the bottom of a darkened closet. In either case, it presented a temporary problem. A problem of clearly seeing until your pupils dilated, allowing more light into the eye.

Imagine, at mid morning, marking fish under the boat at levels of 50 to 70 feet down. With that information, several adjustments are made to the baits. Lines were fished directly off the rod tips on the uptide side of the boat. Carefully measured, the weighted lines fished at those depths, with the hood-bait and a good portion of the leader, hopefully, in the shadow of the boat. It was obvious that a bait presented in the upper levels of the ocean under conditions of high light intensity elicited only few strikes. But, hide the bait in the shadow and the leader becomes much more difficult to see. Fish swimming up into the current see the bait first, with the sinker weight and start of the leader well uptide. With a bait set in this manner, the bites came with a very high frequency. However, this situation is dependent on the existing conditions, and can change quickly due to current velocity, direction, wind velocity and direction.

My competitor never figured it out, never saw the clues that gave this trick away. How about you?

4 TACKLE AND TECHNIQUES

Fish On!

A squirt of liquid soapy water is applied to the seat surface of the giant tuna chair as the distance of the bucket harness above it increases. With the drag lever of the Penn International 130H on FULL, the angler is forced to lean back, nearly standing on the footrest of the fight chair. The soapy water makes the bottom of the bucket harness slippery so the sliding motion of pumping up a fish becomes easier. By applying heavy pressure, so heavy that the braided Dacron line begins to make crackling noises, the swimming momentum of this giant bluefin tuna is slowed considerably.

Not being able to swim rapidly prevents the fast exchange of respiratory gases from the blood of the gills into the surrounding sea water. Carbon dioxide production from muscle contractions during the battle quickly reaches maximum levels in the blood. More importantly, oxygen levels diminish rapidly. Simply put, muscle contractions necessary for swimming require tremendous amounts of oxygen in the blood stream. As the tail beat frequency increases in an attempt by the fish to attain maximum speed, the demand for oxygen in the muscle tissue skyrockets. Bluefin tuna, like many other fish, are ram ventilators relying on their forward swimming momentum to pass seawater quickly over their gills. Their demand for dissolved oxygen in the water is so great, they cannot simply rest motionless on or near the bottom like many other fish. In fact their design prevents it. These huge animals simply could not maintain an upright position if stationary. Their size and bulk is mostly a result of muscle tissue composition, one type of body tissue that has very high oxygen requirements, with nervous system tissues having the highest. They simply aren't built for slow movements.

Maintaining a good sliding motion with the bucket harness, leaning back in the chair, applying heavy pressure and getting line back onto the reel are some of the main angling techniques needed to land a giant bluefin.

Their internal body temperature averages 10 degrees C higher than the ambient sea water temperature; elevated so that muscles can operate faster, producing high speed, power and stamina. Anyone who has slowly examined the outer body surface of these animals can see they are magnificently streamlined. With anterior dorsal fins retracting and pectoral fins slipping into underlying depressions, nature has designed an animal with a much reduced drag coefficient. This is highly significant when an animal must constantly swim forward. If it did not, it would be unable to maintain its orientation in the water and because of its weight, it would sink to the bottom. Slowing or stopping a bluefin swimming in the water has been the traditional way of killing it. As the drag pressure from the reel and the shock absorbing effect of the rod tip continue to work, the muscle tissue of the fish goes into what is called oxygen dept. At the same time the lever action of the rod brings the fish even closer to the transom while the body weight of the angler, connected by a bucket harness to the reel, produces the force that will kill the fish.

You are mistaken if you believe brute strength of the angler kills the fish. With today's relatively sophisticated tackle, the simple mechanics of lever action does much of the job. Properly executied, the pull of gravity on the angler's body opposes the pulling force of the swimming fish. As the fish tires, swimming speed slows, stride length shortens and tail beat slows. The use of their pectoral fins for stabilizing diminishes and they begin to lay over on one side as the pulling force of the hook and line overcomes righting movements. The fish begins to swim in a circle, the line connecting it to the rod describing the shape of a cone.

The behavior of the fish passes through several stages of fatigue. Circling behavior allows the angler to pump the fish up from the depths, applying a lifting force at the head end of the animal. Many times the fish will respond to this lifting force by breaking stride and surfacing, frequently accompanied by erratic swimming behavior. Whether due to confusion, fatigue or possibly both conditions, the fish then attempts to seek safety by diving to the ocean depths. If the tackle and equipment hold together and the angler continues his efforts, this fish will soon be within reach of those attending in the cockpit.

As many know, the tail wrapping of a fish usually allows one to subdue a bluefin quickly. Although not a technique in the strictest sense, it is a situation giving advantage to whoever is at the other end of the rod and reel. In this case, the fish is prevented from rapidly swimming in a forward motion, thereby allowing for little gas exchange between gills and the water. Tiring rapidly, the fish is easily taken. Inexperienced anglers not recognizing this phenomena have spent hours chasing a fish around while applying only enough pressure to keep things tight.

I recall one incident a few years back when a crew was on a giant tuna for nearly 24 hours. In fact some people were taking bets on the fish killing, drowning or losing the crew at sea. Swimming at what must have been a labored pace but fast enough to stay alive for this length of time, it was later overcome when an experienced angler was placed aboard the following day. Needless to say, it was quite a few miles away from the spot in which it was hooked. Oh, I've been in that situation a few times myself with a party. Not that I planned it that way, you see, but then everything doesn't always go as planned.

With a bow mounted fighting chair and a good drag, a fish will actually tow the boat around. This extra pressure will slow down his ability to swim and increase your chances of boating the fish.

Like the day we were diamond jigging for school fish and a giant jumped on. Right then and there I should have made it perfectly clear to the angler he had no chance at all of landing the submarine he was connected to. But a "What the heck, let's give it a try" attitude was adopted as it was early in the day. A glance at the reel spool indicated it was time to chase the fish, which we did. Time and time again we chased for most of the day. It's been my experience, not just with bluefin but with yellowfin as well, these fish will spend a good amount of time near or at the surface when only little pressure is being applied. And so it was that day, racing to the surface, plodding along.

Then, when the situation no longer became any fun, another attitude developed. Yup, you guessed it—"Time to get serious." A lot of time and energy had gone into this fish and the crew felt we had gone past the point of no return. A Penn 6/0 Special Senator with 50 pound test line tied straight to an 8 ounce diamond jig offered no chance in the world, right? Wrong! Nearly eight hours later we were about to take the fish. Imagine, not making a serious mistake in that time period which would have quickly ended the battle. My mistake was hooking the fish in the first place, although we had enough fuel left to get back to Montauk Point and then refuel, if necessary.

The angler remained on the fish, threatening anyone who even suggested giving a helping hand. I suspected then he really didn't know what he was in store for but who was I to say anything? Finally, on another run, having lost count hours before, the fish turned and settled. Another run, and the angler turned it again. It was at this point in time I began to think we might get a chance to see the fish. I didn't dare entertain the notion we might ever get it.

One of the things you come to expect in situations like this is that when it's all over, you won't have any voice left and people on the dock won't understand what you're saying. It was rapidly coming to that point when the circling motion of the fish just under the surface brought its nose to the side of the boat. Remember, there was no leader to pull on. This fish had to commit suicide, which it did. In case you're wondering, it was a 352 pound fish.

The angler never got out of bed the next day and returned to work only after another agonizing day. The fish paid fifty cents a pound, dress-weight, of course, and was shy of the 50 pound test IGFA men's world record by only a mere 545 pounds as the existing record was a fish of nearly 900 pounds.

Another behavior pattern that intrigues me is one in which young school bluefin gravitate to the 2nd, 3rd or 4th wave behind the boat when in the high speed trolling mode. Focusing on the behavior of seven different tuna and bonito species that visit our waters each summer, I indicate to audiences, in my TUNA BEHAVIOR seminars that the only tuna species that hit this close is the bluefin. I advise that if one-, two- or three-year-old fish might be around, it would be a good idea to put out a few small lures close in the wake. For whatever reasons, yellowfin tuna rarely swim into that area behind the boat, with longfin albacore doing it only occasionally. It's my opinion the behavior of various tuna species varies greatly and changes significantly within each species as the fish ages and grows.

Years ago I told Captain Greg Metcalf, founder of Smoker Baits, that it wasn't so much what you put in the water for school bluefins but where in the wake behind the boat you put the lures. Perhaps, as most of us believe, these young fish are attracted to the noise, turbulence and white water of the wake, thinking a feeding spree is in progress. This same situation, in my opinion, extends to other tuna species, which I'll save for another time.

High speed trolling lures presented on the 2nd, 3rd, and 4th wave behind the boat will often produce good action from school bluefin.

Another unique behavior pattern, much more strongly exhibited by bluefins than other tuna species, is their strong schooling behavior. Not just in school-sized fish, but with the giants as well. On more than one occasion fighting a giant, we would see the line jump as if the line were bumping into something. One day, looking down from the tower, so many other giants swam along with the one hooked I wasn't quite sure which one had the hook in it. For years, many captains took advantage of this schooling tendency when trolling school fish by keeping one on the hook behind the transom.

"Hey Captain, look at all those fish down there following mine," was the signal to put the diamond jigging outfits into play. Slowing the boat to idle speed was something already done, with the next step putting the boat into a hard turn. This acts to slow the boat down even further, particularly the inboard stern chine at the transom. Looking down into the depths, sure enough, a small school of bluefins following below and behind the one hooked.

"Just keep your fish swimming along like it is, without putting any more pressure than is necessary."

Grabbing a diamond jigging rod, similar to one previously described, the jig is flipped up ahead of the boat, out wide enough so that, being in a turn, we don't run over the line. With the line premarked at 40 feet, it's stopped there on this first try. With a slight jigging motion, the diamond passes right in front of the school and several dart out after it.

"Bingo! Here, you take it and hang on."

Passing the rod off, another diamond jigging outfit is pressed into action. Thumbing the spool ever so lightly, this next diamond flutters to just below the level of the fish. With another easy jigging motion, a bump, another bump, with a fish locking on a split second later. Round and round we go. The first fish hooked is brought into the boat as the second one is brought into view along with the remaining fish of this school.

You know, watching the fish swim along was as exciting, if not more so, than actually hooking and landing them. It was like being in an aquarium and on some days members of the party were just content to watch these fish swim along. Content, of course, being that there were a few fish in the fish box. On these days, I had little or no trouble in tagging and releasing a few fish.

Someone once said, "Dim light is an ally to those who seek tuna." It's well known by experienced tuna fishermen that these fish bite more readily in the early morning and late afternoon hours. On the grounds it's referred to as the morning and afternoon "bite." Typically, mid day finds these tuna deep in the ocean depths where light levels are low. Surface trolling success tends to diminish as late morning hours approach with fish marking at deeper levels as the sky gets brighter. Dark, overcast days usually finds the morning action extended for a longer period of time with afternoon action commencing sooner.

Recent research suggests that the behavior of bluefins as well as other tuna species may be controlled by light intensity affecting the pineal gland, located deep in the brain of the fish. Chemical messengers, called hormones, act to modify the behavior of the fish, perhaps affecting threshold levels for aggressive feeding behavior. One thing is for sure, their typical feeding behavior pattern is very familiar to those who routinely fish for them. Being on the ocean every day and offshore during the summer months has acquainted me with a situation in which a number of physical factors affect the behavior of tunas, particularly that of bluefins.

Of particular interest to me has been the sea state and its affect on feeding behavior, especially after a prolonged spell of settled weather. The first day of a back door cold front or dry Northeaster has the fish eating the bottom out of the boat. Rough sea conditions are not favored by my clients, but if I can get to where the fish are, there's a good chance we'll have some action. However, if sea conditions severely worsen, the chances of landing a good fish diminish due to the increased strain on the tackle. By then most clients are too seasick to care about catching a fish anyway. Lots of different kinds of fish are turned on to feeding when sea conditions roughen. The most commonly expressed opinion is that this gives the larger predator a better chance at catching its smaller, wave tossed, confused, prey.

But I think several other factors come into play at this time as well. Early in the day trolling, the wind roughens the sea surface making the line less visible to these fish. Secondly, during periods of settled weather with calm seas and bright sun, these fish may not have fed strongly and are hungry. Their strike zone, as I call it, has expanded greatly. On a day with rough conditions, they'll travel farther and faster to swipe at a bait.

Now, I have a question for you. Why when the wind direction is easterly and variable to moderate do the fish develop lock-jaw? Not only don't they show on the fish finders, they frequently refuse to bite. How do these fish know the direction of the wind, and if they do, how and why does it affect their behavior in this fashion? Many of us know this happens, but we are at a loss to explain the reason for it. The prevailing summer wind is southwest with white water by the early afternoon hours. It's my favorite wind direction for the offshore tuna fishing. Allowing for all the other variables, if I can find the fish I can usually get a bite or two.

HOW TO CATCH 'EM
-------SUMMARY-------

FISH SIZE	METHODS	BAIT / LURES

FAST TROLLING (6 to 8 knots)

School/Medium	Flat lines - 1st to 3rd wave Outriggers - 3rd to 4th wave	feathers, cedar plugs, Hex-Heads, spoons, squids, artificial lures

SLOW TROLLING (2 to 3 knots)

School*	Jigging rods- 2nd to 3rd wave	sinking jigs diamond or butterfish
Medium/Giant	Flat lines - 1st to 3rd wave Outriggers - 3rd to 4th wave	Natural or Artificial mackerel Daisy Chains herring Spreader Bars squid Swimmers

CHUMMING

School, Medium Giant	Drifting or Anchored	Natural or Live Baits whiting, herring, mackerel butterfish, bluefish, bunker, squid

JIGGING

School, Medium Giant	Drifting or Anchored	diamond or butterfish jigs

* = Fish on, boat in slow hard turn.

A few years back while trolling the bars and chains for early season bluefin, we experienced a good day's fishing, as did a number of other boats. It seemed that all one had to do was get a rig close to a fish, after which it was promptly attacked. Relatively new to the game of slow speed trolling, I figured there was little or nothing to it and future days would prove to be equally as successful. Was I ever mistaken! Many days thereafter were full of frustration. But one particular day back at the dock carefully examining the stomach contents, I discovered something I wasn't prepared for. This particular fish had a diminished stomach with bits and pieces of Sargasso weed along with several handfuls of sea horses (Hippocampus sp.) that live in various sea weeds for camouflage, transport and safety. Could it be these tuna had just pushed into Rhode Island offshore waters from the edge of the Continental Shelf, the only area where water of this nature/character can be found in late June? Is it possible that on their northward journey from the Gulf of Mexico and Straits of Florida, these fish had eaten little or nothing and were so hungry they had foraged on those sea horses hiding in the weed? So hungry that within a matter of a few hours they traveled to the near offshore waters where we trolled for tuna? So hungry, in fact, their normal guarded feeding behavior was abandoned and the boats trolling had a field day?

Bluefin tuna ask many questions, the trick is to find the answers.

4 TACKLE AND TECHNIQUES

A Little Courtesy, Please!

As a professional charter boat captain, I get the opportunity to watch a lot of antics on the water, particularly those during the summer months on the tuna grounds. Now, I'm certainly no self-appointed critic but almost daily some boat comes along and creates a problem. Usually it involves a nearby boat, not the **Prowler**, but occasionally yours truly has a period of elevated blood pressure. I must admit, I don't always handle the situation with aplomb and coolness. A number of my colleagues, who also suffer under the daily pressure of catching fish for their clients, spoke at length about an increase in poor manners shown by the so called recreational fishermen.

It's becoming more and more obvious that fewer boat owners today demonstrate courteous and responsible behavior when fishing in the fleet. You've already guessed it, the ugly head of greed rears itself more and more frequently as a result of mega bucks for TUNA.

Now, chances are you've seen this obnoxious fisherman. Usually a new boat owner with more money than brains. Knows absolutely nothing so he feels comfortable in having a crew of six or seven. At least the odds are good someone on the boat will know what to do. Unlike yourself, he doesn't choose a likely looking spot (slicks, storm petrels, clouds of bait on the recorder). This character steams into the fleet, slows down only slightly, with considerable wake, and proceeds to look for another boat hooking a fish. Whoever is running the boat figures this is the best way to find the hot spot. None of this requires much talent or brains.

Zeroing in on three or four boats with fish hanging, a search is made to see if another boat is off the ball. What better way to get right into the action? He figures he's got the right to use another vessel's ground tackle. Anyway, the boat is off somewhere on a fish so no big deal. Traditionally, you do not jump on another boat's ball unless given permission or invitation has been extended. I've witnessed a boat owner returning to his ground tackle clearly identified yet with another vessel hanging off it only to be told to get lost. The ensuing argument never should have occurred and simply ruined an otherwise enjoyable day.

Back to our obnoxious friend. With no ball in sight, and no feeling whatsoever for wind and tide or respect of the area immediately around another boat, the anchor is heaved off the bow. Coming tight, they wind up within a few feet of another vessel. What bothers me is that he knows he is screwing up the other guy but he refuses to admit he's made a mistake. The other guy was there first but so what? If he were to re-anchor, he's making an admission. "No way," is his attitude.

Well, you guessed it. The boat our friend is compromising now has to make a move. Sure, the day's fishing is no longer quite as enjoyable. That's the point of this story.

Our friend has no boating talent, probably little angling talent and certainly no respect for others. Shortly thereafter a decision is made to look around. Fish are being baited, fought and landed throughout the fleet, mainly due to talent, technique and hard, hard work.

Up ahead in the tide, several boats are on fish. It looks like another bite is coming this way. A good bet some fish will swim under the boat. Does our friend see it? No way. Hauling the anchor, he does not even bother to look ahead to see if a boat has a fish on as he hauls his anchor way out. You've seen it, the crew frantically waving this boat off course but to no avail. Heck of a way to lose a fish.

Now, instead of moving to the periphery of the fleet at slow speed, our friend, probably due to frustration at seeing others fight and land fish, puts the throttles to the wall. Boats roll violently, soda cans become airborne, tackle, gear and equipment bang and thrash and people become indignant. "Same to you, buddy," is his reply to the shouts and waving fists that blossom in his wake.

Knowing how to anchor under a variety of conditions comes from experience. All too frequently we see improper ground tackle displayed by a boat having problems, or creating them. It's usually some anchor other than a Danforth style or entirely too small for the job. Usually there's little or no chain and most frequently not enough line (anchor rode) to allow for adequate scope. Lastly, there's no means to let go of the tackle.

You've seen this character. Up on the bow, anchor, chain (all two feet of it). Tossed overboard, it soon points straight down. No quick release mechanism is evident, bitter end of line tied to a forward cleat or bit. Yes, you guessed it, no retrieve ball either.

Soon this character is broadside to the wind, now drifting through your chum line. Had you not retrieved line on two outfits, his near vertical anchor line would have taken baits, leaders and floats with it. In his attempts to get the anchor to hold, he interferes with one boat after another on a downward drift, disrupting the rhythm of chumming and working lines.

One of the many tasks necessary to catch tuna in the chumming fleet is paying attention to what is going on around you. All too often a crew is so intent on cockpit duties they fail to see or hear the shouts resulting from a hookup up current or up wind of them. This boat now coming down on them may have a good fish on relatively light tackle. In a gesture of courtesy, lines should be quickly reeled in and action taken, if necessary, to get out of the way. Fewer

Using the popular ground tackle and controlling the anchor from the transom is the best way to anchor when fishing in a tuna fleet.

boatmen today live up to this responsibility of giving the other fellows all the room they need (within reason). In getting out of the way quickly you need a quick release device and it's also a good idea to standby on the local VHF channel. It's a pain for sure as you may wind up loosing a hook bait or two and precious time is lost, perhap while the bite is on. Seriously now, would you want someone to do less than that for you?

Occasionally, even with due consideration to other boats in the immediate area, problems arise. With a change in wind direction or velocity, two adjacent vessels may experience a relative change in their positions. Usually this results from differences in vessel size or amounts of anchor line (rode) in the ocean. Traditionally, the vessel anchored first that day has no obligation to move. Should a boat's changing position encroach on the chumming and fishing area of another, that boat is obligated to move. Again, a pain for sure, but another responsibility that had been traditionally accepted when fishing in the fleet.

Small center console boats with a fighting chair mounted in the bow can effectively take a large fish.

This, off course, raises the question of how close is close. Opinions differ, but if another boat indicates you're too close (perhaps within throwing distance of a 12-ounce sinker), you should strongly consider making a move. Who knows, maybe minutes later with a fish on, you're now going to ask this same boat to drop off the ball. Wonder how quick they'll respond?

Coming into the area of the fleet that is experiencing action and with plenty of room to anchor, keep in mind what happens to a free floating anchor line and ball. It's your responsibility to stay well clear of the ground tackle, which may now be positioned differently in the wind and tide, now that its owner is off on a fish. And to be sure, how many of us have looked to the heavens and requested the fish be boated quickly as the anchor line and ball are now down tide of all your baits. Imagine how someone like myself must feel with the bite going on all around me, customers now anxious, no room to re-anchor and ball and line are just a few yards off the transom of the **Prowler**.

Imagine, if you can, my blood pressure as I watch this boat, with fish now finally along side. Instead of putting a tail rope on the fish and coming back to their anchor to set up, which in effect soon pulls the gear out of the way, they choose to drift down through the fleet. It seems to take forever to get their fish into the boat. The smart thing to do, if they intend to put the fish in the cockpit, is to do so back on the ball. At the same time, they could be getting tackle and gear ready for the next bite.

Just a few years back there was some very serious giant bluefin tuna fishing on the chumming grounds. Braided Dacron quickly did a number on an anchor rode, sawing right through as the line followed a heavyweight bluefin. Heavy mono took only an extra moment or two to achieve the same effect. The heat generated by friction, even under water, is enough to melt the best nylon anchor line. Today, as it was then, if your actions (or lack of them) are responsible for the loss or damage of another boat's ground tackle, you are obligated to make amends. Whether at the Claw, Tuna Bank, Six and Eight or West Bank, traditionally the boat responsible for damage to another's gear either arranges for prompt payment or replaces it.

Hopefully in coming seasons both the pro as well as the novice will be reminded of the responsibilities they have traditionally assumed when out to catch a few tuna in the fleet. If so, those of us involved in both the business and the sport will have a more enjoyable day on the ocean.

5 BLUEFIN TUNA ECONOMICS

Recreational VS Commercial?

Imagine the scene, if you will, at a gathering of sport fishermen where various speakers from the fishing world are talking about tuna; how to catch them, how to locate them, how to use new techniques and methods. During one of the lectures, a speaker asks, ''How many fishermen in the audience have sold bluefin tuna in the past?''

A vast majority of hands go up.

''How many of you, with a fish boat-side potentially worth $10,000, would release it?'' The speaker queries.

One hand goes up in the audience and a comment is heard regarding that individual's intelligence. Lots of laughter follows.

That scenario was enacted in February of 1989. I was one of many in the audience that morning at the Atlantic Offshore Fisherman's Association Tuna Seminar held in Newport, Rhode Island. The speaker was David Borden, chairman of the New England Fishery Management Council (NEFMC) and deputy chief, Marine Fisheries, Division of Fish & Wildlife, State of Rhode Island Department of Environmental Management.

He went on to say, ''I started off that way because the tuna fishery for Atlantic bluefin tuna along the East Coast is a commercial fishery. It can no longer be described as a recreational or sport fishery.''

David then explained that today's regulations are a result of a creation of ICCAT, the International body composed of 23 countries, which essentially has jurisdiction over all tuna species. Collectively, they oversee nine species of tuna, but only one species, bluefin tuna, presently has regulations. The primary function of ICCAT is data collection from worldwide sources, research and, if needed, management recommendations.

"One point everyone should understand is that the bluefin tuna fishery is essentially closed," Borden told us. "We are operating today strictly on a research quota, or scientific allocation, which has been in place since 1982. This was implemented because of general concern on the part of a number of nations that the status of the stocks have precipitously declined to such a degree that serious steps had to be taken."

One of the initial regulations that ICCAT adopted was fishing mortality on bluefin tuna should be maintained at historic levels. Also, minimum size should be established at 14 pounds. They also voted to reduce the impact on spawning fish by curtailing catch rates.

Today, problems faced include a declining spawning stock, based on the best information available. Not just U.S. information, but multi-national data as well. To compound the matter, we are not sure of the strength of the incoming year classes, which is dependent on certain assessment assumptions.

"So, since 1966, ICCAT has been managing tuna species," continued Borden. "The bluefin tuna is one species the regional Councils have no jurisdiction over."

It was back in 1976 that the 200 mile limit went into effect. The Magnuson Fishery Conservation and Management Act (MFCMA) was the law that "Americanized" fishing along U.S. shores. At the same time, this law established eight regional management councils to effectively manage and conserve fishery stocks. September of 1989 the Act expired and Congress held hearings to discuss the strengths and weaknesses of national fishery policies.

"Back in 1976, when the 200 mile limit was passed, tuna was one group of species left out," noted Borden. "Two principal reasons why they can be traced. First was Congress's debate about whether to include tuna, as there was considerable opposition by certain West Coast interests, the tuna seine industry. If Congress included tuna, it was sure to affect the West Coast tuna fishery industry by limiting fishing rights in South and Central American waters, as well as the waters of many Pacific Island nations. Second, the U.S. tuna industry was not very well developed, with the exception of the purse seine industry. The rod and reel fishery along the East Coast was just developing but nowhere near the levels attained in the late 70s and early 80s. Those were the two essential reasons tuna were not included at the time."

"Not to include the tuna is illogical, and I don't understand how it quite came about," confided Borden. NMFS is the U.S. agency for domestic bluefin management. At this time, of the eight regional fisheries councils five agree that tunas should be included under the Act (MFCMA). Among the three not included in agreement is that North Pacific Council regulation fishing in Alaskan waters. Essentially, they don't have too many tuna in those waters so they have taken a position of neutrality in this issue. The other two councils are the Caribbean and the Pacific. The former has a very large tuna cannery in Puerto Rico employing approximately 8,000 people. If tuna were included, there was a threat the cannery would be pulled out by its owners. That was the basis for their opposition. The Pacific Council is opposed to the act of including tuna because of the cannery industry in California. With the Magnuson Act up for reauthorization in 1989, the councils will actively review the aspects of tuna inclusion and jurisdiction."

David then went on to explain about some of the problems the Councils were up against noting: "Every single time we get close to implementing a specific regulation, particularly with the longline fishery, which targets yellowfin, bigeye or bluefin; every time we got close to a decision, if it had any impact on the longline industry, we couldn't get the regulation through the process."

At least NEFMC Chairman Borden was candid enough to explain they suffered problems with certain management issues. I'm sure many of us in the audience were wondering what might happen if Congress included the tuna under the 200 mile limit.

If, in fact, the councils were to get actively involved with the tuna management, I would see a much more direct role for the public." stated Borden "The councils are comprised of both the commercial and recreational fishermen, with the public having a strong voice in management decisions. One of the other benefits would be a whole array of other management approaches that could be applied. We are here to manage a species for U.S. interests, not foreign interests. One major benefit would be improvement on the data base for tuna, which at the present time is weak. There is virtually no agency in the United States that gathers data on tuna on a national basis. In the bluefin fisheries, there are gaping holes in the data that the scientists are forced to deal with, particulalry in formulating assessment figures. A classic example of this is with the recreational fisheries (so called) in the mid Atlantic area of the Delmarva region, as the catches made cannot be determined accurately because there is an inadequate sampling program.

"One of the obvious benefits, if congress authorizes tuna to come in under the MFCMA, would be the establishment of a data sampling program," he continued. "That has to be the first step in any fishery management program, for without it, you have no basis for any action.

"Another significant benefit, some of the U.S. territorial trust properties in the western Pacific have enormous tuna resources within their jurisdiction. In some cases, tuna are the only true natural resources some of these countries have, but they have no control over it. In fact, they have foreign vessels fishing right up to within 12 miles from their shores. If jurisdiction were to be extended to tuna, those countries would reap enormous economic benefits.

"From an international perspective, the current practices of the distant water tuna fleet, basically the purse seniers, have significantly antagnozied a lot of nations in the western Pacific," Borden then explained. "In fact, a group of sixteen nations got to the point where they were prepared to allow the Soviets permission to come in and fish their waters. This caused significant concern with both the U.S. State Department and the Department of Defense. As a result, we negotiated a treaty with those nations, which has affected us all as we had to pay $62 million over a five year period. That action gave U.S. vessels access to those waters and recognized those island nations' rights to those tuna resources. Simple fact, you don't pay for something unless someone else owns it, or has control over it."

Most of the people in the audience that day had an economic interest in bluefin tuna, i.e., harpoon boat owners, handliners, commercial rod and reelers, fish buyers, etc. Many were concerned with the future of bluefin management and health of the stocks, as it played a role in future earnings.

"From an economic perspective, I could see dramatic increases in the economic value to fishermen as a result of policy change," stated Borden "Tuna fishing in the U.S. is at least a $100 million industry. If we extend jurisdiction, it would reserve the principal interests for U.S. fishermen and the industries they support.

"On an International level, the U.S. is the only nation in the world that does not extend jurisdiction to tuna resources in its waters," the speaker concluded.

Every other nation in the world that has tuna swimming in their waters have the right to regulate and manage that resource, but not so the United States. No doubt it is time for the Congress of the United States to amend the MFCMA of 1976 to include tuna under management authority. Tuna fishing in the U.S. is at least a $100 million industry. (A recent survey indicated that direct expenditures in the U.S. related to recreational tuna fishing is now estimated to exceed $250 million annually.)

5 BLUEFIN TUNA ECONOMICS

Selling Bluefin Tuna

This chapter deals with the "behind the scenes" reasons for season variations in prices paid for bluefin tuna, as well as reasons for escalating prices over the years. Undoubtedly many readers will turn to this chapter early in their reading. Ralboray, Inc. is one of the main buyers of bluefin. In his New London, Connecticut office I asked Robert D. Tobin how Ralboray came about.

Tobin: Well, the business started back in 1978, and it came about because Ralph Dupont, Ray Dackerman and I had been involved in tuna fishing for many years. We initially met in 1976 or so and in 1978 we saw that some people were successfuly engaging in the export of bluefin tuna to Japan. We felt that our avocation could become a business so we formed the company eleven years ago.

Anderson: I remember when Ralboray came to Snug Harbor Marina and set up operations there. Quality fish was what you were after.

Tobin: We originally started in Cape Cod as that was where our fishing "home" was, so to speak, and we relied on many of the contacts made there over the years. Quality fish was something we tried hard to emphasize. In our very first year in business, although newcomers, we shocked everyone by being the number one U.S. company on the Japanese auction market in terms of overall price paid. Quality of the fish is the key ingredient, as well as taking care of the fish and making sure it's readily marketable.

Starting with the fish itself, it has certain qualities to begin with, but as soon as it's taken out of the water you can't enhance those qualities. From that point on, those qualities can only deteriorate. Our job was to educate fishermen so quality wasn't seriously reduced.

Tips on Tuna Handling

courtesy of the
Woods Hole Oceanographic Institution Sea Grant Program
Woods Hole, MA 02543

1
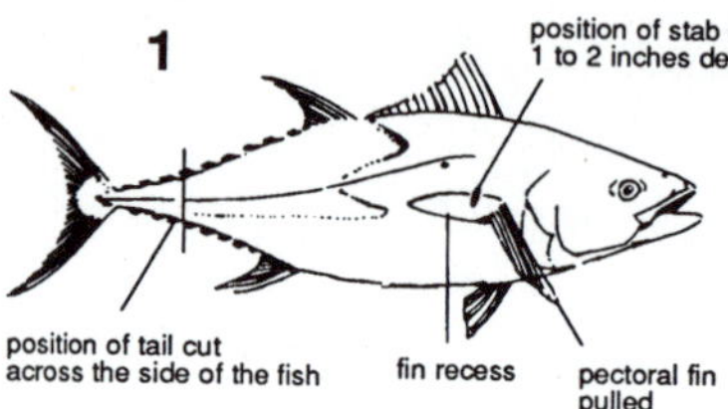

2

*Insert knife 4" in front of the
anus, and then cut toward it.*

3
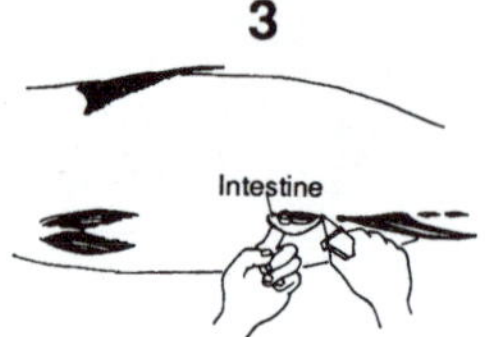

Cut the intestine near the anus.

4
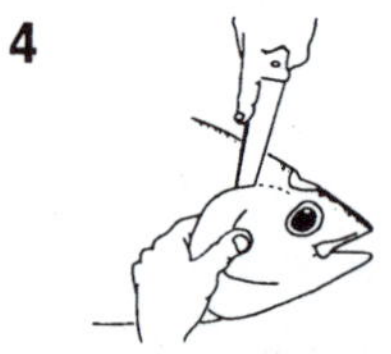

*Insert knife at the top of the gill cover
and slide it toward the eye.*

5

*Cut the main muscle attaching
the gill cover to the head.*

6
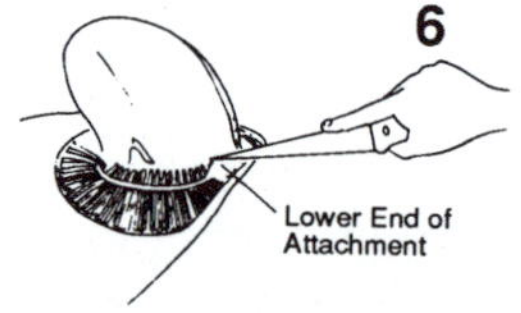

*Cut lower end of gill-to-head
attachment.*

7
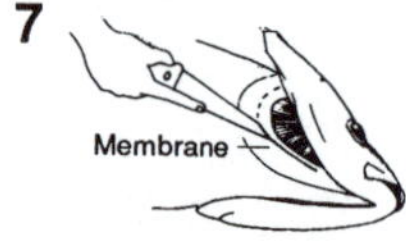

*Cut through the membrane
behind the gills.*

8
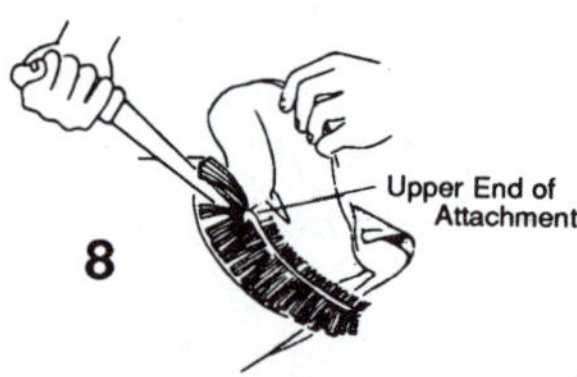

*Cut upper end of gill-to-head
attachment.*

9

*Remove gills & guts and any
remaining attachments.*

10
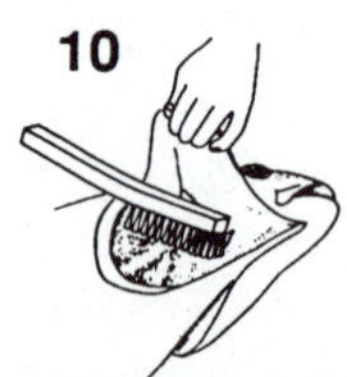

*Scrub spine through
gill openings to
remove the kidney.*

11
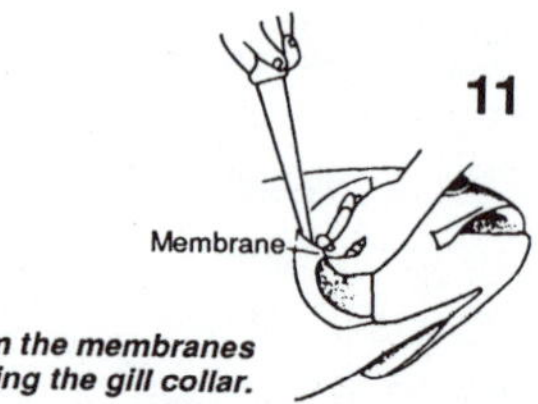

*Trim the membranes
lining the gill collar.*

Acknowledgement. The Woods Hole Oceanographic Institution Sea Grant Program supports research, education and advisory projects aimed at promoting understanding and wise use of marine and coastal resources. This information sheet was prepared with funds from the NOAA National Sea Grant College Program Office, Department of Commerce, under Grant No. NA86-AA-D-SG090 to the Woods Hole Oceanographic Institution, WHOI Sea Grant Project No. M/O-2 and A/S-8-PD. Fig. 1 was taken with permission of New York Sea Grant from "Tuna Handling Tips" by C. Smith and R. Groh, 1983. Figs. 2-11 were taken with permission of Hawaii Sea Grant from "The Management of Yellowfin Tuna in the Handline Fishing Industry of Hawaii: A Fish-Handling Handbook" by R. Nakamura, J. Akamine, D. Coleman, and S. Takashima, 1987. **WHOI Sea Grant would appreciate receiving your comments on this fact sheet.**

Anderson: You mean like bleeding the fish, keeping it wet, getting it back to the dock quickly, etc.?

Tobin: Exactly, we were the first company to give bleeding instructions to the fishermen as well as providing specific information on care and handling. We also dealt with particular fishermen interested in quality—you could see it in their equipment, their boats, their tackle, and their fish tended to be high quality. Other fishermen could care less about quality, and we tried to avoid their "beat up" fish.

Anderson: What can you tell me about the development of the giant bluefin export market? I understand it's been going on for many years.

Tobin: The Japanese have imported tuna fish from the days of the seiners, in bulk as frozen product. It was in the late 1960s or early 1970s that the Japanese export market for giant tuna began to develop, when someone decided to send fish on a test basis, which succeeded. From 1973 to 1977, particularly at Cape Cod and Gloucester, there developed a growing export market. The primary players were companies such as Taiyo Fisheries, as well as several Japanese Trading Companies, who aligned themselves with particular docks or co-operatives in the Cape area and began fish export. Usually this was done on a flat fee per pound basis plus a fee for unloading.

Workmen on the floor of the Tsukiji Market in Tokyo, Japan removing the tail ropes used for hanging fish in quick freezing commercial ships.

One of the larger companies back in those days was Taiyo, which had operations in both Provincetown and Gloucester. Both Stellwagon Bank and Ipswich Bay had heavy tuna fishing activity, and both places were a "hot bed" of bluefin tuna activity. Other payers gradually began to participate in the game, companies such as Marubeni-American Corporation, which was actively involved with the seiners for a number of years and one of the largest fish companies in the world. They also had an interest in the rod and reel, handline and harpoon fisheries.

One of the earliest American players in this game was Mike Purcell, who came from Peabody, and set up in Gloucester as a competitor to the Taiyo group. Mike was probably the leading exporter of tuna for several years and did business with several other companies.

That's how it began, and quality control was not one of the highlights of the early export market. I can remember seeing 9 or 10 whole fish leaving Provincetown to be processed up in Gloucester. The early years were marked by a lack of quality control. Particularly with the seiners early on, and their fish had significantly less quality than that of a rod and reel or harpoon fish. Today, however, the quality of seine-caught fish is much higher, but still not the same. The quality hierarchy would be rod and reel, then harpoon, and then seine fish.

When the fish are in prime condition and the market price is good the Nova Scotia fishermen harvest their giants. These fish have been kept in traps and fed a good diet to increase their fat content.

Anderson: Is that because the fish beat themselves to death in the seine net?

Tobin: That's true, but it also involves excitement levels of the fish and so forth, because they can get in a frenzy which causes internal body temperatures to elevate substantially, I recall visiting the traps up in Nova Scotia where they kept giant bluefin in "farms." I was told by one of the Japanese technicians who was feeding these fish that if they sensed they were about to be trapped and killed, they would go into a swimming frenzy. The result was a higher body temperature with a corresponding lower price on the market in Japan.

(Author's note: Apparently muscle contraction not only produces heat, which is retained and carried by the blood to all parts of the body, but waste products of activity as well. Combined, over time, they work to reduce the freshness and hence the flavor of the muscle tissue.)

Anderson: I understand fish are graded according to a number of factors such as fat content.

Tobin: That's correct, and basically fish are graded on three criteria many times over by the people along the distributive chain: (1) freshness, (2) color, and (3) fat content. Those three factors determines the price paid for a fish. Freshness is critical, and color follows somewhat with freshness, and these two factors are linked to some extent. If you don't have freshness, no matter how much fat it has, the fish is just not suitable for shipping.

The Japanese tuna buyers spend countless hours inspecting the tuna before they bid on them. Their hard work ensures that only top quality fish are purchased.

Anderson: Fish caught in June or early July usually don't pay very much, how come?

Tobin: Early season fish in New England generally do not have a high fat content, and we can experience some difficulty with marketing. These fish are generally not suitable for Japanese or Japanese-American raw fish consumption. Early fish are often what are called KONYAKU, or "water in the meat," and simply not suitable for much of anything. These fish are found after they leave the Gulf of Mexico usually in a post spawning condition, and have had only little chance to fatten up during migration here.

However, not all fish are in that condition, and we can see considerable variation in their fat content, which is reflected in the price in the auction market. Those three factors are probably more important than even supply and demand. Many times I've seen where a fish shipped to Japan, perhaps one of only a few fish available on the auction market, paid very little. You would have anticipated a very high price, but in this case it simply was not a quality fish. Correspondingly, we've sent a few good fish and were surprised as to what the fish brought, even with a lot of fish there.

Recent developments around the world in terms of the bluefin tuna market in Japan have affected the supply and demand. For an example consider the raising and farming of some bluefin in Spain and Tunisia, with more Mediterranean fish now going to Japan. As a result, the Japanese are now becoming more and more selective. Traditionally, the fish from the northeastern part of the United States and Canada have been the best fish in terms of quality in September and October. However, fish are now coming from other parts of the world that rival our fish in quality.

Anderson: You mean that fish from the Mediterranean are beginning to compete with both Canadian and U.S. fish in the marketplace?

Tobin: One of the significant things about that is their season tends to be slightly different than ours, and our fall fish have not seen a lot of competition, with the exception of the Canadian fish. Over the years, Canadian fish have tended to be larger, dressing 700 to 800 pounds. But larger fish tend to bring a little lower price, probably as a result of the risk involved in the substantial investment in just one fish that a wholesaler might have in Japan.

Anderson: Would you take some time to profile the fish price escalation that has occurred these last several years?

Tobin: Foremost, you have to consider the exchange rate of the yen against the dollar. As we sit here today, the rate is 138 yen to the U.S. dollar, and this year and last the rate has been at about the same level. Years ago, the yen was as high as 250 to 260 to the dollar, but when the yen is down to a level of 125 to 130 against the dollar it translates to a lot more dollars when you sell a fish on the Japanese auction market. This is an important factor as to why the price is significantly higher than just a few years ago. Another factor is the Japanese auction market prices are a lot higher now, compared to 7 or 8 years ago as a result of inflation and demand.

One has to understand that bluefin tuna is a commodity in Japan that has a certain status associated with it in terms of marketing, and is a delicacy for those who can afford it. In the auctions, people can get involved with spirited bidding and the price tends to get driven up. All those factors together have contributed to increased prices for the fish.

The tuna buyers on the floor of the Tsukiji Market in Tokyo, Japan examine the giant bluefin very carefully so only the freshest are bid on.

Captain Al Anderson (C) with a high export quality giant bluefin. This fish was taken very quickly and no ''holes'' were caused by a gaff or harpoon.

Anderson: Has the demand for bluefin tuna in Japan increased?

Tobin: Yes, but the quantity of fish we are sending there is less than a number of years ago because of the NMFS quotas in effect.

Anderson: There appears to be an increase in the domestic demand for bluefin, due to familiarity, education, etc.

Tobin: Absolutely correct, as 90 percent of our product would go to the Japanese market when we first started out in business. That's now no longer true, as the Japanese-American of American businessman eating in a Japanese restaurant has created a significant domestic demand.

Anderson: Would you trace the series of events from the time the NMFS tag goes into the fish at the dock to when it gets to the Japanese market?

Tobin: Let's say someone arrives at the dock sometime Monday afternoon with a fish at Snug Harbor Marina. At that point following NMFS tagging the fish is processed by heading and gutting it, along with the removal of the tail and other fins. (Approx. 18 to 25 percent of the gross weight of the fish can be lost in this process.) At that point in time the first assessment is made of the quality of the fish by inspection, along with taking the body temperature, which should be somewhere under 21 degrees or 22 degrees C (68 degrees to 70 degrees F). Body temperature above that suggests the possibility of YAKE, meaning ''burning of the meat.'' You might be able to see it at that time, but we've got to be concerned with it then and anytime thereafter. Fish with a lower body temperature are less likely to have the condition whereby it begins to ''burn from inside out.'' Basically, it's overheating, which usually results from either long-time fighting of the fish, improper handling in the cockpit or warm ocean water temperatures. Many of the American technicians these days, and not just Ralborays, are as capable as the Japanese in judging quality. From a meat sample they will look for color, fat content and freshness of the fish in appearance. Dried and torn skin, wrinkles, multiple holes (gaffs, harpoons), are signs of poor quality.

If everything looks good after cleaning, the fish will then be placed in an iced salt water solution (not brine). Along with other good fish, it will be left to chill to get body temperature down to retain freshness. A number of years back when I was actively catching and selling fish to Ralboray, I would announce over the VHF radio ''Japan fish'' following the boating of a giant tuna. This indicated to the charter fleet a fish taken in short time, of high quality, suitable for the export market. I would then run up a bluefin tuna flag with a Japanese flag under it on the center rigger. At that time Ralboray had a very serious tuna technician inspecting dockside fish. Following weighing he would inspect it, usually smile, and state ''Japan fish.'' Then one day,

Once a giant arrives at the dock, the local buyer starts the export process by removing the head, gills, dorsal fins and tail with an electric saw.

no more smiles and refusal to acknowledge our fish even after weighing. Asking why, I was told by his assistant that I had insulted him by placing the Japanese flag underneath the bluefin flag on the center rigger. Assuredly, that never happened again.

The next day, Tuesday, the fish is checked again, primarily for color. The look of the fish on the second day can be a better indicator than when it immediately came off the boat. Keep in mind that from the time a fish comes off a boat until auction time, the quality of a fish is not improving. It can only go downhill, and if you have to truck a fish several hundred miles prior to processing, its quality will be significantly different.

A decision is then made about what to do with the fish, whether domestic or export fish. The fish may stay in the tank another day, as the optimum temperature prior to shipping is 2 to 3 degrees C (34 to 35 degrees F). Let's say the decision is made to export this fish, along with others of similar quality on Wednesday. Early in the morning the fish is crated and put into a "coffin" and trucked either to Boston or New York. Today, most of our fish fly out of New York, but in earlier days they left from Boston.

After the bluefin has been cleaned, the body is placed into the cooling tank. The fish will remain in the chill tank to ensure freshness till shipment is arranged.

This bluefin has been processed and is ready for export. The fish will be placed into a styrofoam insulated box with ice, then into a ''coffin.'' In a short time this fish will arrive at Narita Airport in Tokyo.

(Author's note, Bob Tobin took a few minutes to profile some of the shipping disasters that have befallen RALBORAY, ie., fish sent to Anchorage, Alaska, left overnight on a Chicago airport unloading dock, etc.)

With luck, the fish arrives at Narita Airport in Tokyo where it is re-iced, clears customs and is inspected by another technician. From here, it might go to either one of five auction companies in Tokyo, or to local companies in Sendai, Osaka or Sapporo. The fish could be either trucked or flown to these other markets.

On Friday night our time, or Saturday morning their time, assuming it went to Tokyo, the fish would go to one of the fish auction houses there. If you can, imagine on display both frozen and fresh tuna alone that might cover half a city bock. Thousands of bigeye, yellowfin and bluefin in one area, which are now being uncrated and prepared for display. Our fish might be only a few out of 25 to 30 giant bluefin on display that morning. Around 4:30 a.m. or so the wholesalers arrive to look over the fish and its quality before doing their bidding.

The opportunity to look at fish quality varies from city to city, based on traditions of the market. In Sapporo, for example, the fish is cut into quarters (loined) and a lot more of the fish can be seen in terms of its quality. In the Tokyo market, a tail sample is allowed, or taking of an inner core sample with a Sashibo. Once a decision is made, a bid will be offered using hand signals (Tokyo). In other cities they use a different system of bidding, using cards (written bid). In Tokyo, as many as 15 or 20 wholesalers may be involved in the bidding, which as one might expect can become fervent at times. Fish purchased are then taken by carts from the auction section to the wholesale section where they're cut and quartered and from where the restaurant buyers pick up their fish for the day. Fresh tuna has a good shelf life and may be served for several days after purchase.

But our involvement may not end at that point. If a wholesaler who has given the fish only a cursory look prior to purchase cuts it open and finds something wrong, he may return to the auction company and try to negotiate a discount. If they cannot agree, an established arbitrator becomes involved, one who may discount the price by up to 15 or 20 percent.

Anderson: So, to summarize what you've told me, a fish landed at Pt. Judith on Monday afternoon could be served to a patron in a Tokyo restaurant Saturday morning our time?

Tobin: That's right, assuming transportation and flight connections go as planned.

Anderson: Do you have to fill in a log for NMFS?

Tobin: We have to fill in a number of reports for them such as a card for fish taken on a daily basis, along with a weekly overall summary.

We communicate almost daily, particularly during the height of the season and when time comes near for quota attainment. They indicate to us when they're considering closing a category in the fisheries long before the notice comes out.

Anderson: In terms of American dollars, how high would you estimate the value of the fish per pound through the 1989 season?

Tobin: It varies, of course, for reasons already mentioned. But let's take a fish on the auction market caught in early season. It might bring up to $4 or $5 a pound, and in late season could go as high as $20 a pound, even higher.

Anderson: Do you think we'll see a continuing trend toward consignment of fish for the future?

Tobin: There's a trend toward that these last several years, no doubt. Certainly less of a gamble on the Japanese market, and it's a marketing decision being made by an increasing number of companies. It's relatively new, and so far has had mixed reviews.

5 BLUEFIN TUNA ECONOMICS

Longlining Bluefin Tuna

"Sure, it's a tough business. We had been fishing just off the bank of Hudson Canyon for three days, just after Thanksgiving. It was the third, or possibly the fourth section of gear, I'm not sure which, and instead of yellowfin or bigeye we had a string of bluefin tuna."

"All of us in the industry knew the longline quota on bluefin was closed, happened sometime back in July I believe. To make a long story short, we cut off a total of 28 bluefin tuna from that section of longline. No way was I going to have any fish in my possession after closure of the fisheries. Fellows on deck knew it too."

"Many of the fish, after being pulled to the topsides for identification, just settled away when cut off. A few of the fish showed some signs of life and may have survived."

It was back in early March when I got the chance to speak with and interview Captain Brigs Endt of the F/V **Catherine E**, a longliner out of Montauk Point, New York. Although relatively new to this industry, he has already made a name for himself as a highly successful fisherman. His crew was back on Long Island since he had the boat at Pt. Judith for several days of minor repairs. His comments serve as the basis for this story.

Today, tuna longlining is probably the fastest growing commercial fishery here in the western North Atlantic, and most certainly in the Gulf of Mexico. Since the early 1980s, many people came to realize they didn't have to go to California or Hawaii or Bermuda to catch a yellowfin tuna or longfin albacore. Along with these fish, the prized bigeye tuna that had tremendous value in the Japan marketplace received immediate attention. Just a few years back, rod and reel fishing along the edge of the Continental shelf was a major source of these species that eluded commercial fishing pressure in the eastern South Atlantic as well as the Caribbean and Gulf of Mexico by a rapidly growing Japanese fleet. For various political and economic reasons, the Japanese agreed to the ICCAT recommendation for cessation of longlining in the Gulf of Mexico so as to spare impact on a declining Atlantic bluefin tuna population. The bluefin tuna was, and still is, a significant by-catch of longliners. With the concentrated Japanese longline effort gone from the Gulf, the numbers of yellowfin tuna in southern waters rebounded quickly.

With the Gulf of Mexico full of tuna fish, it was only a matter of time before this resource found its way northward to the summertime offshore grounds of the New York Bight area and southern New England. In other words, the Gulf of Mexico "cup" ran over and the northeast "saucer" caught the spill. Much of what we catch today results from a temporarily strengthened resource in the early and mid 1980s, a resource which is due to the Japanese longline fishery pull out and the interim period before the rapid development of our domestic longline fishery.

Another aspect of this story, one that has received little or no mention in fishery science circles, is the belief that the decline of the Atlantic bluefin tuna stocks has left an increased "biological niche" for other tuna species along the East Coast. Years back, in the late 1950s and early 1960s, the school bluefin tuna fisheries were very strong. Old timers tell of trolling for schol tuna and days when they returned to the docks with 25 or 30 fish on deck. On days when conditions allowed, school after school of these fish could be seen "pushing along."

Time and again, in discussions over the VHF radio, Captain Michael Potts told that if over the years yellowfin or albacore were around, either Captain John or Captain George Potts (Montauk) would have caught them. The tuna fisheries in the late 1950s and early 1960s were strictly bluefin. For several seasons fish were everywhere until the seiners came in during the mid and late summer seasons those years.

Today, with a resource in severe decline, the bluefin leaves behind a very fertile area for other tunas and many believe the yellowfin and albacore have quickly filled this "niche."

"You didn't see these fish years ago, possibly due to the extreme abundance of bluefin."

"Competition between bluefin and these warmer water species prevented them from being common inshore."

"No one had any idea of their availability offshore or in the Canyons back then..."

These opinions have been expressed more than once in past

sportfishing circles and may certainly be valid. Basically, many feel the decline of the bluefin tuna stocks may have opened the door for the other tuna species. Now when water temperatures reach the high sixties (F) and lower seventies, we're seeing an abundance of other tuna species. Twelve to fifteen years ago, when school bluefin tuna were still very common, little or no effort was made to go "way offshore." Most of the boats of that time had neither the speed nor range to fish outside forty fathoms on a day trip. However, I'm convinced that when the number of bluefin in the waters of the New York Bight and southern New England were so strong, they may have effectively prevented other species from encroaching on the grounds because of simple competition. With bluefin tuna in decline, other tuna species now take advantage of summer squid, sand eels, juvenile mackerel and butterfish when water temperatures allow.

Let's take a quick look at the NMFS data on the growing longline fisheries for Atlantic bluefin tuna. It was back in 1980 that an attempt was made to stop longlining activity for bluefins, as it was not a traditional fishery. Instead, a limit of two giants per day was established south of Cape Hatteras and a percentage of total catch to the north. Lest we forget, in 1982 a moratorium was established by ICCAT and fishing for Atlantic bluefin tuna was closed. Quota allotments, supervised by the National Marine Fisheries Service, in the various categories are supposedly for scientific purposes only. As one can see from the accompanying table, the majority of longline-landed giant bluefin these last few years are (1) coming from the Gulf of Mexico, and (2) are significantly larger in size than fish landed north of Cape Hatteras.

GIANT ATLANTIC BLUEFIN TUNA LONGLINE REPORTS (NMFS)

Year	#Fish Landed	Average Weight	Percentage (Total)
1984	502	570 lbs.	11%
1985	580	606 lbs.	10%
1986	464	614 lbs.	13%
1987	North 39	458 lbs.	
	South 475	605 lbs.	14%
1988	North 13	410 lbs.	
	South 519	632 lbs.	14%

A typical longlining fleet along our coast reloading supplies, bait, gear and goods before leaving for another trip.

At the present time discussions are being held by NMFS to decide the possibility of putting a season on longlining, as it has become a directed fishery in the Gulf of Mexico.

Technically, the Gulf of Mexico is closed to fishing for Atlantic bluefin tuna and fish landed are allowed under regulations as a by-catch only in the directed yellowfin tuna fisheries. At the present time, no means exists to accurately tally the numbers of discards of Atlantic bluefin tuna in the longline fisheries. Log books maintained by permitted vessels are submitted to NMFS show only fish landed for market.

So much for the regulations and statistics involved with this type of fishery. Over a seafood dinner at George's Restaurant in Galilee, the following discussion occurred.

Endt: We fish the gear differently in southern waters as opposed to up here. Down south, we fish 30 to 80 fathoms down with much longer leaders. Up north, we fish shallow, almost floating the bait. We can't fish as many hooks down south as here because of the long leaders. Here, 9/0 hooks are no problem. Hooks are typically 9/0 Mustad, leaders and Hi-Seas 400 pound test mono. The shortest leader is a 5 fathom leader, with some going to 30 fathoms. In the Gulf, because of long leaders, hydraulic leader carts are used. An empty leader is rerieved with a hand cart but with a fish on we pull the leader by hand. And very carefully at that, as one runs the risk of finger loss if not careful."

Anderson: What do you put on the hooks for bait?

Endt: The biggest squid we can get. Sometimes mackerel, and we buy all our bait frozen and then thaw it out. Some is imported, some domestic. Eight or nine inch tubes on the squid, 3½ inch diameter or whole mackerel with a single hook.

Anderson: Are these trade secrets you're divulging?

Endt: No, not really. We even take the time to dye the squids various colors and we use light sticks attached with rubber bands. Cyalumes run us about a buck a piece but the newer stick, smaller in size, is much cheaper.

Anderson: What does it cost to get ready for a trip?

Endt: Well, for an 18-day trip it's not uncommon to spend $8,000 to $10,000. We make 15 to 18 sets a trip, one each day, with a trip each month.

Anderson: What do you mean by a set?

Endt: Well, just before sundown, we lay out the gear letting it drift all night long. At first light, following our "beepers," we home in on the gear. We might move as far as forty-five miles in the night current down south. Takes 6 to 7 hours to haul it back. We cut a lot of gear and then retie it.

Anderson: What do you find on the hook?

Endt: Lots of sharks, particularly hammerheads, blues, makos, threshers, duskies. Fellows down south see a lot of blacktips.

Anderson: What area did you fish mostly last year?

Endt: Just north of Cape Hatteras to the "fence" (Hague Line) at the U.S./Canadian boundary. "We're looking primarily for swordfish, 40 to 55 pound average. Lots of yellowfin. We brought the most fish into Montauk last year in total head count.

Anderson: How about bigeye tuna?

Endt: Well, we never catch them in shoal water, always off the edge of the shelf to the east (Hydrographers) as the summer progresses, and then back to the west (Hudson) in the Fall. We catch them deep but they can be caught at any level in the water column. The Japanese catch bigeye tuna real well but of course the gear has to be right, and the bait, water temperature, etc. Best fishing for us was from 500 fathoms to 1200 fathoms, basically 15 to 20 miles outside the edge of the Continental Shelf.

If we're fishing close to the bank, we've got to keep an eye on the currents. The gear can wind up in the lobster trawls real easy with an inshore "set." Up here, gear might drift an average of 6 to 10 miles in a night. Down south, maybe upwards of 50 miles in a night in the current.

This past year our very last set was in the snow just outside the Hudson Canyon area. Small bluefin worth over $8 a pound, mediums quite a bit more. The quota was filled for longliners and we knew we'd go directly to jail if we had these fish in our possession. I can tell you, the crew was not happy watching those fish settle away.

We really are looking for bigeye tuna and fish of good size and quality can bring up to $18 a pound. We sell all the tuna to Great Circle fish buyers, out of East Hampton, New York. They'll come to Montauk where we home port to buy the catch.

As we get into the summer, most (90%) of the longline boats come north into our area. The whole fleet, including the Merrit boats, up to 300 vessels. At times, and I've seen it in the Hudson, maybe 12 to 15 boats abreast. Tangles with three or four other longline boats are not uncommon. You can't imagine how a big turtle can really screw up the gear or what happens when a pilot whale gets snagged. But nothing like the mess a dolphin can make if the loop is around its tail. The last time it took us two straight days just to clear, cut and untangle.

Typical Longline Section

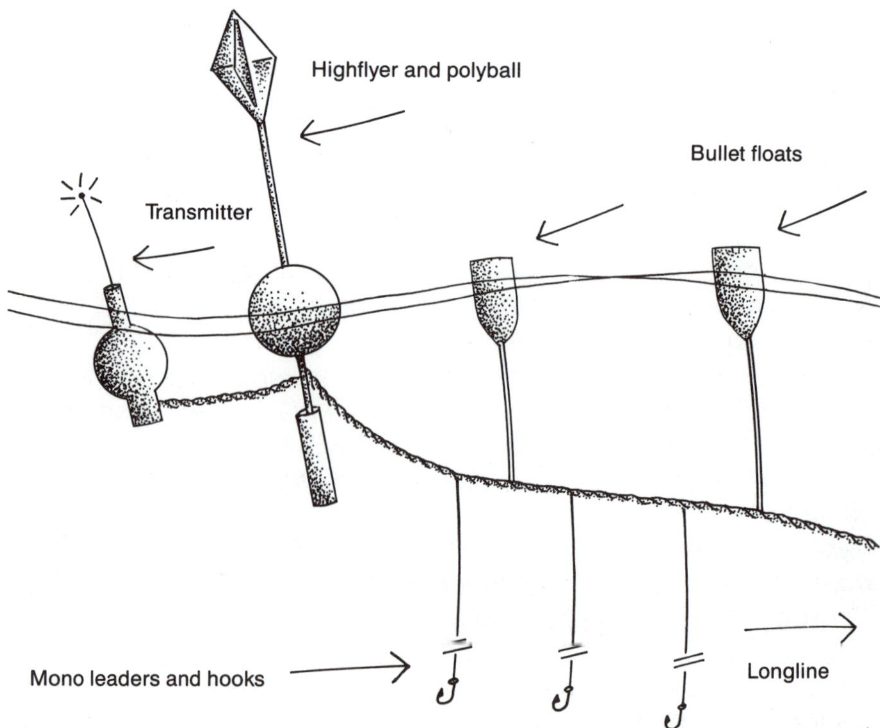

A longline catch of bluefin, yellowfin and bigeye tuna being washed and made ready for inspection on the floor of a Tokyo market.

After the fish are washed, the tuna buyers examine every fish very carefully before they bid on them.

There is the chance, for any variety of reasons, that a boat rod and reel fishing in the canyons this season may come across a section of longline gear. Many longliners monitor the standard offshore VHF radio channels as well as SSB. With most gear marked with the vessel name and number, it can be readily identified.

One set may have eleven high flyers and five radio beepers, a combination of sections. With special frequencies, it can be "homed in on" and easily located when time to haul back. All the gear carries the boat name and numbers, with some of the Norwegian polyballs pushing 90 inches. Usually beepers at either end, with as many as three more interspaced.

Longline fishing is going to continue to attract new fishermen into the fisheries simply because of the possibilities of several "hot trips" back-to-back during the season. With escalating prices being paid to the boat for high quality swordfish, bigeye and yellowfin, there is the chance for very serious money. For example, a nine-day longlining trip out of Montauk, New York during 1988, with 28,000 pounds of swordfish, bigeye tuna, yellowfin tuna and albacore paid close to $250,000.

5 BLUEFIN TUNA ECONOMICS

Spotter Planes

As I talked with Roger Hillhouse over the phone about an interview for this book, he told me why his fish spotting airplane is called **Tony Boy**. Seems a few of the oldtime Portuguese commercial fishing captains had a problem with the English language, so the words **Tony Boy** made it a lot easier for them. He has been flying for 34 years, spotting tuna fish from California to Peru and from the Gulf of Mexico to Maine. He went on to explain that the airplane may range out as far as several hundred miles from the fishing vessels. When schools of tuna are spotted, the airplane radios their position to the boats. If the boats are near the plane, it will wait until they arrive, at which time the plane guides the setting of the net around the school of fish by radio. Payment to the aircraft is usually a percentage of the catch and if no fish, no pay.

Anderson: Tell me a little about the early days of tuna spotting and how you got started in the fishery.

*Willhouse: In 1962 I joined Captain Leonard Ingrande and pilot John O'Conner in the purchase of an old and slightly more than worn out tuna seiner named the **North Queen**. I had been following the happenings on the East Coast concerning tuna exploration by NMFS. I also knew of the success of Captain Manny Philips with his small seiner the **Silver Mink**, who was the original pioneer of East Coast tuna seining. If he was catching fish inshore, we thought there had to be larger bodies of fish offshore. We decided to move our operation to the East Coast, anticipating a large virgin fishery.*

*In June (1962) the **North Queen** and its Captain Leonard Ingrande sailed through the Panama Canal towards New Bedford, Massachusetts. Also transiting the Canal that year to wet their nets in East Coast waters were two other small seiners, the **A.A. Ferante** and the **Western Star**. Captain Frank Cyganowski, who ran the **A.A. Ferrante**, later joined Leonard and myself as a partner, and is well known as a leading spokesman for East Coast tuna fishermen.*

Anderson: Tell me, Roger, how does one learn about catching bluefin tuna?

Willhouse: Well, we knew a little about the migration habits of bluefin along the Jersey Coast and that the Block Island and Montauk areas were traditional summertime sportfishing spots. Not really knowing that much back then, we probably sailed right past several boat loads that year as we made a "bee-line" for Rhode Island waters. Shortly thereafter our airplane located the large schools that frequented those areas and we felt vindicated in the decision to come to New England. Many of the schools were too large to set on with our small boats, schools of 50 pound to 120 pound fish. As the hold of the **North Queen** *would only accommodate 125 tons of fish, the deck would often be loaded as well. However, it was only a few hours to the waiting freezer in New Bedford, as we were typically fishing between Block Island and the Dumping Grounds south of Nomans. Later in the summer we fished on the medium sized 150 to 220 pound fish off Chatham or in Cape Cod Bay.*

Unlike the West Coast bluefin, which are generally fished in clear water along the 100 fathom curve out to 1,000 fathoms, the East Coast fish are caught well inside the 100 fathom curve in dirty, off-colored water that most West Coast fish wouldn't even think of swimming in. We spent countless hours scouting offshore, in waste effort, while the fish passed inside in 15 to 20 fathoms of water.

After a year or so we waited off Cape May, New Jersey, usually around July 1st and then followed the fish up the coast until they concentrated in areas south and east of Block Island in August. There were seasons when the entire body of fish missed New Jersey and came in over the Continental Shelf around the fish tails (Block Canyon) and Hudson Canyon, to make their first appearance in the Shinnecock area.

In the fall, usually in early September when the northeasters turn the water over and begin to cool it from Nomans to Montauk, the fish backed up toward the 30 to 50 fathom lines off Shinnecock. It isn't long after that they disappear over the Shelf but if we had a spell of good weather, we could put a plane in the air and evaluate the population size and composition for the coming year. Some years we had seen what we estimated to be 4,000 to 5,000 tons in the departing group, the smaller 10 to 15 pound fish do not join this exodus. They depart some other place or time.

Anderson: Did your success that first year bring the West Coast fleet to New England?

Willhouse: Success always breeds competition and in its first year of fishing the **North Queen** *caught 900 tons of fish which was exceptional, even for today's modern super seiners. The following year*

A successful set made around a school of bluefin. The water has actually turned red from the blood of all these fish.

(1963) saw a fleet of some 15 boats arrive from the Pacific that would normally have been fishing off Central America. In this fleet was another small seiner (140 tons) belonging to my partners and me, called the **Sea Rover.**

Most of the fish we caught that year were in the 20 to 80 pound class. Many of the schools of fish were in the 125 to 150 pound size and because of their darker color, the canneries had placed a size limit on the fish they would purchase. We had problems estimating their size and many sets had to be released, resulting in some mortality.

Anderson: How did you get involved in the WHOI tagging program?

Willhouse: In 1963 Frank Mather was soliciting help in tagging bluefin and he realized the seiners were the logical ones to get great numbers tagged and released so he offered us $10 per fish. Unfortunately, in the early years the fish were released while our fishing was taking place. A great number of fish released one day were caught and became statistics the very next day. However, we felt this was a worthwhile project as his tagging program verified growth rates and established migration patterns. We are proud to have worked with him and believe that his contribution to bluefin went much further than the call of duty. It was, in fact, a matter of dedication on his part.

Anderson: How fast can these fish move from one area to another?

Willhouse: Bluefin, when traveling from one area to another, usually do it deep underwater and at the rate of about fifteen miles a day. A rule of thumb for us is if you have not seen much sign of a large body of fish for six or seven days, you should start looking 90 to100 miles further up the coast. Skipjack (oceanic bonito) will also disappear deep underwater and then show up in a new feeding area miles away, generally at the same pace of fifteen miles a day. When bluefin or skipjack are bunched up in schools, it indicates they are in a feeding area and they will generally show mid-day after a morning's feeding.

Anderson: When did you first realize the impact of the seining operations in the mid-sixties?

Willhouse: The fishery began to show the strains in 1968, as our small 125 ton seiners were catching from 1,000 to 2,000 tons each prior year. In 1968 that catch dropped to around 200 to 250 tons, and 1969 was not much better. The larger boats from the Pacific and Puerto Rico became discouraged but the Canadians entered the fishery with five new 1,200 ton seiners along with a cannery in St. Andrews. Keep in mind these boats, though fishing in the Pacific, unloaded their catches in St. Andrews. Consequently, they had to pass along the U.S. Atlantic Coast and they timed their unloading so they either entered the fishery with some available hold space still left on the way north, or they came down empty to fish before going on to the Pacific. We always stayed off the small seven to ten pound fish (one year old), but not so the larger Canadian boats that passed our shores each year. They fished any size of fish and when we complained it did no good. With quotas established in the mid 70s, this Canadian fleet became a significant factor in the decline of our school fish stocks. Often there would be as many as four Canadian boats along the coast for a small quota of five hundred some odd tons of fish. It seemed poor business to us to tie up so much fishing capacity for so few fish, unless, of course, they were over-fishing their quota. Years later, in talking with former captains and crew members our suspicions were borne out.

Anderson: Tell me about your involvement with opening the foreign export market, Roger, as I've been told you got it started.

Willhouse: In 1972 we began the export of giant bluefin tuna for the Japanese market. The abundant 125 to 150 pound fish of previous years had moved on up into giant status. The limited amount of school fish just wasn't sufficient enough to support our endeavors. Leonard and I flew to Japan to do business with the trading company of Maru Beni-Michiro Fishery. They asked us to deliver a total of 1,000 tons of giants a year to their motherships. We told them we would *deliver no more than 400 tons (a small number compared to today's quotas), as we were concerned over putting too much pressure on the reproductively mature fish. We detailed only one boat **(A.A. Ferrante)** to fish for giants in the fall, with the Japanese freezer ship returning home with its frozen cargo for the Christmas season market. Our first year's price was a long, long way from that of today's.*

Anderson: How did you become involved with the conservation of bluefin tuna?

Willhouse: In 1974 with the Canadians continuing to catch small, one-year-old fish, along with our observations of fewer fish passing through the school fishery, my partner and I became disturbed. This concern prompted us to fly to Madrid, Spain, to attend an ICATT scientific meeting. Previous discussions with Frank Mather verified our concern for the future of the resource and at that meeting we recommended a minimum size for bluefin tuna along with an overall tonnage quota based on our experiences. It was an astounded U.S. delegation that listened to our request, as they were not accustomed to having commercial fishermen initiate conservation regulations. A year later saw establishment of a 1,100 ton quota and a minimum size limit (14 pounds or smaller) entered into law. Perfect or not, a proud moment for us, but a frightening one, as it now put us at the mercy of NMFS.

Author's note: At this point in our conversation Roger Hillhouse particularly asked that I describe and mention their action in formulating these conservation measures.

Willhouse: Tell readers we weren't forced into following the rules. Tell them we were leading advocators of protection to the bluefin once we saw the effects of fishing on a long but late-life spawning fish. Not many people who shout for our heads these days are aware of our involvement in the history of tuna conservation.

Author's note: Willhouse described their voluntary termination of fishing the following year, as Congress had yet to finalize bluefin regulations.

Willhouse: We had already caught our 1,100 tons and could have continued to fish legally. Instead, we returned to Pt. Pleasant and Cape May while the Canadian fleet continued to fish unmolested. We remained at the dock to show good faith in what was yet to be law.

Take a moment to consider our side of the situation. With our contribution of voluntary action on behalf of the bluefin, we feel that it is only fair we share in the results years ahead as stocks rebuild. We had struggled for a number of years and barely survived until the price of the fish rose to a point of profitability. Our sharing these results today is certainly justified, don't you think?

Medium and giant bluefin tuna taken by a purse seine. Their posterior body and tail damage is due to "Beating Themselves." These fish had to be transferred to private boats because the seine quota was grossly exceeded by many tons that year.

202

Author's note: Roger had alluded to spending quite a lot of time in the air over schools of fish, so I asked him to tell me a little about schooling behavior.

Willhouse: I can fly over a school of 50 pound fish and they will all be 50 pound fish. The same goes for 70 to 100 pound fish except for the one- and two-year old fish, which will mix together size wise. If a small bunch of odd size fish, say a group of 100 pound fish, should join in with a larger school of 50 pound fish, they will remain in a separate congregation of their own and will not mix or intermingle. They will either remain at the left side, right side or behind, but always in a small separate group. Sometimes a small bunch of giants will join a school of mediums, but will stay separate in the school. Later, invariably if you watch long enough, you will see the larger fish move away as a group from the main body and go their own way. Often, when waiting for a boat to arrive, we have the opportunity to watch the interaction of schools for hours at a time.

I also had a lot of time to watch the ''sport'' boats fishing and over the years when school fish are up and pushing water, the ''sport'' boats have little or no luck catching them. It's rare to see a fish hooked from a bunched school of fish that have eaten well in the depths and then come up to ''sun themselves'' and regroup.

The exceptions is the small one- and two-year old fish that bite readily even when schooled. I've seen ten to twenty pound fish turn and follow the trolling jigs for quite a distance. For whatever reasons, the larger fish don't do that.

If we are attempting to set on a school of fish and a ''sport'' boat comes in on the school, as they often have, we know better than to set if it's a school of small fish. They will turn on a dime and follow the trolling boat right out of the net.

Anderson: I've heard that NMFS was considering banning the use of aircraft for spotting for safety reasons. How bad is the air space problem over schools of fish?

Willhouse: Well, years ago the seiners had the air all to themselves. However, we developed rules amongst ourselves as to air safety. The number of planes in the air now make this impossible when fishing giant tuna. The rise in fish prices has made it practical for many harpoon boats to use a plane. Pilots who had never seen a giant tuna from the air crowded near our planes as they circled a school of fish. Crowded so as to be wing tip to wing tip. The only way that we could operate when most of the fish were congregated in a small area was to immediately stack our planes both above and below the aircraft directing the boat. That way no one could crowd him while he concentrated on the fish, which demanded TOTAL concentration when they are deep under the surface. To take your eyes off the school, even momentarily, is to lose sight of them. One pilot reported the wing tip of another plane banking overhead was actually between his windshield and his propeller. To this day he does not know how the other fellow maneuvered away without a crash.

The past couple of years have matured most of the beginners and the situation is greatly improved. Today we tend to fish different areas and a code of conduct has developed among the more professional pilots, including that of remaining clear of a working plane.

Anderson: Would you care to voice a few opinions on other aspects of the fishery, seeing that you've been involved with it for so long?

Willhouse: One thing that bothers some of us is that the Gulf of Mexico spawning grounds has a longline fishery which continues to be a major threat to the bluefin. I don't know why, but the presence of heavy fishing has always disrupted the numbers of small fish spawned in the Gulf. The 1973 year class was the last dominant year class proceeded by many normal year classes. This all took place prior to major Japanese fishing efforts which began in 1974, at which time less and less small fish were seen off New Jersey even though the giant population was still very high. Today, U.S. longliners have taken their place and the disruption continues. Longlines may just keep the fish from congregating in sufficient numbers at the right time and place. For whatever reasons, a disruption continues.

On the encouraging side, there has been an impressive increase in the signs of medium fish and small giants (400 pounds) along the New England Coast. It becomes more impressive when you realize the magnitude of the fishery off Canada the last few seasons. Nova Scotia was bustling with bluefin tuna activity for the first time in years. I heard some pilots describing sights never seen before, such as counting fish in a school by the hundreds or thousands. In the past, they were accustomed to counting in the tens and twenties.

The sightings of the past two years have eased any apprehension I may have harbored. Though the "jury is still out," we are seeing indications that the past years of conservation may bloom into a healthier resource, allowing a modest commercial fishery.

5 BLUEFIN TUNA ECONOMICS

Handlining For Bluefin

The VHF radio was on again and the morning coastal marine forecast indicated northeast wind and rain for later in the day. The chances of taking a fish tomorrow didn't look good, certainly not with that forecast. The ocean swell from the previous day was gone but the wind, now southerly, had come up with the first light in the eastern sky. Not a dark red but a brassy red, suggesting wind, and a lot of it. All the handlines were now set, with the fish baskets and remaining coiled line neatly arranged along both sides of the boat. The remaining totes of chum, bait and ice were stacked on deck just aft of the empty on-deck lobster tank, a doubled piece of tarplin laid over top to act as an overnight insulation barrier.

All there was to do now was wait, cut the chum and dribble it over, with an occasional check of the hook baits. The bait was fresh; in fact, alive and swimming the morning before, taken by a local dragger. It is interesting how a number of draggermen were quick to focus on the demand for fresh chum and hook bait. In fact, you could count on certain draggers having four or five totes of well-iced chum bait ready to sell to whoever was willing to pay the price. And along with the chum, a special bucket of well-iced hook baits, usually large or jumbo butterfish. You couldn't come aboard to hand pick them out while dragging but back in Galilee you could come over to get what you needed, provided of course your name was on the wheelhouse note pad. Along with the handful of bills, payment included a cold double six pack of beer; a thank you to the crew for their effort and a reminder for the next time your voice was heard over the VHF asking if bait was available.

Back now on the deck watching the old paper machine, fish after fish were marked 40 feet down. Again, another definite mark while glancing from the fathometer to the floats well aft of the transom, knowing that at any moment…

The block styrofoam float was well down and as the lightweight cord of the ''snap line'' parts, gloved hands take hold of the handline. The shocker section is all overboard and the quarter-inch nylon is grabbed. Not just held, but yanked on hard, again and again, setting the hook deep in the mouth of this giant tuna. A pair of wet, thin cotton gloves is between you and the line now firmly attached to this fish. At this moment several handfuls of small, cut bait pieces are thrown as far up as possible by the other crew member. Thrown as far as possible so as to extend the time available to help at this crucial point in time.

When this baited hook set at forty feet ''went off,'' it took two of the other lines on that side with it. Lines that had to be quickly untangled, so that you could hang on and put some pressure on the fish. Untangled so that the trailing hook, torn right out of the bait on the adjacent line at the strike, would not impale itself into you as the line was worked. Untangled so that the fish didn't take you over the side. The other crew member throws more chum overboard, on the theory that ''once they are in the slick, don't stop.'' A moment later, a tangle is cleared quickly with the sharp, serrated-edged, short bladed knife kept handy for just this kind of situation.

Another bucket of sea water douses the remaining handline in the ''basket,'' to make it soaking wet to keep the heat generated by friction to a minimum. More bait overboard. With the tangles cleared, this fish has moved off to the side of the boat allowing a chance for the other crew member to switch jobs. The strain of holding a fish quickly causes fatigue which can prompt a mistake, possibly injury and loss of the fish. There is no question that handlining a giant bluefin tuna is dangerous and those successful at it pay particular attention to the details of this technique.

You pull, then hang on for dear life. You have visions of going overboard, as had happened on another boat. Fortunately the handliner only got a soaking as a result of losing his balance but also the loss of a really good fish that would have paid top dollar.

Pulling hard now, so hard, in fact, there is the temptation to bend the line over the coaming but to do so would result in parting the fish right off. You pull so hard one wonders how the gear can hold together. But it stays together because of the stretch characteristics of nylon. Such line is a real plus when fighting a fish as it's more forgiving when compared to the shorter, single strand wire leaders popular just a few years back.

With another switch of the crew on the line this fish begins to come closer because it's prevented from swimming at speed and replenishing oxygen levels in its blood. Now it's swimming on its side, in circles, straight down, coming closer with each timed pull.

Closer and closer to the poised, aluminum shafted harpoon, with its deadly dart and 3/8 inch nylon line. More color with each circle. Out wide now, then lost for a moment under the chine, then circling back out clear of the boat once more. Timing by the glove man, timing by the harpoon man, so as to hit the fish at just the right time and in the right spot. Taking that little extra time to ensure a high quality fish, which, if coupled with other variables, will bring top price from the buyer.

A moment later the fish is stuck with quick successive thrusts on the harpoon handle ensuring deep penetration of the dart. The harpoon line is then quickly taken in hand. Once more under the boat, this is the final effort to reach safety. All it accomplishes is the discoloration of its snout as it bumps the keel and carries away some of the soft bottom paint.

The handy straight gaff raises the tail out of the water and a moment later the loop of the tail rope comes tight. Now head down in the water, the last futile attempts at escape are made, with its tail beating sharply against the rust stained fiberglass of the transom corner. Then the head is pulled up and the gill plate jabbed as the last remaining heart beats assist in the routine bleeding of the fish which leaves a blossom of rose-colored water.

With the fish soon to be in the boat, the continued chumming action is abandoned and the remaining gear is retrieved, carefully checked and put away for the next time out. A reinforced length of ¾ inch plywood is readied at the transom to prevent the sharp edge of the deck at the transom from damaging and softening the side of the fish as it comes aboard. Not very important a few years back, this is vital with today's prices. A few quick incisions and the bleeding procedure is completed.

Contributing to today's success are recent changes in the typical "handline." Today, the typical basket contains 400 to 500 feet of ¼ inch or smaller nylon Nygold line with a 100 foot shocker line of 400 pound test #60 net mending twine. Attached to this is 24 to fifty feet of 300 to 400 pound test monofilament with a 10/0 or 11/0 Gamakatsu hook. Sinkers are used, taped in place as needed, to gain depth. The whole handline including basket would cost $50 to $60 wholesale. The handline industry, like the rod and reel industry, has come to recognize just how well these fish can see. No longer do they fish heavy gear that causes the fish to shy away and the chumming aspect has risen to more sophisticated levels involving the amount of chum, how to work the bait and adding fish oil scents. However, the basic idea is still the same: small pieces of chum in high quantity until one fish makes a mistake and grabs the overly large, fresh, dead bait or actively struggling live bait.

Other changes have been made, not just with the handline. Changes such as more cooperation between the boats on the grounds when a boat gives way, to do it quickly, since the fish have become so valuable. Years ago, the common attitude was not getting off the hook, not moving for another boat. If you lost a fish, it was no big deal because you could go right back and get another one without too much trouble. So you didn't get off the hook for fear of stopping or interrupting your own chum line. Those attitudes resulted in a lot of bad feelings but as the yearly price rose and with most of the boats now on the grounds for profit, and not fun, a growing spirit of begrudged cooperation developed among handliners.

Changes have been seen on the traditional tuna grounds as well. Today, the ''crank boats'' and harpooners are way off chasing the fish following wherever the planes tell them to go. No longer do you see the fierce chumming competition of years ago. Boats move from one traditional handline area to another because of the lack of fish, the dogfish problem, the weather, size of fish, etc. There are better fishermen handlining today compared to just a few years back, particularly since the price has escalated well over the $10 a pound mark.

Years ago, as the first signs of a commercial fishery for giant bluefin tuna appeared, the Unification Church ''moonies'' precipitated a lot of resentment on the part of other fishermen, particularly with those looking for some fun and to cover expenses from the sale of the fish. As the number of boats in the ''moonie'' fleet grew, it became obvious they were in their own little world as most ignored others around them. On more than one occasion retrieving lines to avoid interference but only getting off the ground tackle at the last possible moment.

But as they became better fishermen much of the resentment waned. Perhaps because they too had to buy a boat permit and frequently paid a better price for fish brought to them, as well as being able to supply fresh hook and chum bait. And so what if most of the proceeds went to the church.

Today, most of those in the handline fishery, like all the other fisheries, will agree that 10 percent of the fishermen catch 90 percent of the fish. Most will also agree that in 1989 medium sized fish abounded and there appeared to be more fish than ever before but considerably smaller in size. In fact, just a few years back the average handlined fish weighed nearly 650 pounds, a real brute compared to today's fish.

5 BLUEFIN TUNA ECONOMICS

Harpooning

Looking out the window again for the third time in the last 10 minutes, it was obvious the smoke emitting from the smoke stack went straight up. There was absolutely no wind. In fact, the smoke rose to about 1,800 feet where it then mushroomed horizontally due to its being trapped under a layer of cooler air. A temperature inversion was in place along the coast, a result of a massive high pressure system over the New England and mid-Atlantic regions.

Even before he got to the ringing phone the harpooner knew instinctively who was calling, and knew also his response to the question.

"Looks dead calm here, what do you say to giving it a try?" asked the caller. "Not a breath of wind this morning, for sure."

"See you down at the boat," he replied. "I'll bring the lunch. Make the call."

Having idled only long enough to cast off the dock lines, the captain pushed the gear shift lever ahead and the engine RPMs were brought up to allow clearing the end of the dock in the ebbing current. With that the stuffing box packing rotated for just a split second and then stopped. Hot from the previous trip and with little or no time to gradually cool off on the spinning shaft, it had adhered in one spot to the bronze shaft. Breaking away, the drip, drip became an unnoticed dribble soon to affect the day's success.

At about the time the boat cleared the breakwater the starter in the Cessna 180 was being engaged and in a moment the engine came to life. Low RPM roughness soon faded into a steady roar as pre-flight cockpit procedures were attended to. All along the coast light aircraft such as Super Cubs, Citabras and Cessnas would soon be in the air. These aircraft were ideally suited to the spotting of fish and the addition of a belly tank fuel gave them the cushion of another six to eight hours air time. Most of these aircraft carried VHF radios with either private frequencies or scramblers, CBs and portable cellular phones. The cost of this electronic equipment was negligible, considering a pilot might get 25 percent of the fish sale monies. It was understood by most that this percentage extended to fish taken jointly or by the boat alone, as fish were frequently taken coming and going to the area covered by the spotter. Some even got their 25 percent share plus the cost of fuel but this agreement was limited to but a few of the better pilots and the highly successful stick boats they routinely worked for. This was going to be a VFR day and the chances of several aircraft bunching up over pods of fish were high. This had the looks of one of those days with potential airspace congestion where one small mistake could spell disaster.

Several of the lead fish in a pod of giant bluefin were now swimming steadily at a sustained rate just under the surface in the warming upper levels of the thermocline. Solar radiation promised to raise the sea surface temperature another full two degrees before mid day providing there was no wind to mix the surface layer. Muscle contraction in these huge fish was producing constant levels of heat, some of which was being used to elevate stomach and intestine temperatures which hastened the enzymatic reactions of the digestive process. Bluefin are one of several fish species that can maintain a body temperature up to 10 degrees C above the temperature of the water they swim in. The bulk of heat production was being used to warm the muscle used for swimming as only swift predators can catch fast swimming prey like squid, mackerel and herring. It is this near-surface swimming behavior that creates potential danger.

Swimming along on roughly a northwest heading, the fish in this school are all hearing the sounds of the open ocean through their lateral line system. The noise is similar to that described by astronomers of outer space, perhaps best described as hash. But now, a new noise, growing ever so faint and distinct.

''There they are,'' comes the matter-of-fact shout from the deck.

Coming down the tower, the harpooner made his way forward to the root of the pulpit, now extended over the ocean surface with the foot brace almost twenty feet from the stem of the boat. Hinged at the bow, it could be swung upward and back coming to rest against the upper ring of the tuna tower, close to twenty five feet above the ocean surface. It was hinged so that it would not extend the overall length of the boat and was constructed of light weight aluminum so as to not drastically nose the boat down at the bow. Folded back, it would allow this thirty five foot boat to be charged only at the dockage rate for a thirty five foot slip and no more. Folded back it was safe from becoming torn off in rough sea conditions.

Well behind the pod of fish the boat matched their turning movements while plastic trash barrels lined up at the transom were filled with sea water from the wash-down pump hose. Five barrels totaling over 1,500 pounds squatted the stern of the boat down, overcoming the weight of the person standing nearly twenty feet off the bow and slowly raising the height of the pulpit over the sea surface. This boat, relatively narrow for its length, has no spray rails forward. No spray rails to splash water and make noise, and is now well up in the bow, reducing any hint of a bow wave. This quiet boat becomes deadly silent as all electronic equipment is turned off. Only the sound of the propeller noise remains.

Closing to within fifty yards of the fish, preparations have been completed. Beginning with the harpoon, the dart has been completed. Beginning with the harpoon, the dart has been fastened to the pike and trails about forty feet of plastic-coated outboard motor tiller cable ending in an electrical plug. A permanent wire cable and socket now connected to the plug is lashed to the deck, traveling back to an inverter and the bank of batteries connected in series. A basket, lashed forward, holds a warp, ball and highflyer line also connected to the harpoon.

Following the fish's wave or bauble the harpooner must wait till "color" is seen before letting the harpoon go.

Bronze Harpoon Dart

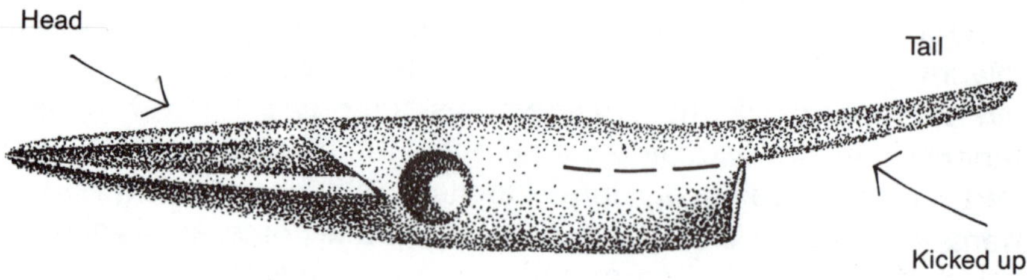

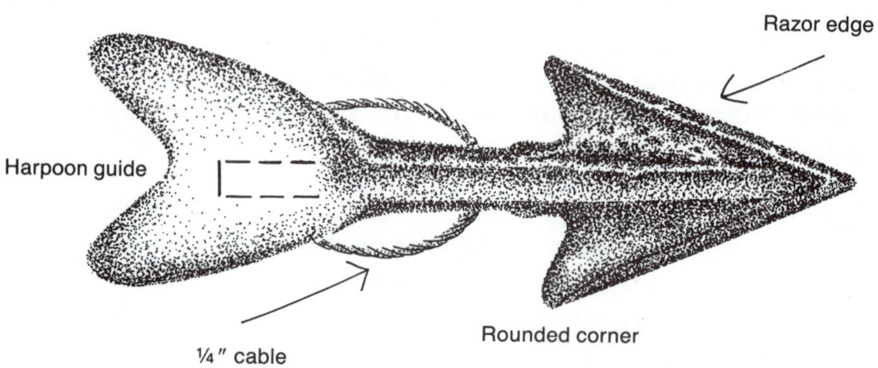

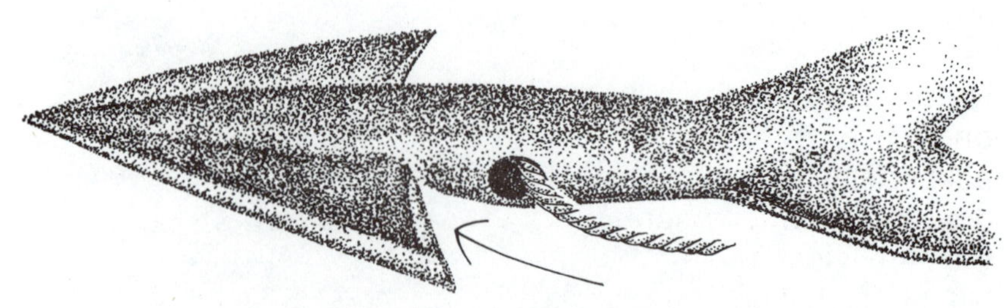

In the tower, hands deftly turn the wheel to keep the boat directly behind the last fish in this pod. Propeller noise has slowly and steadily increased as the distance between boat and fish closed, but this particular boat had now been transformed into a "sneaky" boat, a term given to a special kind of boat that can easily approach to within a few yards of a swimming giant bluefin tuna. Not that the fish couldn't sense this growing danger, it simply had never experienced it before.

Pushing along now, the fish create a flow of water over themselves that disrupts the sea surface, forming a wave of water called a bauble. This wave behind each fish fades away to nothing; hence, the term. Coming in behind the fish the throttle has been set and will not be changed. To do so would spook these fish into frenzied flight.

"Color, I see color," is heard from the tower. This height advantage along with Polarizing sunglasses enables the tower man to see the fish first. The angular body, beautifully streamlined, is being pushed along with a steady, constant tail beat. A tail beat that could, if maintained, carry this animal around the world at the equator in a period of one year.

With a different perspective, the man in the pulpit strains to see "color," as they move closer, ever closer to this swimming fish. A constant directive and description of the fish comes from the tower man and with eye contact imminent a final visual check is made of all the harpoon equipment. The key piece of equipment, the dart, has seen special attention. The forward broadhead edges have been carefully ground to a razor sharp edge for easy penetration. The rear edge of the head has been blunted and the corners rounded to reduce the cutting and tearing of tissue when pulled backward. The tail of the dart has been bent or kicked up to facilitate the turning or toggling into the flesh underneath the tough skin. Should the dart carry through the body of the fish in the area of its tail or obliquely through the back coming out on the opposite side of the fish, the fish is said to have been buttoned. The ideal shot sends the dart deep into the back of the fish to the level of its backbone. A boned fish, suffering from a damaged spinal cord or severed backbone, lapses into fits of shivering and shaking with uncontrolled swimming movements. It offers only little fight and frequently beats the water into a froth before quickly expiring.

In the basket and on the foredeck attached at one end to the dart and cable, is a length of warp over 300 feet long with a ball at the far end showing the boat name and the NMFS Permit Number. This length of line (warp) is needed should a fish die and sink. At a depth greater than 300 feet, the taut line from fish to ball could tear the dart out, particularly when surface conditions roughen, and the ball begins to bob on the surface. In some areas, the warp is lengthened to nearly 800 feet. In shallow waters, care must be taken to add a mid-line cork to suspend the warp in the water column. If not done, the warp could sink along with the fish and foul itself on the rocky bottom with little or no chance of recovery. To reduce the time need-ed to tire a fish, several plastic milk crates are ready to clip to the warp, their addition creating slightly more resistance in the water. Should a green fish come back to the boat, a bang stick is ready to dispatch it with a head shot. But this scenario is not likely today as the dart connects to an insulated cable, called a ''shocker.''

The bow and pulpit turn off from the fish ever so much and all at once the body of this fish materializes into reality. The rhythmical tail beat, the golden finlets twitching from left to right with each beat, the bauble now only several harpoon lengths away are a beautiful sight. A mental note is made to lead the fish a little bit less as it is swimming perhaps only 3 feet beneath the oily calm surface. Pois-ed, the harpooner is ready for the right moment to throw or lob the stick. Many refer to a swimming giant tuna fish as a ''teflon coated ice cream cone,'' and the angle of the fish is critical for penetration.

This ''sneaky'' boat has made all of the necessary preparations and is within a few yards of a small pod of swimming fish. This is the time for patience.

At the last possible moment, the harpooner must lead the fish a little bit and throw the harpoon at just the right angle so that penetration is made.

Deep in the bilge of the boat the water level continues to rise ever so slightly as the stuffing box dribbles. Unnoticed earlier because of get ready procedures, the bilge water level is again pushing the arm of the float switch even higher. Another fraction of an inch and the mercury flows down the tube and the electrical circuit is completed. With a ''shir,'' the bilge pump motor, still set to automatic having been overlooked earlier, spins the impeller. The noise of the gushing water from the topside outlet, along with that of the impeller, reaches the lateral line of the bluefin almost instantly.

At that very same moment the stick is thrown, arcing in mid air.

Within several tenths of a second impulses from the tuna's brain reach the white lateral muscle bundles controlling the tail oscillations and in a flurry of speed this fish jumps to almost 30 miles per hour.

The dart, aimed for the broad expanse of the body, passes harmlessly by the narrow (peduncle) tail and the reaction from the pulpit is one of anger and profanity as it becomes obvious the fish has been missed.

The original shocking device came down to New England waters from Canada where it was used to take large swordfish in short time. Immediatley after being stuck the current would be applied, resulting in muscle spasms and finally its death throe.

A good harpoon boat can land up to 15 fish in a single day. During this time the processing docks are kept busy preparing the fish.

In the case of giant bluefin tuna, this allows a greater number of fish to be taken in the course of a day and the Harpoon Category quota for 1989 was reached about July 14. Understandable, when some of the permitted boats landed 12 to 15 fish in a single day. From just a few years ago when only 30 boats had NMFS permits, boats now number over 250 in this fishery and attainment is achieved sooner than ever before. The 60 short ton (sT) quota for this Category had a 15 short ton buffer which was fiiled, bringing the total tonnage landed to 75 sT.

A while back I had a chance to talk with Ralph L. "Trigger" Watson from Beverly, Massachusetts. Having fished for swordfish and tuna for 25 years and flown for close to 30 years, with much of that time over the waters of the Dumping Grounds and south of Block Island, he was obviously qualified to answer a few questions. I asked him to explain why there is such a rush to harpoon fish in the early season even though these fish have nowhere near the value of late season fish.

"I think quite a few of the people in this industry are afraid that if they don't get them somebody else will," Watson stated. "There's a limit to the number of fish tonnage that can be taken so a lot of fellows focus on taking as many fish daily as possible. This means taking them quickly and that's where the "shocker" comes in. Oh, a few fellows are in it for an ego trip, people with absolutely no need for the money, people who want to be able to impress others with tales of how many fish they took. These people sport the best equipment possible, simply looking for something to do. Most, however, are in it for the money. Greed is the reason for setting up "shocker" equipment. A few fellows from Maine, highliners, grossed between $150,000 to $200,000 a season. You know, back in the 1950s and 1960s these fish, if left on the dock, would be used as lobster bait."

6 BLUEFIN TUNA TAGGING

Frank Mather: How It Started

Frank J. Mather, III (Franko by his friends) was responsible for initiating one of the world's oldest and largest game fish tagging programs. His work on bluefin tuna led to a gathering of scientific knowledge that influenced the thinking on many important fishery issues. Today we have information on migratory cycles, geographical range of populations, growth rates, estimations of population size and mortality, as well as the ability to determine the effects of fishing pressure on Atlantic bluefin tuna populations. I looked forward to my interview with him and the chance to ask a few questions. He is unquestionably an interviewer's delight. No sooner had I pushed the ''record'' button than he said, ''I talk too much and sometimes get off the track. If so, shut me up and go on to the next question''. There was no need to do that and what resulted was an eye opening question and answer conversation.

Anderson: Tell me a little about the studies on bluefin tuna.

Mather: Aristotle (384-322 B.C.) wrote quite a bit about bluefin tuna. There were lots of stories all through the Middle Ages as different writers told about their habits and what not. They repeated a lot of superstition about this fish, and a lot of facts also. The history of many fish traps in the Mediterranean goes back well before Columbus's time. In fact Columbus's journal mentioned seeing tuna in mid-ocean heading east and he speculated they were heading toward their demise in a fish trap.

For years, scientists believed that bluefin tuna didn't go anywhere, that they were non-migratory, like they never moved. Then an article by M. Sella in 1930 examined fish hooks which at that time they were handmade and characteristic of different areas and by that method he determined tuna moved all around the Mediterranean and eastern Atlantic areas. He was correct in his belief and the sad part was he died just before we got our first trans-Atlantic migration tag returns. Many of his critics also died just before we got those trans-Atlantic returns, and I was sorry for that, as they thought they knew it all.

Anderson: When did you first begin to study Atlantic bluefin tuna?

Mather: I kind of worked into a general program on the biology of bluefin tuna in the late 1940s and early 1950s, and at that time the tagging of bluefin tuna was considered to be nearly impossible. The Pacific scientists made a breakthrough with the dorsal loop tag, which allowed small tuna to be tagged. We did some experiments with that technique, which turned out to be fairly successful, as we got the first trans-Atlantic migrations ever recorded with those tags in 1959. We were anxious to tag the larger fish, but use of the dorsal loop tag just wouldn't do, so we started experimenting with the dart and streamer tag. In essence, it's a miniature harpoon with a spaghetti type streamer attached. Thus, it was possible to tag a much larger and more powerful fish such as a giant tuna. All that was

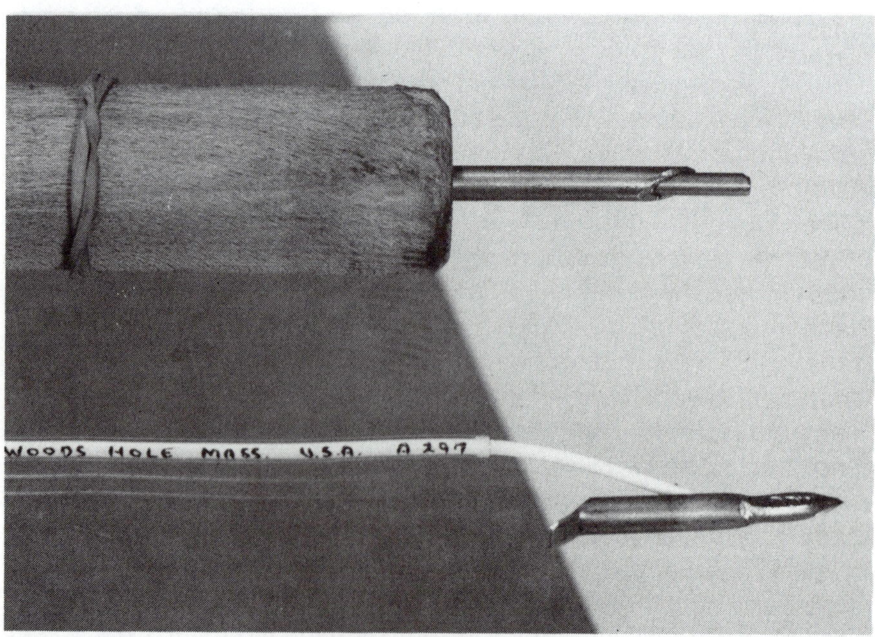

In the early 1950s, this was the first type of dart tags to be used on giant Atlantic bluefin tuna at Bimini in The Bahamas.

In 1954 Frank J. Mather III (L) demonstrated on local television how to use the dart with spaghetti streamer and dorsal loop tags.

required was to get the fish within reach of a long tagging pole, jab the tag in it and cut the leader as close as possible. In my opinion, removing the hook can do more damage than leaving it in the fish, especially with big fish.

We still had a problem with numbers and a bit of skepticism but in 1959 a couple of sailfish returns along with a white marlin return from Havana, which was tagged out of Ocean City, Maryland and the trans-Atlantic bluefin returns got a lot of people interested in the Cooperative Game Fish Tagging Program (CGFTP). We were almost ready to give up at that point and we had various psychological and emotional reactions to fish tagging. As long as there were no returns everything was great but when a Japanese longliner caught a white marlin tagged out of Ocean City, Maryland, everyone was absolutely horrified that the Japanese were going to learn they had marlin there. Remember now, Ocean City had spent millions of dollars promoting and advertising that fact. So in effect, all the Japanese had to do was watch TV, listen to the radio or read a newspaper or magazine. Just how stupid can people be?

Anderson: What actually happened to the school tuna fishery in the 1960s?

Mather: When the super seiners came in from the West Coast, I was sure that was the end of tagging. There was, at that time, a local seine fishery of just up to four small boats, which the stocks probably could have sustained. I believe they started in 1963 and returned again in 1964 and 1965. They had massive impact on the stocks in which several generations of bluefin were wiped right out. Not only did they catch the small ones but they took medium sized fish whose darker color the American housewife was "educated about" and did not prefer. Many of that size fish simply went overboard (dead) because they knew they couldn't sell them at a good price. They also lost many tons of fish through fishing technique accidents. For instance, when they needed, say, another 8 or 10 tons, they would make a set and have as much as 100 tons in the nets. Those extra fish never survived. Also accidental breakage of nets lost up to 100 tons at a time. The impact on the stocks was much greater than assumed from the actual catch data.

Anderson: What was public opinion like early on in the tagging program?

Mather: The sportfishing fraternity was skeptical but the need for conservation on the basis of tag returns was pointed out. The commercial interests also became skeptical because they felt there was no justification. We had to fight a public relations battle all the time with people not returning tags, false information, whatever. On the whole, however, we've accomplished very significant results over the years. When push came to shove for conservation, this (tagging) was the most convincing evidence available that the stocks were being extremely heavily fished.

It's quite interesting that some of my peers with NMFS and other institutions claimed the evidence was inconclusive but I later came across a report which some of these same individuals had signed that agreed completely with what I said. I think it's a safe bet to say that if it were not for the tagging program, there would be very little bluefin tuna available today.

This is interesting from a personal standpoint. I got a letter this past Thanksgiving from a fellow who is a chief boat owner in the local seine fishery and an air spotter who I know is a very intelligent observer. He had previously written a letter about how devastating the seine fishery was; they caught 90% of the schools they sighted. During the entire 1967 season, they sighted only two schools of fish which they had not caught. In this particular letter he indicated that every Thanksgiving he's grateful for something and this year he was thankful for my efforts because the last five years they have had pro-

fitable fishing. He added that such success would probably not have occurred had I not taken a strong stand on this issue. Remember now, this letter came from a commercial seine fisherman.

Anderson: How do you see the fisheries today?

Mather: Once the price developed on the fish, sportfishing transformed into commercial fishing. Sportfishing tackle changed as well and line test went to 200 pounds or more, and double lines far exceeded regulation length. There is practically no such thing as a sporting catch today, with the exception of a very few individuals.

Anderson: How did you manage to get so many fish tagged in the early years of the CGFTP?

Mather: In the early years we tagged most of the fish ourselves, which was considerable, and we got a few good cooperators. In Chatham with school fish, we had Charles W. Brown & Sons, along with a number of outstanding people from Long Island, New York and with the giant tuna most of the early ones were tagged in the Bahamas, as they had no commercial value there. In fact, it was considered a waste to bring those fish into the dock and a lot of tag and release was done there.

To continue with how we got fish tagged, when we realized at the peak of the seine fisheries there was a real crisis with bluefin survival (mid 1960s), we knew the number of fish being tagged by the sportfishermen and cooperatives was inadequate to secure convincing results. So we made arrangements to pay for fish and have our people tag them from the seiners. That way, we got large quantities of fish tagged over a short period of time. The year before we started this program we had 29 tag returns, with most fish being tagged by members of the Atlantic Tuna Club. We became alarmed by the high rate of recapture, maybe close to 30%. In 1964 we got approximately the same rate of return when we tagged fish out of the seiners, with over 500 fish tagged and released. In 1967 we had 48% of the tags returned from fish tagged the first two summers and since we knew there are so many ways tags can be lost, the recapture rate had to be considerably higher. Tag losses can occur for several reasons. One is shedding the tag, another is a fish can die from natural causes, another is people simply don't notice the tag, and another is people are too lazy or opinionated to return a tag. Shedding experiments indicate it could be as high as 20% in fish tagged.

Anderson: Have the tags always been the same?

Mather: Today the present tags are stainless steel and plastic and progressive improvements have been made over the years. For example, the information sleeve was supposed to have been glued in place to the heavy mono by the tag manufacturers because the metal crimp at the end sometimes let go and the information on the tag was lost,

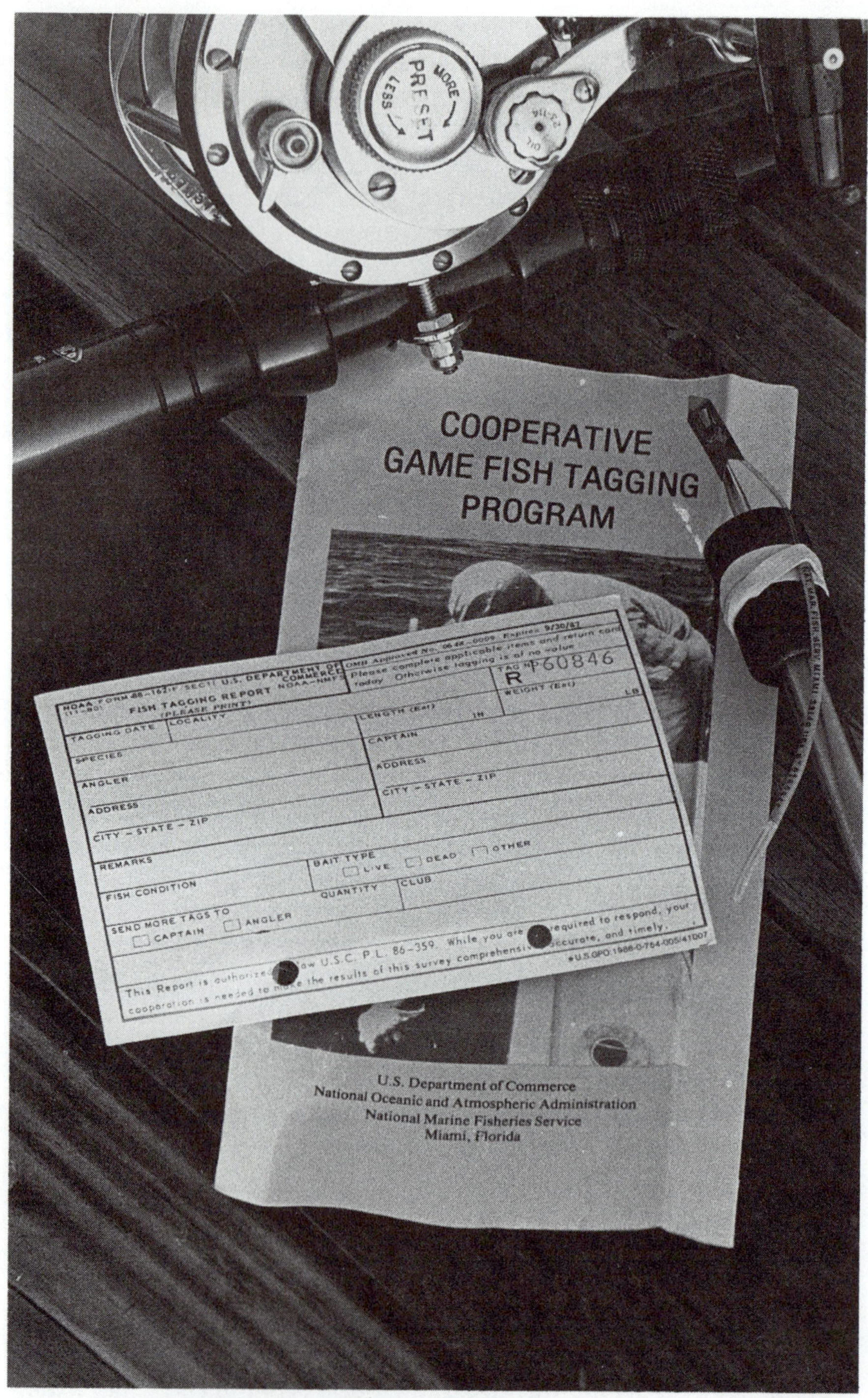

The Cooperative Game Fish Tagging Program made the latest changes to the tags. Today they have a stainless steel barb crimped to a heavy monofilament leader material along with an information card.

224

but this was not always done. A plastic crimp is used today.

Anderson: There seems to be a lot of evidence whereby a fish tagged in a given area is frequently recaptured in that same area at a later time, suggesting fish return to that area for a number of years. What's going on?

Mather: The migration of bluefin tuna seems to vary greatly with age. Fish spawned in the Gulf of Mexico are assumed to move up to the mid Atlantic regions, the New York Bight and lower Cape Cod area in their first year of life. These fish (up to about 75 pounds or 4 years of age) don't appear to move very far in the winter, perhaps out to the edge of the continental shelf where the longliners have a chance to catch them in considerable quantities.

The medium fish, as well as larger sized school fish (75 to 300 pounds) have been pretty much lacking and we have much less information on this size fish. When NMFS (Gloucester Station) was running offshore experimental longlining operations, they found very large concentrations of these mediums along the northern edge of the Gulf Stream, from off Long Island, New York to south of Newfoundland. We weren' t sure just how far these concentrations extended but we had fantastic catch rates on these fish. One set of taggings we did in Oceanographers Canyon just before the start of the season in June provided four returns out of 29 from Long Island to Provincetown, which gave us a clue as to their possible migratory pattern. It appears that instead of going much south of the Gulf Stream in the winter, these fish go east. For whatever reason, this size fish is not caught in the Gulf of Mexico or in the Bahamas. For these areas the minimum size seems to be around 275 pounds.

Anderson: I've read where fish tagged in our waters have been recaptured in European waters but I suspect this is a rare occurrence, correct?

Mather: The giant bluefin seem to make extremely long migrations, with some going as far as Norway and others going to the south Atlantic off Brazil and Argentina. These are extreme migrations, of course. Fish that have been tagged at 15 to 20 pounds in northern waters have been recaptured years later in the Gulf of Mexico weighing well over 300 pounds. There seems to be some trans-Atlantic interchange for small as well as giant fish but it appears to be an occasional or small scale event.

(Ed. note: The author's daughter tagged a school size fish off Block Island, that was recaptured two years later off the coast of Spain from the Bay of Biscay.)

Anderson: Some of the larger bluefin make their way up into the Canadian Maritimes in the late summer or early Fall where the water temperatures are quite low. Is this due to the fact the larger

ATLANTIC BLUEFIN TUNA
TRANSLANTIC & TRANSEQUATORIAL
MIGRATIONS

Lines joining releases and recaptures are diagramatic and do not necessarily represent migration routes.

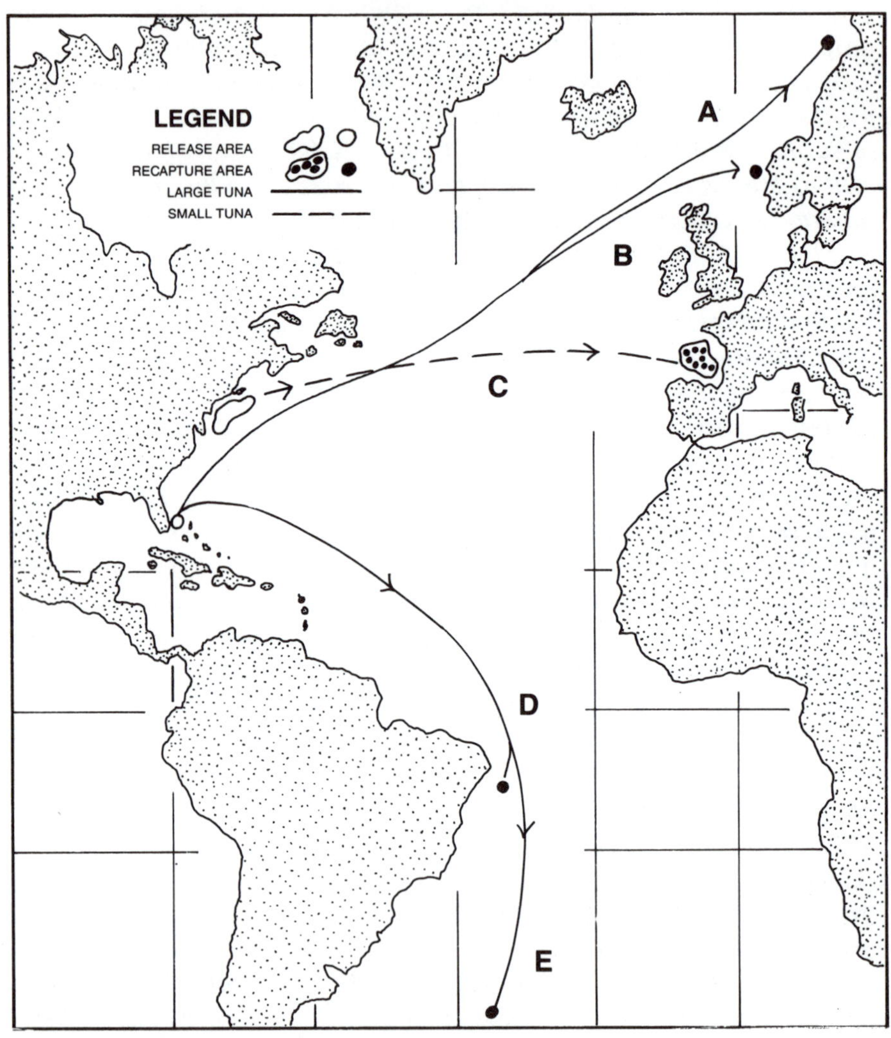

RELEASE & RECAPTURE KEY   The month and year of release are listed first and the recapture date second.

A: 1 return
June '60—Sept. '62

B: 8 returns
June '60—Aug. '62
June '61—Sept. '61

June '61—Oct. '61
June—Aug. '62
May—Aug. '67
June '69—Aug. '76
May '72—Aug. '73
June '73—Aug. '76

C: 44 returns between
1956 & 1979
D: 1 return
May '63—March '65
E: 1 return
June '69—Feb. '73

fish develop a strong thermoregulatory ability?

Mather: Yes, in fact for some years, in the late 1960s and early 1970s, practically all the giant tuna fishing was off Newfoundland and I fished for them right next to icebergs. Incidentally, those same fish seemed to shift their pattern and went into the Gulf of St. Lawrence and attained enormous sizes. Those fish that were in the 500 to 600 pounds range off Newfoundland grew to be 1,000 pounds and more.

Prior to 1972 there had never been a 1,000 pound bluefin caught on rod and reel and very few by other methods. The 1970s data by NMFS with bar graphs indicated distinct classes of fish over 1,000 pounds involving several hundred fish. Since there were very few medium sized fish, it's quite possible the giant bluefin had little competition with feeding and could attain larger size. This is just a hypothesis, of course.

Now that there is a representation of all the age groups of bluefin, I believe the 1,000 pound fish is something of the past. Fishing pressure is very high now and that may be responsible for some fish never getting the chance to attain that size. Year ago, conditions had to be different to allow so many of them to get so big.

In the period of the middle 1970s, it was difficult to catch a bluefin tuna between 17 and 700 pounds due to the seiners killing all those generations of fish. Years ago when I complained about the lack of medium sized bluefins (135 to 310 pounds), I had a call from one fellow in Gloucester who said he had just caught a couple. I asked what the fish weighed and he said over 500 pounds. Not quite mediums.

Anderson: What about the high price being paid for fish today?

Mather: In my opinion, the development of a high price had the greatest impact on the larger fish (giants) but actually I think it's more efficient, conservation wise, for the seiners to get thousands of dollars for one large fish than thousands of dollars for several hundred of small school fish.

Anderson: When does a bluefin tuna become able to reproduce?

Mather: NMFS has concluded that sexual maturity in bluefin tuna occurs at a time when the fish is approximately ten years old and weighing about 300 pounds. However, I find it extremely hard to believe. We know in Europe (Mediterranean) that bluefin begin to spawn when they reach 80 pounds or so and we've seen many ripe males in the 60 pound range here in our waters running milt. We've also seen ripe females here in the 100 pound range. If the government scientists are correct in saying the only place bluefin tuna spawn is the Gulf of Mexico, only a fragment of the population are actually spawning. It is interesting to note that Japanese longlining data indicate there are many bluefin distributed throughout the warm

If more tagging data was available back in the late 1950s, the migration pattern of this fish caught by Murray (R) and Lillian (L) Cianciolo might have been known.

waters of the Atlantic during that spawning period. Although the Gulf has spawning fish, it may not be the only area where it is going on. It could be that spawning in bluefin is a lot more random than we think but keep in mind some concentration of spawning fish is needed for successful spawning.

It is a very difficult situation to figure out and there are a lot of question marks in this equation. In the Mediterranean, at least with the eastern stocks of bluefin, they used to think the fish spawned in a lot of areas but now it seems there is a main spawning population in the Tyrrhenian Sea, north of Sicily. They have a different situation there, as the fish spawn on the surface and it's easy to find spawning fish with air spotting. Which, incidentally, also makes it very easy to wipe them out. In the Gulf of Mexico it's an entirely different story. The western Atlantic bluefin spawn well below the surface, some deep, and are not visible to aircraft. Interestingly, we have two totally different spawning behaviors in these populations.

The fish in the Mediterranean and eastern Atlantic approaches to the Mediterranean have another behavior pattern that is totally different. The trap fishery there depended on the periodic run of tuna, either pre or post spawning runs, but the fish always went through each area at a given time so they just put out traps and caught those fish. This trap fishery dates back to the time of Julius Caesar or so. In the western Atlantic, the only comparable run of tuna we know of has the fish (giants) going by Cat Key and Bimini in May and June. Yet, in the Mediterranean and its Atlantic approaches, there are hundreds of areas that trapped fish successfully. There is a very distinct difference in behavior between these two stocks of bluefin, at least with the giant fish.

Anderson: What have we learned from tagging studies?

Mather: Tagging has indicated a number of things to us, such as migratory patterns, growth rates, and most importantly, estimates of fishing mortality and catch rates, particularly in the seine fishery. This was the principal factor leading to the conservation measures of bluefin, of moderate measures in the whole Atlantic, and on a more radical basis for the western North Atlantic. I think that without these measures, if we hadn't lost all the fish by now, we would certainly be in the process of doing so.

Anderson: How do you feel about the escalating prices being paid for bluefin tuna?

Mather: One thing that disturbs me is the continuing development of a higher price paid to boats for the fish, and it's created a mind-set in a lot of people. They use this as reason for justifying fishing and boating expenses, by catching and selling Atlantic bluefin tuna. I see this going on as long as the price continues to escalate and there is a resource to catch. As long as the demand remains and with fewer fish, the higher the price paid will be. With prices pushing twenty dollars a pound now, the guy who didn't give it a try last year will do so this year. Another thing that disturbs me is that along with the Japanese, the U.S. is developing a taste for Sushi and Sashimi. Another thing is the growing popularity of Cajun blackened fish, which enables a lot of tuna, some previously undesired, to command a very good price today.

I'm also disturbed, if they're true, by reports that bluefin tuna loins, if not too large, have been passed off by fishermen as bigeye tuna to avoid restrictions. Bigeye tuna can get up to 300 pounds or so, and how do you tell a bigeye from a bluefin, especially after it's been headed and gutted and had the fins cut off? Some of these same fishermen talk about their feeding the public with their efforts. Actually, this is a fad. Who do they think they are kidding at $20.00 a pound or so? Prestige, luxury items and fads is all it is. One thing for sure, poor people aren't eating a lot of tuna at that price.

Anderson: Do you believe the future holds any promise for the bluefin tuna?

Mather: Today there seems to be greater awareness by the marine angler that tuna stocks in general are not unlimited and conservation might not be a bad idea. Programs like the AFTCO Tag A Tuna and Tag Flag using NMFS tags is sure to gain in popularity. Many billfish tournaments now are strictly tag and release for reasons of conservation. There has been a definite change in attitude and people realize they can capitalize on the opportunity to tag fish today. The mere fact of releasing fish puts many into the ''in crowd'' so to speak, more so than flopping fish after fish up on the dock. But don't get me wrong, when fish are bringing close to $20,000 each, releasing is a little bit difficult.

6 BLUEFIN TUNA TAGGING

The Tagging Programs

''What do you mean, put a tag in 'em and let the fish go? You must be out of your mind. Why, the next fellow who catches this tuna, if I let it go, is going to hustle it up the dock to the fish buyer. Now, don't forget, I've spent thousands of dollars for this boat, electronics, tackle, and what not. Tell that to someone else, not me.''

This response is typical of too many ''sportsmen'' today who venture offshore for tuna. In my home waters of New England the attitude of the majority of anglers is ''kill, and sell all they can.'' Back at the dock these fish are marketed to help pay the cost of fuel, bait, tackle and equipment.

The number of owners and anglers with offshore outboard powered rigs to fancy ''mega yachts'' who have this mind-set has grown tremendously these past few years here in the New York Bight and southern New England area. Seems to me that if one can afford a fully equipped sportfisherman and all the trimmings, they have no real need to kill and sell every last fish.

What really bothers me is a question typically asked by someone who has never been fishing before in their life, ''If we get to keep all the tuna, how do we go about selling them?'' Oh, I can just hear the comments now, but someone has to speak out about this attitude of today's angling public.

Don't get me wrong, I'm no hypocrite. If you've got a giant Atlantic bluefin tuna on only yards from the transom and worth thousands of dollars in the Tokyo market, by all means, take it. If you're fast to a bigeye tuna and are holding hundreds of pounds of ice aboard to insure quality by all means take it.

On the other hand, if you've just returned from a canyon run and the cockpit has upwards of a couple of dozen small yellowfin tuna, none of which have been headed and gutted or seen any ice whatsoever, this part of the book is aimed at you, my friend.

Of course you might find a buyer willing to unload your catch, however, inspection would probably indicate the fish as being too soft and tainted. If so, you will shortly hear there is little or no demand for fish this size or of this quality so the market price, if any, is far less than you imagined.

It's obvious, even to the casual dockside observer, that some fishermen are responsible for a considerable amount of waste of a rather valuable resource. Today, more and more people are beginning to recognize the recreational value of this fishery. Tackle sales, marina slip rentals, bait, fuel sales (dockside and on the highway), motel rooms, charter bookings, boat and equipment sales, etc., far and away exceeds the value of fish sales. Think about it; the resource is worth hundreds of times more alive than dead.

Recognizing the real value of this resource, more and more anglers are becoming equipped to tag a tuna. So off you go, with tags and tagging stick but instead of finding a few young of the year yellowfin, you find a few bluefin tuna in the 125 to 140 pound range. Back at the dock, headed and dressed, with ice in the body cavity and covered with a wet blanket, the fish buyer says "OK, I'll take them." Most of us in the sportfishing community don't have a problem with this. However, sometime this coming season the New

Today's Game Fish Tagging Program makes it easy and fun to tag school bluefin tuna like this one.

York Bight area or southern New England may experience a short period in the offshore fishery when either small bluefin or yellowfin tuna abound. With these fish having little or no commercial value, hopefully the hard core "catch 'em and sell 'em" attitude will diminish. Placing a tag into a one year old bluefin tuna of 10 to 14 pounds or a yellowfin of 25 to 30 pounds will not severely impact your pocketbook and perhaps will help the fish that makes your fishing such a great sport and challenge. Today, more than ever before, researchers need as much information as possible on tuna stocks in the western North Atlantic.

The primary tagging program for tuna species is the same Cooperative Game Fish Tagging Program begun by Frank Mather 35 years ago. Headed by Ed Scott today, the program uses dart tags that are free to the fishermen. The tagging results help plot the tuna populations, growth rates and longevity as well as seasonal migration routes. This tagging information can be used to assess population dynamics, a valuable tool as it becomes more important to manage all tuna species for the future of the fish. The tags are available in packs of five from:

> Game Fishing Tagging Program
> Southeast Fisheries Center
> Att: Ed Scott
> 75 Virginia Beach Drive
> Miami, FL 33149

There are several secondary tagging programs across the country that also encourage the tagging of tuna. A neat program initiated by AFTCO brings them all together in an annual fun tournament called the Tag Flag Tournament. The program is supported by many major fishing conservation organizations who award prizes in several categories as well as many fishing publications that publish updates on who won awards for tagging tuna and billfish. Fishermen who tag a certain minimum number of fish of the qualifying species win commemorative Tag Flags and the chance at the overall awards. For more information contact:

> AFTCO Mfg Co., Inc.
> Att: Ben Secrest
> 17351 Murphy Avenue
> Irvine, CA 92714

An earlier program promoted by AFTCO, the Tag A Tuna for Tomorrow Program also encourages tagging of bluefin and continues to operate as part of the Tag Flag Tournament.

OK, so write to NMFS and get your tags. Check all the enclosed info, make a note to collect the following equipment and put it aboard for the upcoming season: tags, a tape measure, a scale weighing fish up to 50 pounds, a tagging stick, a Tail Gaff (AFTCO, SOLO) and a few rubber bands. A few years back when larger fish had only little value, long tagging sticks were necessary. Today, however, smaller fish require using shorter sticks (24 to 48 inches), especially as the smaller fish may be tagged chine side or even topsides. A spare tagging needle is a good idea and may be gotten from several sources (SOLO, AFTCO, CGFTP). This is an item most local tackle shops do not carry, so plans are best made now to secure an extra needle.

Consider a situation in which you're inside 40 fathoms. With a few fish already in the boat, the next hookup comes rather easily to the transom. It turns out to be a small yellowfin or bluefin of 15 pounds and easily handled. Check to get a "sure, go ahead" nod from the crew. Idle along, letting the fish "catch its breath" and lead it along to the side of the boat. Use a gloved hand to grab the tail or use a tail snare to quickly lift the tuna aboard by both head and tail onto a wet towel.

All tagging equipment should be laid out and at the ready, tag affixed to the needle, rubber band holding the other end to the tag stick. At arms reach are a tape measure and scale. The tag is inserted following weighing and measuring.

If the fish is a bleeder, hold off on tagging or release. Occasionally, a fish has a torn gill raker and is bleeding profusely. It's a poor decision to waste a tag on this animal, as chances are it may become too weakened by blood loss to survive when put overboard. If, however, the bleeding is mild and if the fish is handled carefully, it has an excellent chance for survival.

Enter weight and length on the tagging data card. Quickly lift the tuna overboard by gloved hand at the tail and allow it to plunge into the depths head first. It is very important you do not just flip the fish overboard. Landing tail first, it has no swimming momentum and cannot quickly pass water over its gills to carry oxygen to body tissues. In fact, the animal may lapse into shock and simply settle away with you having nothing to show for your efforts.

Take it from me, fish in the 35 to 50 pound category are a little tougher to tag and release successfully. They do not come to boatside as easily as a 15 pound fish. With two people involved a fish can be quickly lifted aboard, measured, tag inserted and data double checked. Picked up by the tail with a head first drop overboard, the disappearing fish is a good sign of success.

Fish over 50 pounds only rarely have little or no market value. If so, tagging and release is a different story. With one person having a leader in hand, a second individual has tag stick duties. As the boat idles ahead slowly the fish will lay over on one side or the other as it tires. Getting the dorsal (back) side toward the tagger is critical. Once the fish is properly oriented, the tag can be inserted quickly adjacent to the dorsal fin. Patience is required as the fish may reorient itself several times while being towed alongside. However, as the fish is guided along with some water moving over the gills, more time can be taken in getting the tag into the meaty area of the back.

Keep in mind that along either side of the fish, running under the lateral line, is a major blood vessel. If the tag goes into this blood vessel, death of the fish will occur quickly. Should this happen, and you have a heavy bleeder, it's best to keep the fish.

At times, some blood is evident from the hooking and tearing of tissues in the mouth area. In most instances this is superficial unless a gill is torn. Small blood loss can be disregarded. A critical judgment for sure but do not let a little bleeding prevent you from making a release.

Over the years the majority of tuna fish tagged and released from the **Prowler** have been one to three year old bluefin caught in the trolling mode. Not too difficult a job to lift the fish up onto the gunnel, twist the hook out, take quick measurements and then push the animal headfirst back overboard. Hook removal, if done quickly and cleanly, appears not to traumatize the animal. As proof of this, in 1985, 80% of all the CGFTP recaptured bluefin tuna that year from the western North Atlantic had been tagged by parties aboard the **Prowler**.

With larger fish, particularly if time does not allow ample tiring, simply reach down and snip the leader as close as possible to the hook. It's a good idea to grab the lure and slide it up the leader before you do this, of course.

Tuna taken in the chum slick with the hook deep in the gullet are easily released by simply cutting the leader as close as possible to the hook. Be sure to double check for a tell-tale flow of blood from the gill area, indicative of a badly injured fish.

Again, the tagger should double check to see that all pertinent information has been recorded on the Tag Report Card and is accurate. Filling in the information required several days later, trusting to memory and perhaps with some inaccuracy, is not helping the CGFTP program. Although most of us now think in loran TDs, the

CGFTP prefers the location of the fish to be filled in with latitude and longitude, instead.

With cards filled in at day's end, your responsibility has not ended. The next step is to make a copy of the data for personal records, perhaps in the boat log, and get the postage paid cards into the mail.

Once received by the CGFTP Southeast Fisheries Laboratory personnel, tagging data is entered into their computer system. Now, should a fish you tagged be recaptured, the tag in the fish will display a message of reward and address, as well as the number corresponding to the data card information now on file.

Oh, one more point. Make a note to purchase a few tag flags, those red pennants with a capital T (Tag) on them. On the way home for the day you can have someone in the crew run up one for each fish tagged and released. Someone is sure to come down the dock before the day's cleanup is completed and ask what they're all about. I'll even bet you'll be more than ready to tell 'em.

6 BLUEFIN TUNA TAGGING

The Cooperative Game Fish Tagging Program

Over the years, I've been involved with a number of major fishing tournaments here in Rhode Island either on the executive board or as a committee member. As the Director of the New England Offshore Sportfishing Tournament, I can usually be found at the captains and anglers meeting the evening before the fishing starts explaining tournament details. What continues to amaze me is the number of members of the angling community who have no idea what tagging is all about, how one goes about tagging and releasing a fish or gets hold of a few tags should they decide to release a fish. In this tournament, SOLO Marine products offers an award for tag and release in an effort to promote conservation. Along with this, the tournament recommends that tuna under 50 pounds not be brought to the scales. Instead, consideration is given to the tag and release of smaller fish for obvious reasons.

A while back, I had a chance to talk with Edwin L. Scott, director of the CGFTP, who sent off a copy of a recent report "History Of The Cooperative Game Fish Tagging Program In The Atlantic Ocean, Gulf of Mexico, and Caribbean Sea, 1954-1987."

At the present time, there seems to be a trend by anglers to tag and release small fish and we are seeing more articles in the various saltwater fishing magazines describing this activity. Let's take a quick look at the CGFTP, started back in 1954 by Frank J. Mather III, while at the WHOI. Frank's primary interest was bluefin tuna but the program expanded to include billfish and amberjack. In 1973, the program became a combined effort between WHOI and (NMFS). After Mather's retirement in 1980, the NMFS Southeast Fisheries Center (SEFC) Miami Laboratory assumed sole responsibility for funding and operation of the program.

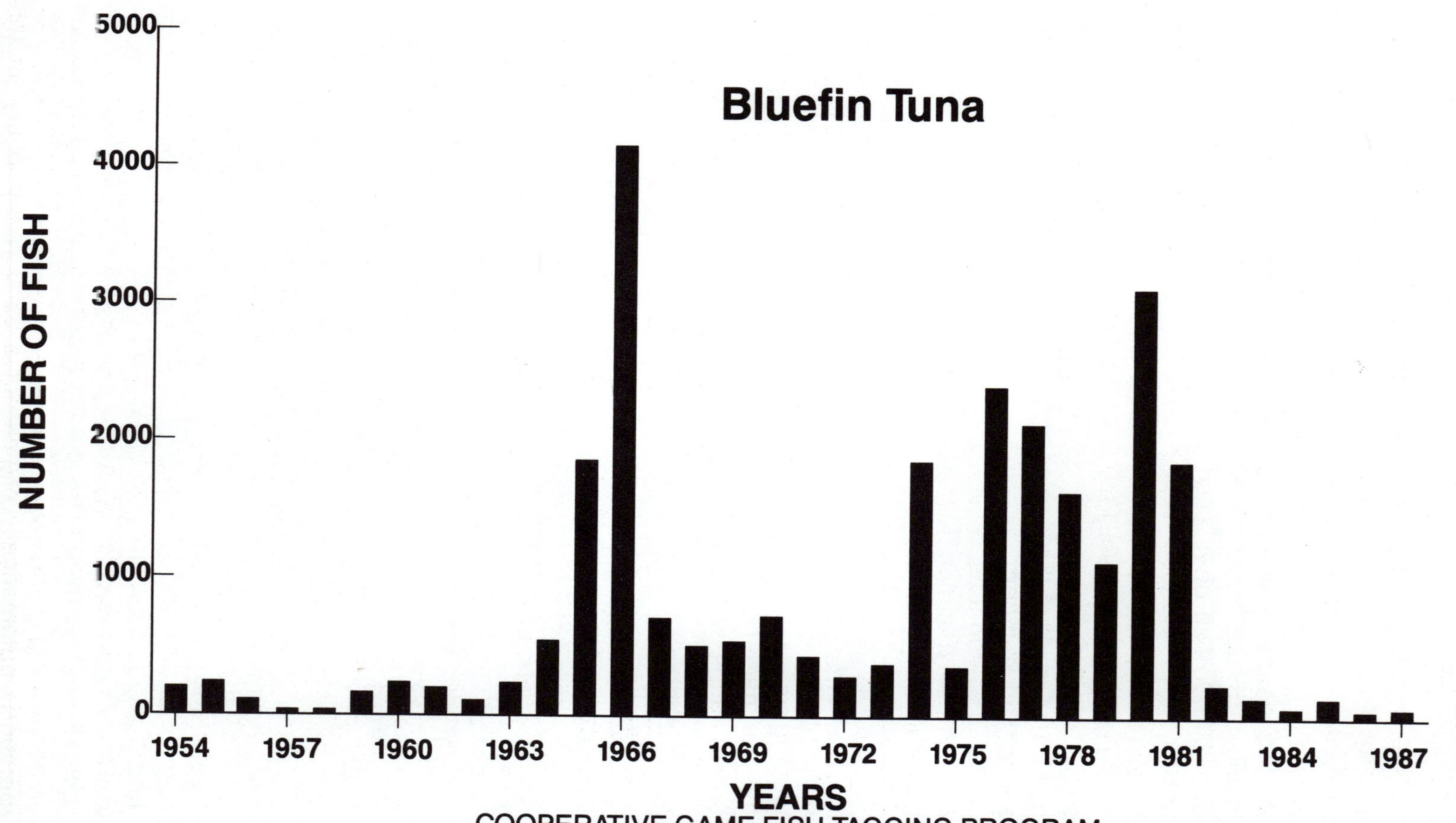

Bluefin Tuna
NUMBER OF FISH
5000
4000
3000
2000
1000
0
1954
1957
1960
1963
1966
1969
1972
1975
1978
1981
1984
1987
YEARS
COOPERATIVE GAME FISH TAGGING PROGRAM

Over 10,000 individual anglers, charter boat captains and commercial fishermen have participated in the CGFTP since 1954. At present, about 2,500 persons are listed as active cooperators in the program. Participants reside not only in the U.S., but also Canada, Mexico, South America, Africa, Europe and various Caribbean Island countries. Through 1987, cooperators tagged and released over 118,000 fish of 78 species. More sailfish have been tagged (39,800) and released than any other fish species, followed by bluefin tuna (26,795).

You must write directly to NMFS to get a pack of tags, Ed Scott says, "We have found we increase the probability that a tag will be used if we restrict the distribution of tags to individuals who personally request them."

Within a short time, a pack of five tags will be sent off containing a brochure explaining the CGFTP, instructions on how to tag a fish and how to fill out the important tag release card. A few rubber bands are included to help hold the plastic portion of the tag on the tag stick and a tagging flag, all within a plastic ziplock pouch for convenient storage of these materials. Should you desire a fancy tagging stick, you can visit your local tackle shop to see if they carry the one made by AFTCO. Otherwise, you can make one up from a broom handle with a hole drilled in its end to take the tagging pin.

The tag by itself is a stainless steel dart tag, basically a slotted metal barb with a yellow vinyl stream with a tag identification number imprinted on it, the word "REWARD," and the Miami laboratory address.

Ed is careful with requests for bulk tags. "Fishing clubs, tournaments, and other groups often make requests for large numbers of tags. In these cases, we ask that the individual club members or tournament participants personally contact us for tags." Since 1982, clubs may not purchase bulk tags and equipment from the manufacturers and the tagging data goes into the CGFTP computerized files.

Getting a tag into a bluefin is only part of the job and careful attention must be paid to the completion and return of the tag release card, which corresponds to the tag identification number. Data requested from the tagger includes: species of fish, date, estimated weight and length, location released, angler's name and address, captain's name and address, condition of fish at release, type of bait and club affiliation along with additional remarks.

There's a reward for capturing a tagged fish. "The CGFTP has always provided incentives to encourage tagging and the return of recovered tags," says Ed. "If one recaptures a bluefin tuna, that person is automatically eligible for a $500 yearly lottery for this species conducted by the International Commission for the Conservation of Atlantic Tunas.''

Since 1982, the CGFTP has provided additional incentives to cooperators who tag billfish and tuna. Recreational fishermen are eligible for annual trophies such as, for the most bluefin tagged, awarded by the International Game Fish Association.

Each year the CGFTP publishes an annual report that summarizes the numbers of releases and recaptures of the various program species, including bluefin tuna. The CGFTP feels that public recognition provides an incentive for future efforts by tagging and those individuals who tag and release ten (10) or more fish are listed by name with the number of fish species tagged.

Bluefin tuna have strong migratory behavior as evidenced by nine fish tagged and released off Cat Cay, Bimini, and recaptured off the coast of Norway (10,000 km). According to Mather, trans-Atlantic movement was first recorded in 1959 when a fish tagged and released off Massachusetts was recaptured in the Bay of Biscay off the coast of Spain (Mather 1960). Additional recaptures during the next few years demonstrated trans-Atlantic movements by both large and small fish, often with times at large of only a few months (Mather 1962, 1969; Mather et al. 1967).

Later recapture records have been great enough to document migration patterns of most size/age groups of bluefin in the North Atlantic.

The longest time at large for a bluefin tuna was 18 years for a fish tagged off Montauk Point and recaptured off Nantucket Island. However, a bluefin tuna at large for 16 years provided more valuable information because skeletal structures from this specimen were successfully used to validate the vertebrae method of age determination for this species (Lee et al. 1983; Prince et al. 1985).''

As you might have guessed, tagging has provided scientists with information on age and growth of many species, including bluefin tuna. For example, a tagged fish of small size that has been at large for an extended period of time and then recaptured and retained to allow various skeletal structures to be examined can validate the accuracy of aging techniques.

This is facilitated by the Save It For Science program started by the Miami Laboratory in 1982 (Prince 1984). Through this program, fishermen participating in the CGFTP are encouraged to retain carcasses of tag recaptured fish and to notify the Miami Laboratory so scientific staff can retrieve the skeletal structures. This program has also been recently adopted by ICCAT since many of the billfish and tuna tagged through the CGFTP are recaptured by foreign long-line vessels.

There are a number of problems associated with tagging of fish and the program's major problem is the inaccurate estimation of a fish's size when it is tagged and released. This is because the program is dependent on commercial and recreational fishermen who volunteer to tag or return tags from recaptured fish. These people are not trained scientists and with the fish in the water at the side of the boat can only *estimate* its length and weight. With smaller fish, scientists can make actual measurements but with larger fish this is nearly impossible to do. Hence, the chance of error can be high, particularly in light of the level of excitement and enthusiasm of a successful angler.

Needless to say, if a fish is recaptured several years after being tagged and its weight is less than estimated, this could prove to be quite embarrassing for the cooperating tagger, for sure.

Over the years I've had considerable opportunity to watch tuna being brought into Snug Harbor Marina to Ralboray, the major buyer. On a number of occasions, I've seen bluefins with tags in them as the fish is hung up for weighing or picture taking. In most instances the crew of the boat was totally unaware of the significance of the yellow tag streamer in the back of the fish. If it had not been brought to their attention, I'm sure the recapture data would have been lost. I find it amazing how unobservant and uninformed the fishing public is in these matters.

On another occasion, a worker for the fish buyer pointed out a tag in a giant bluefin and suggested the angler remove it and contact someone at the address printed. The reply was they, "couldn't be bothered."

7

THE INTERNATIONAL GAME FISH ASSOCIATION

What, you might ask, is a chapter on the International Game Fish Association (IGFA) doing in a book that attempts to profile the changes that have recently occurred in the bluefin tuna fishery. I suppose it's particularly puzzling in light of such common attitudes as, "Better get all the harpoon gear ready. Tag 'em and let 'em go? Man, you're crazy. The heck with the other guy. What do you mean the fish is only worth that much?"

Sad to say, much of the angling public has lost the ethnic of sport-fishing because of the high prices being paid for giant bluefin tuna, as well as several other species. This has led to the loss of respect and appreciation of the rights of others, as well as inconsiderate behavior on the fishing grounds. The reason is bluefin tuna (giant) have become big business for many people. It's the reason why they purchased an expensive boat along with costly tackle and equipment. With today's dockside prices, several good fish will take the "sting" out of their financial outlay.

On the opposite side of the coin lies the philosophy and objectives of the IGFA, basically unchanged since its founding back in 1939. Compared to today, rod and reel fishing for bluefin back then could be considered unsophisticated, with nowhere near the number of tools presently available.

IGFA president Elwood K. Harry (in the chair) preparing to tag a bluefin tuna off Cat Cay in the Bahamas in 1963.

After crew member Harvey Dotten wired the fish, Norris Rollie successfully tagged Elwood K. Harry's bluefin.

Let's take a quick look at the major objectives of the IGFA today.

1. To encourage and further the study of game fish angling, the related species, and the habitat requirement of such species.

2. To work at all levels of government and industry for the preservation of the species and the protection of their natural habitats.

3. To compile and distribute game fish information to all IGFA members, the general public and scientific and legislative government bodies for the furtherance of education in the wise use and conservation of the species.

4. To ensure that the recreational angler is adequately represented at all meetings where the future of the game fish population and the angling sport is being determined.

5. To assist and participate in domestic and international game fish seminars and symposiums where the expertise, data and purposes of this organization may be helpful in assisting other organizations with similar objectives.

6. To develop and support game fish tagging programs and other scientific data collection efforts, and to aid scientific and educational institutions which provide vital instruction and research in ichthyology, the fishery sciences, and related studies.

7. To maintain and promote fair, uniform and ethical international angling regulations, and to compile and maintain world record data for game fish caught according to these regulations.

8. To develop and maintain an international museum and reference library on game fishes, the sport of angling and related subjects.

9. To accumulate and maintain a worldwide history of game fishing for the use and benefit of the public.

Most of the anglers in the saltwater arena know what the letters IGFA represent and would probably venture to indicate they were aware of its record keeping activities for both fresh and saltwater fish. However, many are unaware of the International Library of Fishes and Museum operated today. Founded in 1973 by the IGFA, it is to be the most comprehensive reference library in the world on rod and reel fishing and related subjects. The library now contains over 9,000 books on fishing worldwide. The IGFA assist with, or initiates the publication of, over 2,000 fishing articles in the U.S. alone. Along with this, the Library maintains a current listing and file of outdoor and fishing magazines from both U.S. and foreign countries, as well as a file and copies of scientific papers on fishery research worldwide. Many of the IGFA member clubs send off yearbooks with top catches and awards to be included in the file, which is later indexed and maintained for data reference historical purposes.

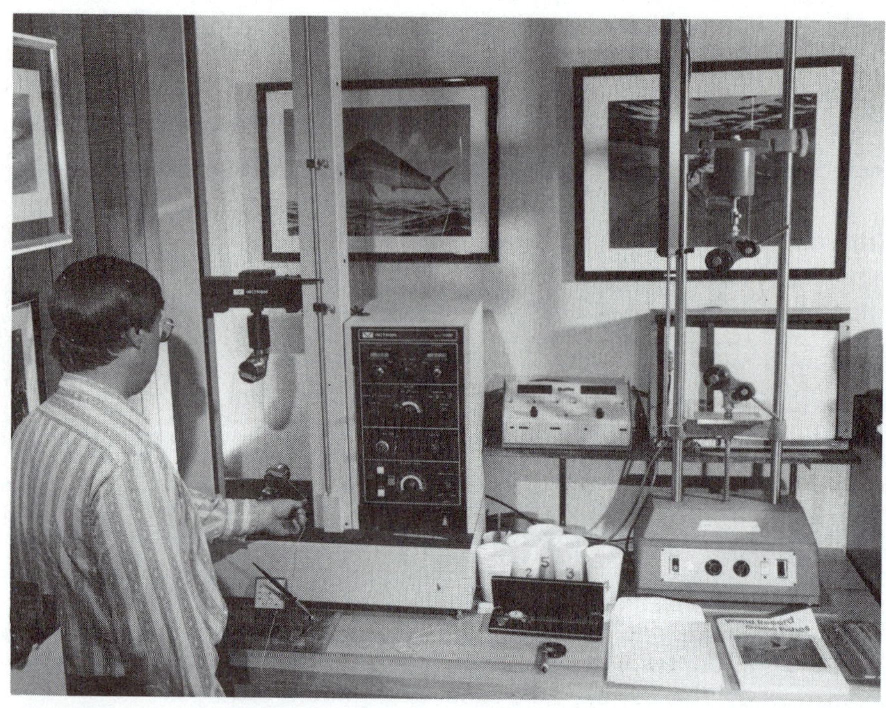

To qualify for an IGFA line class record, these machines carefully check and double check line strength and size before issuing a new record.

Michael Leech (L) and Elwood K. Harry examine some of the many antique fishing reels which were donated to the IGFA's museum.

The IGFA's library is compiled of a general public reading and research section and an International Library of Fishes.

The film and video library has some of the oldest fishing films ever made.

Perhaps one of the most difficult tasks facing the IGFA today is the development of its section on the history of angling. Books, papers and news clippings from worldwide "pioneer" anglers have been compiled and will be added to as time progresses. "History is being made every day in the angling world, and the IGFA intends to document, compile and preserve this history," reports Elwood Harry, president of IGFA.

Anyone interested in donating superior quality fishing films or videos, as well a photographs, should contact the IGFA, as their archives of films, photographs, and artwork date back to the turn of the century. Their video collection contains more than 500 action films on fishing. "Many anglers have all kinds of collections but are not aware of the IGFA facility, and wait too long to ensure that their data and memorabilia will be permanently retained in good hands," says Harry.

Let me warn you that if you should decide to visit their office at 3000 East Las Olas Blvd., Fort Lauderdale, FL 33316-1616. (305) 567-0161, be prepared to spend a great deal more time than you had anticipated.

Back in 1980, when I turned to a full-time charter fishing for a living, I decided it would be a good idea to become a member of the IGFA. Several years later the waters offshore had large numbers of longfin albacore only a few miles south of Block Island. On one particular day I had a group with a female angler aboard and we had taken a number of these fish. Instead of the usual 30 to 50 pound fish, we had boated several close to 70 pounds trolling "plastic," as we say. Finally her turn came and we had a savage strike. On 30 pound class tackle she had her hands full with this fish but she was experienced and did a very good job. I recall that at boatside it took two members of the crew to gaff and lift the fish aboard. On the trip back to the dock I realized this fish she landed was much larger than I was accustomed to seeing so I decided to weigh it on the state certified scale at the marina. We all watched as the weights were moved to balance the arm of the platform scale at 77 pounds. Not thinking to take any pictures, this fish was then expertly steaked out by yours truly, cut into chunks, bagged and put into the party's ice filled coolers. Once home, I went to the den and pulled the latest (1983) IGFA World Record Game Fishes edition off the shelf. A few minutes later I realized I had filleted a potential world record albacore as the women's 30 pound line class record at that time stood at 62 pounds, 6 ounces. Imagine! I cut up a fish bettering the existing world record by approximately 15 pounds. From that day on, my copy of the IGFA annual Record Book has been on the boat!

A couple of years back, when the idea of doing this bluefin project began to take shape, I went to the University of Rhode Island Library in Kingston and the School of Oceanography Library in Narragansett expecting to find a book or two written about bluefin tuna. Instead, I only found listings of reports and scientific papers in the card catalog. I then made a mental note to visit the IGFA Library in Fort Lauderdale when on vacation in Florida. Surely, there would be a listing of a book or two devoted to telling about this great fish. Instead, I found only a few chapters on bluefin in books devoted to offshore fishing. On that visit, I had a chance to speak with Elwood K. Harry, president of the IGFA, and he indicated that if there were such a book, he would know about it and a listing could certainly be found in their card catalog. It seemed incredible that no one volume had been written on fishing for bluefin tuna in U.S. waters, so I contacted the Reference Department of the Library of Congress in Washington, D.C. Guess what, Elwood Harry was absolutely correct. The only thing I could find that might even remotely be considered a book was a 75 page report done by the Department of Fisheries, State of Massachusetts, in 1978, on the Economic Impact of the Atlantic bluefin tuna.

However, before I had to leave the IGFA Library that day, I did look at what Zane Gray, S. Kip Farrington, and Van Campen Heilner wrote about bluefin tuna fishing. It's hard for us to imagine the numbers of fish back in those days.

Along with the previously mentioned activities of the IGFA, most people are familiar with the World Record Game Fishes book published each year. This book alone is worth the cost of membership. A recent edition boasted 320 pages and contained a wealth of information about the IGFA, its international representatives, philosophy and goals, library of fishes and the membership program. Another section contained up-to-date, in-depth stories about fresh and saltwater fishing by noted authors. Another section listed International Angling Rules, World Record Requirement, the IGFA Fishing Contest, and Club Requirements.

There's close to 70 pages devoted to all-tackle, line class, and fly fishing world records. The Guide to Fishes illustrates the world's fishes and charts help identify major game fish species. There's also a section on knots.

Patricia Kuhnle held the Women's Record for 130 pound Class for two years. This huge fish was taken in North Lake, Canada.

INTERNATIONAL GAME FISH ASSOCIATION
LINE CLASS WORLD RECORDS FOR BLUEFIN TUNA

LINE CLASS	WEIGHT	PLACE	ANGLER
Men's Records			
1 KG (2 LB)	Vacant		
2 KG (4 LB)	Vacant		
4 KG (8 LB)	17.69 KG 39 LB	Montauk New York	Chuck Mallinson
6 KG (12 LB)	30.84 KG 68 LB	Montauk New York	William Collins
8 KG (16 LB)	85.27 KG 188 LB	Montauk New York	Stephen Sloan
10 KG (20 LB)	53.97 KG 119 LB	Montauk New York	Stephen Sloan
15 KG (30 LB)	97.97 KG 216 LB	Ocean City Maryland	Byron Phillips
24 KG (50 LB)	407 KG 897 LB 4 OZ	Gran Canaria Canary Islands	Charles Chtivelman
37 KG (80 LB)	506.21 KG 1116 LB	North Lake Canada	Dr. J.M. Steffey
60 KG (130 LB)	679 KG 1496 LB	Aulds Cove Canada	Ken Fraser
Women's Records			
1 KG (2 LB)	Vacant		
2 KG (4 LB)	Vacant		
4 KG (8 LB)	18.82 KG 41.8 LB	Virginia Beach Virginia	Mrs. William DuVal
6 KG (12 LB)	22.22 KG 49 LB	Montauk New York	Lynnette Pintauro
8 KG (16 LB)	24.72 KG 54 LB 8 OZ	Oregon Inlet North Carolina	Laura Bostwick
10 KG (20 LB)	42.18 KG 93 LB	Provincetown Massachusetts	Willia Mather
15 KG (30 LB)	53.29 KG 117 LB 8 OZ	San Diego California	Gladys Chambers
24 KG (50 LB)	234.96 KG 518 LB	Bimini Bahamas	Mrs. Phyllis Bass
37 KG (80 LB)	400.97 KG 884 LB	North Lake Canada	Patricia Kuhnle
60 KG (130 LB)	530.71 KG 1170 LB	North Lake Canada	Colette Parras

SOME SELECTED REFERENCES

Anonymous. *Tuna Migrations in the North Atlantic Studied by R/V Crawford.* Commercial Fishing Review. Volume 24. Number 2. pp. 41-42. 1962.

Anonymous. *Environmental Impact Statement of the Proposed Listing of the Atlantic Bluefin Tuna as a Threatened Species.* U.S. Department of Commerce, National Marine Fisheries Service, National Oceanic and Atmospheric Administration mimeo report. pp. 1-136. 1975.

Aristotle. *History of Animals,* Ten Books, trans. R. Cresswell (London, 1897).

Arrington, Joel. "Tune Up for Tuna," *Salt Water Sportsman*, May 1988. p. 92.

Baglin, Raymond E. Jr. *Length-Weight Relationships of Western Atlantic Bluefin Tuna.* Fisheries Bulletin: Volume 77. Number 4, 1980.

Baglin, Raymond E. Jr. *Reproductive Biology of Western Atlantic Bluefin Tuna Thunnus-Thynnus.* National Marine Fisheries Service, Fisheries Bulletin Volume 80. Number 1. pp. 121-134, 1982.

Beckett, J.S. *Swordfish, Shark and Tuna Tagging.* Technical Reprint of the Fisheries Board of Canada. (193): pp. 1-13. 1970.

Berry, F. *Identifying Bluefin Tuna.* Underwater Naturalist. Volume 10. Number 2. pp. 8-11. 1970.

Bigelow H. and W. Schroeder. *Fishes of the Gulf of Maine.* United States Fish and Wildlife Service, Fisheries Bulletin: Volume 53. Number 74. 1953.

Bond, C.E. *Biology of Fishes.* (Philadelphia: W.B. Saunders, 1979).

Bullis, H.R. Jr. and F.J. Mather III. *Tunas of the Genus thunnus of the Northern Caribbean.* American Museum Novitiate, Number 1765, p. 12. 1956.

Butler, Michael. "Plight of the Bluefin Tuna," *National Geographic.* August 1982. pp. 220-239.

Carey, F.G., Kanwisher, J.W. and E.D. Stevens. *Bluefin Tuna (Thunnus Thynnus) Warm Their Viscera During Digestion.* Journal of Experimental Biology, Volume 109. pp. 1-20. 1984.

Carey, F.G. and K.D. Lawson. *Temperature Regulation in Free-Swimming Bluefin Tuna.* Journal of Comparative Biochemistry and Physiology. Volume 44A. pp. 375-392. 1973.

Carey, F.G. and J.M. Teal. *Regulation of Body Temperature by the Bluefin Tuna.* Journal of Comparative Biochemistry and Physiology. Vol. 28. pp. 205-213. 1969.

Crane J. *Notes on the Biology and Ecology of Giant Tuna Observed at Portland, Maine.* Zoologica, Volume 21. Part 3. Number 16, 1936.

Cunningham, Rip. "Maritime Monsters" *Salt Water Sportsman* April 1986, p. 92.

Dizon, A.E. and R.W. Brill. *Thermoregulation in Tunas.* American Zoological, Volume 19. pp. 249-265. 1979.

Dragovich, A. *The Food of Bluefin Tuna (Thunnus Thynnus) in the Western North Atlantic Ocean.* Trans. Amer. Fish. Soc. 99: pp. 726-731. 1970.

Farrington, S.K. Jr. *Atlantic Game Fishing.* New York: Garden City Publishing Company Inc. p. 298. 1939.

Farrington, S.K. Jr. *Fishing the Atlantic Offshore and On.* New York: Coward McCann Inc. p. 312. 1949.

Farrington, S.K. Jr. *Trail of the Sharp Cup.* New York: Dodd, Mead and Company. p. 176. 1974.

Farrington, S.K. Jr. *Tony the Tuna.* Southhampton, New York: The Yankee Peddler Book Company. p. 19. 1975.

Freeman, Bruce. "Thunnus Thynnus: The Bluefin Tuna." *The Edge Canyon Fishing Annual.* pp. 85-87. 1988.

Funakoshi S., K. Wada and T. Suzuki. *Development of the Rete Mirabile with Growth and Muscle Temperature in the Young Bluefin.* Bulletin of The Japanese Social Science Fisheries. Volume 51. Number 12. 1985.

Gaffney, Rick. "Tuna Alley." *Salt Water Sportsman,* May 1986. p. 43.

Gibbs, R.H. and B.B. Collette. *Comparative Anatomy and Systematics of the Tunas, Genus Thunnus.* United States Marine Fisheries Service. Bulletin Volume 66. Number 1. pp. 65-130. 1967.

Gifford, Tom. *Anglers and Muscleheads.* Illustrated. Dutton and Company. Inc. p. 186. 1960.

Goldstein, Bob. "Bluewater Giants." *Sportfishing.* April/May 1986. p. 50.

Gordon, B.L., *The Marine Fishes of Rhode Island.* Watch Hill. Rhode Island: The Book and Tackle Shop. p. 136. 1960.

Gray, Zane. *Tales of Swordfish and Tuna.* New York and London: Harper and Brothers. 1927.

Hayashi, T., T. Koto, G. Shingu, S. Kume, and Y. Morita. *Status of the Tuna Fish Resources in the Atlantic Ocean 1956-1967.* Far Seas Fishing Resource Laboratory, Japan: Journal Series. Number 3. pp. 1-72. 1970.

Heilner, Van Campen. *Saltwater Fishing.* Philadelphia: Penn Publishing Company. 1937.

Heilner, Van Campen. *Saltwater Fishing.* New York: Knopt. 1953.

Hinman, Ken. "Bluefins: Troubled Times." *Salt Water Sportsman.* March 1988. p. 84.

Hinman, Ken. "U.S. Tuna Policy: Time For A Change." *Salt Water Sportsman.* March 1989. p. 90.

Hutchinson, Bob. "Bluefins by the Numbers." *Salt Water Sportsman.* May 1983. p. 70.

Joseph, J., W. Klawe, and P. Murphy. *Tuna and Billfish-Fish Without a Country.* Inter-American Tropical Tuna Commission. p. 45. 1980.

Levine, J.S. and E.F. MacNichol, Jr. Color Vision in Fishes. *Scientific American.* Volume 246. pp. 140-149. 1982.

Lozano, Cabo F. *Critical Study of Echo-Sounders Used for Tuna Selection.* Proceedings of the General Fishing Countries of the Meditteranean. Volume 5. Number 8. pp. 91-99. 1959.

Lyman, Hal. "The Cup Recollected." *Salt Water Sportsman.* October 1985. p. 58.

Lythgoe, J.N. *Visions in Fishes.* Edited by M.A. Ali. Published by Plenum Publishers. N.Y. 1980.

Marr, J.C. and M.B. Schaefer. *Definitions of Body Dimensions Used in Describing Tunas.* United States Fishing and Wildlife Series. Fish Bulletin, Volume 51. Volume 47. pp. 241-244. 1949.

Martingale, Inc. *Economic Impact of the Atlantic Bluefin Tuna Fishery in Massachusetts.* Massachusetts Department of Fisheries. Illustrated. p. 75. 1978.

Mason, J. *Food of Small Northwest Atlantic Bluefin Tuna (Thunnus Thynnus) as Ascertained Through Stomach Content Analysis.* University of Rhode Island (Masters Thesis). 1976.

Mather, F.J. III and H.A. Schuck. *Growth of Bluefin Tuna of the Western North Atlantic.* United States Fish and Wildlife Series, Fisheries Bulletin. Volume 61. Number 179. pp. 39-52. 1960.

Mather, F.J. III. *Recaptures of Tuna, Marlin and Sailfish Tagged in the Western North Atlantic.* Copeia. Number 2. pp. 149-151. 1960.

Mather F.J. III. *Tons of Tuna, Closing a Gap in our Knowledge.* Oceanus. Volume 7. Number 3. pp. 15-19, 1961.

Mather, F.J. III. *Transatlantic Migration of Two Large Bluefin Tuna.* Journal of Conservation. Volume 27. pp. 325-327. 1962.

Mather, F.J. III and M.R. Bartlett. *Bluefin Tuna Concentration Found During A Long-Line Exploration of the Northern Atlantic Slope.* Commercial Fishing Review. Volume 24. Number 2. pp. 1-7. 1962.

Mather, F.J. III, M.R. Bartlett and J.S. Beckett. *Transatlantic Migrations of Young Bluefin Tuna.* Journal of the Fisheries Research Board of Canada. Volume 29. Number 0. pp. 1991-1997. 1967.

Mather, F.J. III. "They Went Thataway." *Salt Water Sportsman.* 29(7), 40-3. 72-3. 1968. Volume 29. Number 7. pp. 40-43, 73-73.

Mather, F.J. III. "The Atlantic Bluefin Tuna Situation." *Sportfishing.* Volume 4. Number 12. p. 55. 1968.

Mather, F.J. III. "Long Distance Migrations of Tunas and Marlins." *Underwater Naturalist.* Volume 6. Number 2. pp. 6-14. p. 46. 1969.

Mather, F.J. III. *The Bluefin Tuna Situation.* Proceedings of the 16th Annual International Game Fish Research Conference. October, 1973.

Mather, F.J. III. *Game Fish Tagging: What has it Taught Us?* IGFA World Record Game Fishes. pp. 79-96. 1980.

Maul, G.A., F. Williams, M. Roffer and F.M. Sousa. *Remotely Sensed Oceanographic Patterns and Variability of Bluefin Tuna (Thunnus-Thynnus-Thynnus) Catch in the Gulf of Mexico.* Oceanology Acta. Volume 7. Number 4. pp. 469-480. 1984.

McClane, A.J. *McClanes Standard Fishing Encyclopedia and International Guide.* Holt, Reinhart and Winston. 1057 pages. 1965.

Meyer-Waarden, P.F. *Relation Between the Tuna Populations of the Atlantic, Mediterranean and North Seas.* Proceedings of the General Fishing Countries of the Mediterranean. Volume 5. Number 22. pp. 197-202. 1959.

Moss, F.T. "The Case of the Subway Tuna." *Sportfishing.* Volume 3. Number 6. p. 10. pp. 47-49. 1967.

Moss, F.T. *Successful Ocean Game Fishing.* Maine: International Marine Publishing Company, p. 245. 1971.

Moss, F.T. *Bluefin: A Modern Sea Adventure.* New Hampshire: Perigree Press. p. 288. 1985.

Murphy, R.C. *The Structure of the Pineal Organ of the Bluefin Tuna (Thunnus Thynnus).* Journal of Morphology. Volume 133. pp. 1-15. 1971.

Murray, Paul. "Deliverance." *Salt Water Sportsman.* March 1987. p. 68.

Nakamura, H. *Tuna Distribution and Migration.* London: Fishing News Books. p. 76. 1969.

Nicholson, Paul. *Atlantic Tuna Club, Then and Now.* Private Printing. p. 48. 1954.

Partridge, B.L., J. Johanson and J. Kalish. *The Structure of Schools of Giant Bluefin (Thunnus-Thynnus) in Cape Cod Bay, USA.* Environmental Biology Fisheries. Volume 9. Number 3-4. pp. 253-262. 1983.

Potthoff, T. and W.J. Richards. *Juvenile Bluefin Tuna and Other Scrombirds Taken by Terms In The Dry Tortugas, Florida.* Bulletin from Marine Science. Volume 20. Number 2. pp. 389-413. 1970.

Poveromo, George, "Chum Up A Bluefin." *Salt Water Sportsman.* October 1985. p. 54.

Prince, E.D., D.W. Lee and J.C. Javech. *Internal Zonations in Sections of Vertebrae from Atlantic Bluefin Tuna Thunnus-Thynnus and Potential use in Age Determination.* Canadian Journal of Fisheries in Aquatic Science. Volume 42. Number 5. pp. 938-946. 1985.

Reiger, George. *Profiles in Salt Water Angling.* New Jersey: Prentice Hall. p. 470. 1973.

Rich, W.H. *The Horse Mackerel Fishery (Tuna) Of Maine.* United States Bureau of Fisheries Memo. Number 5-339. pp. 1-7. 1935.

Richards, W.J., *Tropical Atlantic Tuna Larvae Collected During Equalant Surveys.* Commercial Fishing Review. Volume 31. Number 11. pp. 33-37. 1969.

Richards, W.J. *Spawning of Bluefin Tuna (Thunnus Thynnus) in the Atlantic Ocean and Adjacent Seas.* International Commission of Conservation on Atlantic Tunas, Standard Commission of Restraints and Statistics. 75/97. pp. 267-278. 1976.

Ristori, Al. "Return of the Tuna." *Salt Water Sportsman.* August 1983. p. 24.

Ristori, Al. "Back to Schoolies." *Salt Water Sportsman.* September 1984. p. 48.

Ristori, Al. "Update: Bluefin Tuna." *Salt Water Sportsman.* February 1985. p. 61.

Ristori, Al. "Chunk Up Bluefin." *Salt Water Sportsman.* September 1985. p. 44.

Ristori, Al. "Schools In." *Salt Water Sportsman.* September 1986. p. 66.

Ristori, Al. "The Lady and the Tuna." *Salt Water Sportsman.* November 1988. p. 74.

Rivas, L.R. *A Preliminary Report on the Spawning of Western North Atlantic Bluefin Tuna in the Straits of Florida.* Bulletin of Marine Science on the Gulf of the Caribbean. Volume 4. Number 4. pp. 302-322. 1954.

Rivas, L.R. *A Comparison Between Giant Bluefin Tuna from the Straits of Florida and the Gulf of Maine, with Reference to Migration and Population Density.* Proceedings from the Gulf Caribbean Fishing Institution, Seventh Anniversary Session. Havana. pp. 1-17. November 1954.

Rivas, L.R. *The Pineal Apparatus of Tunas and Related Scombrid Fishes as a Possible Light Receptor Controlling Phototactic Movements.* Bulletin of Marine Science Gulf and Caribbean. Volume 3. Number 3. pp. 168-180. 1954.

Rivas, L.R. *Preliminary Models of Annual Life History Cycles of The North Atlantic Bluefin Tuna.* The Physiological Ecology of Tunas. Academic Press. pp. 369-393. 1978.

Rodewald, M. *Transatlantic Migrations of the Bluefin Tuna and Anomilies of the Atmospheric Circulation.* Conservation Commission of Permanent International Explorations. C.M. Volume 2. Number 7. p. 7. 1967.

Scott, E.L. E.D. Prince and C.D. Goodyear. *History of the Cooperative Game Fish Tagging Program in the Atlantic Ocean, Gulf of Mexico and Caribbean Sea.* 1954-1987. In Press.

Sella, M. *Distribution and Migrations of the Tuna Thunnus Thynnus L. Studied by the Method of Hooks and Other Observations.* International Review Ges. Hydrobiol. Volume 24. pp. 446-466. 1930.

Sharp, G. and A. Dizon. *The Physiological Ecology of Tunas.* New York: Academic Press. p. 485. 1978.

Springer, V.G. and H.D. Hoese. *Notes and Records of Marine Fishes from the Texas Coast.* Texas Journal of Science. Volume 10. pp. 343-348. 1958.

Stevens, E.D. and J.M. McLeese. *Why Bluefin Tuna Thunnus Thynnus have warm Tummies (Temperature Effect on Trypsin and Chymotrypsin).* American Journal of Physiology. Volume 246. Number 4. Part 2. R487-R494. 1984.

Stillman, Charles K. *Eastern Tuna Fishing.* New York: The American Angler. p. 29. 1921.

Thompson, Peter. *The Games Fishes of New England and Southeast Canada.* Down East Books. 1980.

Wardle, C.S., J.J. Videler, T. Arimoto, J.M. Franco, and P. He. *The Muscle Twitch and the Maximum Swimming Speed of Giant Bluefin Tuna, Thunnus Thynnus L.* Journal Fish Biology. Volume 35. pp. 129-137. 1989.

Westman, J.R. and W.C. Neville. *The Tuna Fishery of Long Island, New York.* Long Island, New York: Board of Supervisors. 1942.

Williamson, Gordon. *An Account of the Bluefin Tuna in Newfoundland Waters with Some Reference to the Tuna Fishes in General.* St. John's Newfoundland Tourist Development Office. 1962.

Wise, J.P. and C.W. Davis. *Seasonal Distribution of the Tunas and Billfishes in the Atlantic.* National Oceanic and Atmospheric Administration Technical Reprint. National Marine Fisheries Service Special Scientific Reprint Fisheries. pp. 1-24. 1973.

Wilson, P.C. *Review of the Development of the Atlantic Coast Tuna Fishery.* Commercial Fishing Review. Volume 27. Number 3. pp. 1-10. 1973.

Wulff, Lee. *Quest for a Record Bluefin.* Gray's Sporting Journal. Volume 3. Issue 2. 1978.

VIDEOS

IGFA Series: Private and commercial films now on video tape, available for use only at the IGFA Headquarters, Ft. Lauderdale, Florida.

IGFA Series #C77: *Giant Bluefin Tuna.* Bimini, VHS, Color, Sound. Minutes 45.

IGFA Series #C119: *Bluefin Bonanza.* Newfoundland, 1969, VHS, Color, Music, Minutes 25.

IGFA Series #C126: *Death of the Bluefin Tuna.* Sportfishing, underwater, commercial netting scenes, VHS, Color, Sound, Minutes 60.

IGFA Series #C128: Part 1: *Tuna Fishing at Wedgeport.* 1935, VHS, Black & White, Captions, Minutes 16.

IGFA Series # C128: Part 2: *Tuna Fishing at Jordans Ferry, Canada.* Michael Lerner, VHS, Black & White, Captions, Minutes 8.

IGFA Series #C167: *Bluefin Tuna Caught by Mike and Helen Lerner.* Bimini 1947. VHS, Color, Sound, Minutes 90.

IGFA Series #C171: *Bluefin Tuna Fishing in Nova Scotia From A Small Boat.* Michael Lerner 1937. VHS, Black and White, No Sound, Minutes 8.

IGFA Series #C173: *Giant Tuna Fishing.* Newfoundland 1960's. VHS, Color, No Sound, Minutes 40.

IGFA Series #C179: *American Sportsman - Tuna Fishing at Cat Cay.* VHS, Color, Sound, Minutes 22.

IGFA Series #C181: *Bimini Tuna and Marlin, 1957.* VHS, Color, No Sound, Minutes 22.

IGFA Series #C187: *Where the Biggest Bluefin Swim.* Lee Wulff, Nova Scotia, VHS, Black and White, Minutes 30.

IGFA Series #C196: *Giant Tuna Small Boat.* Lee Wulff, VHS, Color, Sound, Minutes 30.

IGFA Series #C246: *Nova Scotia International Tuna Match.* 1966. VHS, Black and White, partially in Sound, Minutes 30.

IGFA Series #C311: *Tuna Fishing at Lower Wedgeport, N.S., Canada, 1947.* VHS, Black and White, Minutes 10.

IGFA Series #C354: *Bluefin Tuna Fishing at Lower Wedgeport N.S., Canada.* VHS, Color, No Sound, Minutes 9. Murray Brothers: *Tuna Mania.* First part instruction, second part angling. VHS, Color, Sound, Minutes 90.

FILMS

British Broadcasting Corporation (BBC) "World About Us" Series: *Mattanza-Death of the Giant Bluefin.* 1978.

ABOUT THE AUTHOR

Captain Al Anderson has been charter fishing since 1967 and operates the **Prowler** out of Snug Harbor Marina in Wakefield, Rhode Island. He resides in Narragansett with his wife Daryl Anne. His activities in marine sportfishing have been profiled by many regional outdoor writers over the years.

The experiences of charter fishing have allowed him to author many articles for The Fisherman Magazine and his slide and lecture presentations on bluefin and tuna behavior have become popular seminar programs in the off season in New England.

He has boated well over a hundred giant and medium bluefin for clients in his career. Since 1971 he tagged and released over 300 bluefin tuna. In 1988, he was honored by the International Game Fish Association for tagging the most bluefins that year for the Cooperative Game Fish Tagging Program as well as tagging the most bluefin tuna in the world. He is presently the IGFA representative for the State of Rhode Island.

Previously active on the executive committees of seven major Rhode Island fishing tournaments, he is presently the Director of the New England Offshore Sportfishing Tournament. At the present time he is an advisor on Oceanic Pelagics to the Marine Recreational Fisheries Committee (New England) for NMFS.

He received his Masters Degree from Adelphia University in 1963 and moved to Rhode Island where he has been actively saltwater fishing ever since. His charter business became so successful he was able to leave his science teaching occupation for a more exciting life on the water.